My dear Jim

A biography of
Walter E. Spradbery

An Artist in War and Peace

With commentary by John Spradbery

Editorial guidance Anna Lavigne

Tea and sympathy Elizabeth Spradbery

malet@supanet.com
el.malet@gmail.com

The life of Walter E. Spradbery revealed mainly through a remarkable correspondence discovered some 35 years after his death: part of a huge quantity of penned correspondence, reputed to have amounted to over one thousand letters to a lifelong friend, James Berry. Also, diaries from pre-World War One and later correspondence to a certain Miss Elinor Pugh.

Also diaries, speeches and miscellaneous recollections from times past.

Assembled and commented upon by John Spradbery

First published August 2010

Published by **John Spradbery Publishing**,
Worthing BN11 4SA
email: malet@supanet.com

Distributed by: **John Rule Art Distributors**
40 Voltaire Road, London SW4 6DH
Tel: 020 7498 0115
email: johnrule@johnrule.co.uk

A CIP catalogue record for this book is available from the British Library

ISBN 978-0-9565935-0-4

Design: Mike Blacker, www.blackerdesign.co.uk
Cover design based on a design by Roy Blinston Design, Queanbeyan NSW Australia
With ackowledgement to XCS Consulting, Canberra Australia

Contents

Acknowledgements

The London Transport Museum, Imperial War Museum. The Wellcome Trust, The Epping Forest District Museum, William Morris Gallery, The Buckhurst Hill Community Association, The Buckhurst Hill British Legion Association, The Essex Art Club and the City of Peterborough Central Library

Elaine Berry, Helen Power, John Spradbery (great nephew to Walter Spradbery), David Bownes, Anna Lavigne, Deryck Selby, Carly Hearn, Diana Tredinnick, Heather Thirtle, Tony Oliva, Libby Horner, Sandy Connor, Lynette Laugher, Dr Philip Spradbery (Australia), Roy Blinston (Australia) and Elizabeth Spradbery

Foreword

It was not until the year 1957 or 1958 when by sheer chance on a Bank Holiday Monday I was aimlessly wandering down Whitehall – the London thoroughfare famous and dignified for laying wreathes, mourning the dead, acclaiming royalty, military and national sporting victories – that I caught sight of my father, Walter Ernest Spradbery, among the motley band of people, marching down the centre of that illustrious street, carrying the very earliest banners of the CND. This was CND's pioneer days – when disdain and apathy was hugely apparent among the media and the public. It was the very first Aldermaston to London march, protesting the very real threat at that time of nuclear confrontation with the Soviet Union. It was a time when I was not living at my father's home, and I was truly shocked and moved to see him there in his declining years, struggling with his white walking stick and proudly displaying his first world war medals, pinned ridiculously askew on to his old tweed jacket. This was the moment the Campaign for Nuclear Disarmanent was perhaps truly born, and the first realisation to me that Walter Spradbery was a man not alone with his beliefs, not someone apart; showing perhaps the true meaning of patriotism with his fellow marchers. Lost amongst a Whitehall crowd of gawping bank holiday onlookers, it was the moment that tears filled my eyes and the gathering love and respect for my father for the first time in my life held no bounds. In that awesome historical landmark, with clergymen and other distinguished figures around him, an aura of Christ's children hung around and over him in that sunshine sky like no other day.

This book is fundamentally an account of an Englishman – a working-class Londoner's life and career spanning the late Victorian era to the aftermath of World War Two and some years beyond, when there might have been a glimpse of a better future! This against a background of existence where half-a-crown bought a meal and sustained another day. It also revealed a pattern of life contrasting with the world today. A life and environment at the time untouched by the supposed progress of the modern age: access to lift-off travel, telephonic communications and the needless and unwitting intrusion of such control of peoples' minds and bodies like never before.

Today in the obscene vulgarity of the relentless quest for monetary rewards and fame at all costs, Walter Spradbery would have been a man apart. In his own day, he led the humblest of lives with a clear vision of right and wrong. A vision and a destiny seemingly possessed by very few – and correspondingly only remembered by a very few!

The words conveyed here are predominantly those of the man himself, Walter Spradbery. The essence of his words are linked with those of his son, reflected upon some half a century later. My thoughts, comments and observations are a labour of love and belated appreciation for a father who must have had the highest hopes and expectations of me; expectations alas far beyond me. Nevertheless "Sprad" never wavered or fell short of his fatherly responsibilities towards me – and I owe him some delayed final acknowledgment regardless of the tie of blood.

This is a journal – a chronicle – of the life of a man who happened to be my father. He died on the last day of the year in 1969 and I was present in my late sister's home when life left him. In his last days, his final moments, his mind echoed names of distant colleagues and friends who themselves had left this world long before. I listened in bewilderment to the names that emerged from his dying lips. Medicinal drugs, which all his life he had fought against taking, had seemingly destroyed the last vestiges of the coherent thoughts of his most cherished memories. Even so in his expiring moments, he desperately wanted to hang on to the last moments of his life.

My previous images of him in hospital were not good; an eighty year old man clinging on to a hospital cot-bed like a demented child; undoubtedly the secondary effect of drugs injected into his weakened body as he lay helpless. Was this my father? Some time earlier he had been released from hospital to return to his derelict and deserted home, "The Wilderness", situated in the heartland of Epping Forest. Escorted by my sister Rima, he stumbled into the deserted house only to discover his most precious possession, an oil painting portrait of his everlasting love, his late wife Dorothy, had been stolen from the studio wall from which it had hung since the first days of their married lives together. For the very first time in his life my sister actually heard him speak harshly of another human being. And strangely thereafter, in the intervening days up to his eventual death, I never heard the name of my mother, Dorothy, cross his lips again.

Walter Ernest Spradbery was called by his closest and dearest friends "Walt", "Sprad" or just plain "Walter"; and then others – perhaps not so friendly because of his outspoken views on pacifism, his belief in the preciousness of life itself, his honesty, his values and vision far and beyond their own – called him a "fellow traveller", a "communist sympathiser" and in the simplest of slang "a conchie". Just as today, it is sadly deemed acceptable to patronize, ridicule or ignore the views of those to whom you are totally opposed. Throughout his life, to other human beings, even some relatives or adversaries whose conscience he touched or troubled, he was plainly looked upon as an uneasy figure to be drawn closely to!

However, Walter Spradbery, to a truly select band of artists, humanists and various men and women of exceptional and distinctive vocations of his day, proved someone intellectually gifted and easy to respond to. As his closest surviving descendant, I look upon him today, if patriotism has any real meaning and worth, as the most patriotic of countrymen. He was a lover and upholder of everything of English character in beauty and intellect, and in the minds of his closest and dearest friends and acquaintances, he must have been the most quintessential of Englishmen.

This is the story of his life, told in the main through extracts from a diary and a vast number of letters, amounting to thousands of hand-written pages that he wrote to a lifetime friend, James Berry, whom he met on the battlefields of the Somme in 1918. The diary of his earliest years must have been written in his very last days, before his sight finally deserted him.

Alone and bereft, with the imagined voice of his beloved Dorothy "singing in the Wilderness" in the last fading summers of the derelict surroundings of his home, "The Wilderness", a rambling cottage and a garden that had provided him with his sweetest and most enjoyable years of an extraordinary life. "The Wilderness" must have been an idyllic home to him of glorious summers and cold winters warmed by log fires, in the heart of what was once Queen Victoria's own forest land, historically left by her to the City of London for the people of that great city to enjoy as their very own.

In those woods, a cottage and garden that today have disappeared off the face of the earth – without trace. A place of legend, where music and song flourished and echoed in the treetops, as the menace of German warplanes droned overhead in the desperate years of World War Two. An oasis of almost mythological acquaintanceship for lovers of music and art at a time of grave and disturbing concern for a land in the throes of a European war where danger was never more real.

As his surviving son, I can only look back and wonder that it is only since his death that I am really able to appreciate the legacy that has been left to me to unravel and unfold. This is a testament to a man who led an existence apart from the greyness and hardship of the working class background he was born into and never lost sight of.

John Spradbery

Emily Feltham Spradbery and her son Walter, 1889

Chapter I

The Beginnings

1889

I, Walter Spradbery, like everyone else, was born naked and with a cry for help, dependent at once and forever on human charity and goodwill for my well-being; blessed by the mercy of Providence and the abundance of nature that had created me, and which down the ages has been made more serviceable to man, by human creative and constructive endeavour and inspiration....

It is officially recorded that I was born on the 29th of March 1889 at Dulwich, but I remember nothing of that place of early habitation and my earliest vague memories are of Hackney, an ugly and once Blitz stricken quarter called Amhurst Road where my parents wrestled with financial losses and increasing debts in a miserable Off Licence business to which they had descended from the once prosperous Hambro' Coffee House, Tavern and Hotel, 6 and 7 Water Lane, Tower Street – near the Customs House, London, where, as an old print I have tells me, my grandfather Joseph Spradbery respectfully informed gentlemen and families arriving from and passing to the continent that they would find every accommodation calculated to ensure their comfort and convenience on the most moderate terms and obtain information respecting Coaches and Steam Packets to all parts of the Kingdom....

My father, Joseph Spradbery, had been by his own description, a wine merchant of the City of London, but was nevertheless, a Free Liveryman of the Haberdasher's Company to which he had been bound apprentice, although I think he never dealt in Haberdashery at any time in his life.

My mother was the dominant personality, with no great faith in the powers of the government and the law, socialistic without knowing anything of Socialism, of deep and sincere ethical convictions, rebellious against fate, unbowed, lovely to look at, with the complexion of a girl that remained fresh and clear till her death at 86....

Her reactions to life were dramatic and temperamental. Adored by my father, she gave him an affection most deep for all the upheavals and storms that the violence of her emotions and dramatic intensity inflicted on him and her children....

During these years I attended church school, played street games with the local boys, made friends and grew up. My brothers had left home and much before this found refuge in the army, and the youngest of my two sisters was a "companion help". I was like an only child – made much of and living very much in my own thoughts and imagination. The elder sister was regarded by mother as a lost soul: we rarely saw her. Wild impetuous, clever, in youth she had gone on the stage, taken up palmistry, and somehow maintained herself in a questionable world of society....

My mother deserves a book to herself and it would be as long and complex as a Russian novel – full of tragi-comedy, passion and pathos, and the tangle of psychological problems, and practical problems equally full of difficulty. She loved me with intensity and possessiveness. She would have kept me from a world she distrusted, and she taught me at her knee, the noble and Victorian principles she believed in, and to read and write and simple arithmetic. She taught me to read from bible stories pointing to the words as I followed them....

In my earliest memories, amid poverty I had no fear of it, nor felt I its menace, but was the centre of my own world, only vaguely aware of my parents anxieties or disappointments – only dimly sensible of possible dangers that might beset me but alive to the love and affection which surrounded me, their youngest child, and comforted and content with it....

I think my first contact with the menaces that imperil life was when a half witted cousin led me into a back-yard filled with bottles, and breaking one deliberately cut my arm with it. It was incredible and shocking and stands out alone in a shadowy time. Years later I met another shock when first allowed out alone in a poor neighbourhood, when an urchin somewhat bigger and more aggressive suddenly snatched some coveted trifle I had from my hands, punching me hard and in the solar plexus leaving me gasping, dazed and faint and surprised both by his ferocity and ill-nature. Madness and envy were thus revealed to me....

In our little house in Walthamstow, we had of course as did everyone else, a front room or parlour; in this, with the mahogany bookcase and a circular convex mirror, remnants of more spacious days, was a fretwork-fronted piano, around which on occasions of family reunion we used to gather to sing popular and old fashioned airs....

My mother's tuition in music must have come to an end about the time she mastered "The Maiden's Prayer" and a few Quadrilles, but she had gone on playing from memory, and "by ear" ... and few days passed but she sat at the piano and expressed her more sentimental moods in song; and as I grew up I sang with her similarly. We enjoyed ourselves immensely and let ourselves go. It was an emotional background to life that rose to outbursts of intense feeling: what would not be said could be sung.

...When the family assembled, with a little pressing, everyone else gave voice to some song they deemed suitable to their age and sex. My elder brother, home on furlough (leave) would sing "Soldiers of the Queen" with unembarrassed vigour, and my sister, more apologetically gave us the traditional ballad, "She wheeled her Wheelbarrow through streets broad and narrow, crying Cockles and Mussels alive

alive oh".… But it was my mother who was the most moving artiste: her special songs were "Evangeline" (Longfellow) and "Jessie's Dream", or "The Relief of Lucknow" and I know we were all thrilled and touched by them, and that her singing and playing always had beauty and pathos, so that were I to hear it again now I should feel moved to tears and nostalgic emotion.… She looked lovely and the movement of her beautiful hands fascinated and delighted me – they were expressive. Many songs she sang had intimate associations and meaning for her that she impressed on my young mind.

A song called "The Reaper", for her, concerned a loved child that died in baby-hood; and most poignant of all was "The Bridge", it began: "I stood on the bridge at midnight when the clock was striking the hour, and the moon rose over the city, behind the old church tower" and went on: "my heart was hot and restless and my life seemed full of care, and the burden laid upon me seemed greater than I could bear". And it roused in her the memory of her anxiety and despair at the increasing financial difficulties and the rebellious waywardness of her eldest children, and recalled, to me, how she had hesitated when I was yet unborn, with the thoughts of suicide, upon London Bridge. "How often, oh how often" continued the song, "I had wished that the ebbing tide, Would carry me away on its bosom to the ocean wild and wide" and as she sang it our hearts were filled with grief and pity also – we floated on the tide of those emotions. Fortunately it went on: "But now it has fallen from me, 'tis buried in the sea, and only the sorrows of others cast their shadow over me", and finally: "the moon and its broken reflection and shadows shall appear as a symbol of love in heaven and its flickering image there" and so triumphantly we recovered with tears still in our eyes.

My father, for all his habitual humming, was rarely induced to sing, even on fes-tive occasions; but there were a group of songs that he had sung in earlier days and could be persuaded to try very occasionally. I remember the cover designs of these that portrayed side-whiskered singers in stirring attitudes. The words perhaps characterised his simple philosophy; one went – "Try to be happy and gay my boys, remember the world is wide, and Rome wasn't built in a day, my boys; so wait for the turn of the tide.…"

He was only 59 when, on the tide that there is no resisting, he slipped away, in the enveloping darkness of a London fog. My father died when I was sixteen. We had been with my mother to visit some, to me particularly grotesque, if not repul-sive old friends at Harlesden. They were an old couple, very decrepit: the old lady so palsied that most of the soup shook from her spoon on its way from the plate to the mouth, and he was usually somewhat dazed by the whisky she endeavoured unsuccessfully to keep him from.… On this last visit the maid had left them, got married in spite of their vigilance towards followers, and they were at the mercy of help from a domestic who did not sleep in. However when it was discovered at the time for leaving that a dense fog had descended in the district, it was decided my mother should stay, but my father, who had his work to do in the morning and I my art school to attend must attempt the journey home, so we set out on the long walk to the station. We had to almost feel our way, and when we had gone some distance my father surprised me by saying he felt frightened. I took on courage and reassured him that we were going forward alright, but a little later he suddenly groaned, lent against a fence and slipped to the ground breathing heavily. A wall of darkness, yellowed by the nearest street lamps surrounded us. I tried to loosen his collar and called out for help and one or two men came out of the fog in response, and a lady went off to call a doctor. She returned and the men lifted my father and carried him across the road to a surgery, where a doctor examined him and injected something with a syringe, but in a few moments came gravely up to me to tell me he was dead. To my own surprise dismay did not seize me, but a sudden feeling of responsibility and command – a knowledge that I must take hold of the situation and direct what was to be done. I felt as though a spirit had descended upon me....

My father's body was taken by the police to the mortuary and my good unknown friend, the man who had come out of the fog, accompanied me to the station and I set out for home alone. Money and the ticket for the journey had been given me. It was past midnight when I reached Walthamstow after a dreamlike journey on a wretched branch-line of the Great Eastern Railway, from Gospel Oak, and I went to my brother, who was then newly married, and lived nearby, and broke the news....

Many years later my mother told me that the man who had helped me when my father collapsed, wrote to her, offering, if circumstances were difficult, to adopt me, or, she hinted, to marry her possibly. But she destroyed the letter and never answered or showed it to anyone.

My sister Florrie inherited from my father his kindness and simplicity of disposition, his humble acceptance of life as it came, with a steadfast faith and hopeful optimism in the face of adversity.... I remember an occasion when I was invited to have tea with her at her employers' house, and how she prepared it in the garden, with gooseberries and custard and cakes and my heart rejoiced to find I had one so understanding and regardful for a sister. She had no social opportunities, my mother watched her lynx-eyed that she should meet no undesirable young men, and circumstances were not likely to produce any desirable ones from my mother's viewpoint either. Nevertheless a handsome and attractive young man had his eye on her, the buoyant Len Rix, who delivered the milk, and before my mother was quite aware how quickly true love works, he was taking her out to theatres and had a command of her heart and affection that he has never lost in all the vicissitudes that a lowly fortune and the raising of a large family bring....

...There was my brother Charlie's youthful and spirited adventures, which, at the time of the Acacia Road days, had gone so far as to lead him to join the Devon

Regiment, taken him to India and to the Boer War where he was besieged with Sir George White's forces in Ladysmith. My earliest recollection of him is at Hackney when he sprang over a fence from an adjoining backyard where a bonfire was burning and fireworks were being let off, with his face blackened and a shovel as a banjo – and I was somewhat alarmed by the apparition…. I vaguely remember him looking after us when we were all ill with influenza and bringing us up basins of bread and milk. And I have learned since that there was nothing else to bring in the house, nor money to buy other food, and he was desperately hungry himself. Then for a while he became a legend to me, and I pictured him as the "Absent Minded Beggar" of Caton Woodville's drawing and Kipling's verse and the pictures in the illustrated papers of the day were all associated in my mind with him….

Conditions, with employment by the Singers Sewing Machine Co, had improved, the outings and treats had become possible as I have told and we went to the seaside – the expanse of Great Yarmouth sands were disclosed to me – and the fishing boats, the pier. I remember troops going off from there, seeing them in the marketplace with bands playing and tearful and excited womenfolk running beside them and crowds cheering and singing "Oh it's Tommy Tommy Atkins, you're a good and hearty man, a credit to your country" and all the rest of it – and how I felt it was awful, and waves of pity and distress mingled with my excitement for the pictures of wounded men and horses and the awfulness of war were with me – and the stirring music of drums and bugles had a devilish sound. I thought I was a pacifist from that minute.

School Days

My schooling began at St Saviours Church School to which my mother submitted me after some dispute with the School Board Authorities; successfully delaying it until I was seven; I in examination having demonstrated the effectiveness of her own instruction for the earlier years. We paid 2 pence per week I think to distinguish us from ordinary board school boys. I entered my first class without misgiving and marked all my sums with a cross as I saw the boy next to me do, not knowing that as mine were right and his wrong, mine should have had an "R" written after the answer had been announced. For the second lesson a new master came in, of singularly prim appearance, dapper, with a bird-like countenance and a finicky way that always reminded me of a fowl pecking. Nevertheless I looked at him trustingly and heard him begin a lesson, when suddenly he called a boy to the front, told him to put his hand out and produced a nasty little thin cane and deliberately struck him a sharp blow on the extended hand with it. The boy yelled and tearfully retired to his seat. I fell into a fit of sobbing. The master came up to me, put an arm about me and began to explain that I should not be hurt for I was surely a good obedient boy. But I turned on him – of course he would not hurt me why should he – but he was cruel and wicked to hurt the other boy – that was why I was upset – at his deliberate hurting of any little boy. It impressed Mr Farmer, a most conscientious teacher who retained a distant friendly interest in me until his death long after I left school. My mother watched my schooling suspiciously and was a terror to the headmaster with the criticism and complaints she brought. Having no regard for attendances and their grant-earning value, she kept me away whenever I was a little unwell and took me out to the forest for healthy recreation – and this was often the subject of their dispute. I took full advantage of every opportunity. Mr W.A. Cox became headmaster of the school and choirmaster at the church. Choral singing was his whole delight and St Saviours became a singing school. "Sweet and Low" and "The Minstrel Boy" were songs we learnt to sing with modulated feeling and good tone. I hardly remember other lessons. Drawing and painting had a place on Friday afternoons and I was considered good – and at "composition" but my spelling was atrocious.

I read considerably – my "Chums" with the illustrations in brilliant penmanship by Paul Hardy and Gordon Browne and Marriot, Dickens and other works from my father's collection – including Shakespeare to which again I was attracted by the illustrations. Aesop's Fables in books for the bairns made me realise many a moral lesson made clear by its vivid parables.

Sport did not interest me – I could not be persuaded to take up cricket or football and once when the master who organised games put a football before me and bade me kick it hard, I lashed out vigorously, missed the ball and, overbalancing, sat on it. That so disgusted him that he never tried again.

I played imaginative games – "Redskins and Cowboys", "Robbers and Thieves" (with smoky colza oil lanterns) and a game where one rescued one's side by dashing through a ring of the other boys who kept them prisoners, in the playground at school. Iron hoops that bounced over the pavements either trundled with a skimmer or beaten with a stick were played by us all but I never see them now. Girls had wooden hoops. Leap Frog, Jimmy Knocker, and Hop Scotch were other street games.

I had a number of boy friends who lived in the road – Henry Wilkins, Bert Gore but my first hero-worshipped friend was Henri Baulard to whom I was attracted by his being half French, and a handsome well-dressed and set up lad. I remember he had leather gaiters which I felt were very distinctive and heroic-looking. When he first came to school and I observed him I determined to know him and make him a friend. I followed him and his younger brother and a group of boys on their way home to find out where he lived and to knock up acquaintance. They all had long willow canes they had cut themselves and challenged me as to why I had followed them. Amusing themselves by flicking me hard and often with the canes, which I bore smilingly. They hit me harder and I declared I liked it and so they continued until tired themselves – but I had made myself known and we became friends. I had a hard job to explain the weals on my back to my mother when I washed to the waist as was my habit before going to bed. I was allowed to ask Henri and his brother to tea on my birthday and he brought me my first birthday present from a friend. It was a book called "The Phantom Ship" by Marriot – one not in my father's collection, and to me it was the best of them all….

Sex matters were in those days treated like the Victorian bather; well covered up and made to look ugly, ridiculous and shameful. It was not touched on at school except furtively and suggestively by the boys. What one got to know was as likely as not to be perverting rather than illuminating. Certainly nothing clearly factual was disclosed. Some parents gave their children rabbits or guinea pigs to keep so that they might observe the ways of nature, but I only had a single rabbit for a short time and learnt nothing from that, except it was a nasty job to keep its hutch clean.

Older boys sometimes said lewd things which I did not understand but pretended I did. The growing body had not yet become restive with vague desires, later to become urgencies, perplexing, frightening, mysteriously vital, secretly exciting – but the world was disclosing its complexities, its hypocrisies and pretences, and its uncertainties. I began to realise that I was finding more wisdom and information in books than in the folks around me, and they seemed safer to consult….

Owing to my frequent absences (from school) under my mother's encourage-ment, matters became so strained with the Headmaster that my mother decided to remove me: and to find a better school. I was accepted for the Walthamstow Technical College under Dr Bridges, but what was being taught there was quite unintelligible to me. I arrived in a middle of a term; everyone else seemed to know what the strange signs of algebra meant but I foundered in everything except draw-ing, but even there became the butt of a master who fondled some boys but jeered at me because I showed I disliked that sort of approach. He also taught woodwork – and I was clumsy and completely unused to tools – so he amused himself by hit-ting my knuckles while I tried to plane. His friend the chemistry master took up an attitude of ridicule to me also and I became so miserable (for I was most anxious to succeed and justify the hard-earned money being spent upon me) that I became ill and delirious, after having added to my shortcomings by playing truant several days – again seeking refuge in the forest I had come to love.

My mother took the matter up with her customary vigour, and as a result the Chemistry and Art masters were sent down to our home to explain themselves and apologise. They came, tall-hatted in those days, very bold gentlemen, into the lower reaches of Walthamstow from the superior neighbourhood of Hoe Street but were humiliated in the first round by my mother, who, finding they impudently failed to remove their hats, reminded them she was accustomed to these observances. But it was clear I could not go back and that so far as Bernard Shaw put it in his own case, up to this point my education had been sadly interrupted by my school days. Then my mother heard of a new Upper Standard School as it was then called – The William Morris School and applied that I might enter there, and since I was coming on from the "Tech" no doubt the matter was not too difficult – anyway I was accepted.

There I at once began to learn happily and things opened out for me – confusions melted. Under the skilful guidance and humour of George Bubbers my class master, school became a joy and enlightenment spread apace. He made all clear – the class was alive with endeavour. I began to shine a little – my paraphrase was so good that it was read to the class for dictation. My drawings were displayed. I received prizes and I was encouraged to enter for a scholarship to the School of Art. I was getting on – indeed school-leaving time was not far off. The scholarship results were expected and one morning Mr J.C. Blake the Headmaster came in and after consultation with Mr Bubbers, called me out. "Good old Sprad" said someone "You've got a scholarship!" But this was the position explained to me: "The result of the Scholarship exam is not yet known. The one for one day per week for which you entered will be out tomorrow but there is a better scholarship for the evening classes for which you can sit being 14+ this evening if you like. You can't have both – will you sit for the evening one?"

For the moment I was nonplussed – but I looked at the kind faces of my instructors and said I would sit for the higher, better scholarship. I got it and so entered a career as artist on which my life has been built....

I am eternally grateful to George Bubbers – from him I learned of William Morris after whom the school was named and his artistic importance and purposes. And it gave me direction to my own. He is indescribable – his face always seemed about to break into an amused laugh and it often did – the eyes always twinkled – his mouth twitched with amusement. He understood boys and the sporting ones loved him as much as the studious – he had no dignity nor air of superiority and certainly no pretentions – he was a teacher by nature, a creator of interest who opened ways to information and recognized sincere effort – his explanations, illustrations were easy – like daylight.

His dress was undistinguished – would have been unremarked in a football crowd – probably his family thought him a little untidy – he would have made a grand Headmaster for a public school, but I don't think he ever was a headmaster – we just had the luck to have him for our very own in class 7b – and it made all the difference.

The Walthamstow School of Art

The School of Arts and Crafts was established in one of the fine old houses which remained in Walthamstow from more spacious days, architecturally interesting and picturesque, historic in having been a Court House with a grand staircase, noble hall and lofty panelled rooms, a notable entrance, decorated with carved swags said to be Grinling Gibbons, a magnolia in its garden and wisteria climbing upon its walls. No effort had been made to preserve it as it deserved and it is now a derelict ruin beyond repair. The headmaster was W.H. Milnes R.B.A. and its day students were in the main the daughters of the older and wealthier families who had artistic aspirations, and those who more seriously hoped to earn a living by art, teaching or design. The scholarship classes consisted of school boys of my age being given elementary training in a hopeful endeavour to spread knowledge and practice of arts among all levels of the community.... Large casts of the Venus de Milo, the Discobolus, the Gladiator and the Dancing Fawn were the impressive features of the Antique Room and a great number of casts of ornamental, classic and Gothic, made subject matter for elaborate studies in stumping chalk. There were a large number of excellent books on design including Owen Jones' Grammar of Ornament (an encyclopedic survey of design down the ages) and Meyer's Handbook of Ornament, a much consulted book of reference. Books by Lewis F. Day and Walter Crane supplemented these and Lilly Chridgely's Plantform and Design demonstrated the possibilities of conventionalising and twisting an infinite variety of plants into the ornamental forms favoured by those days and forgotten now.

W.H. Milnes was of aristocratic and dignified bearing and his presence always brought the light-hearted or frivolous to gravity. He was genuinely devoted to his work, an excellent teacher and imparter of his own knowledge; kind, appreciative while critical; the ladies admired him ardently and he was respected by all. He introduced me in my evening scholarship class to the principles of design and it was a very sound and illuminating introduction. His assistant, William Smith, carried on, and we all did homework, exhibited for the headmaster's criticism each week. I was enthralled and enthusiastic and my homework so far demonstrated my response, that in a few weeks my parents had been approached to see if I could not put in full-time attendance for art-training, day and evening. I was all for it, but my parents explained that they looked to me to earn money very soon – that to allow me even with a scholarship to spend a number of years in study was impossible. The headmaster was sympathetic and determined. He proposed I should become a student-teacher with a grant of £15 per year, and that was accepted to my joy, and so, at fifteen I began to teach the principles of design I was just acquiring to those a little less informed and ingenious. So successful was my first class of 16 students that we gained 9 first class and 7 second class certificates in the Board of Education

Early bookplates "Sprad" designed prior to 1914

Exam for Elementary Design in that first year, and I was very proud and happy, and the pleasant young ladies among whom my lot was now thrown congratulated me and smiled on my shy awkwardness. I began to collect the preliminary certificates myself – Model drawing, Geometry, Still Life (watercolours became my delight) and dozens more as time went on, and I laboured on the "Sheets", imperial size drawings for the Art Class Teachers and Art Masters certificate. And then as I have told, my father died.

Fifteen pounds a year did not seem enough to meet the situation now, with my father's earnings gone. I had supplemented this grant by doing black and white designs for the Painters & Decorators Magazine, and small as the return was, I was much encouraged with the publication of those designs and articles I wrote to accompany them. And I consulted adverts in 'The Studio" to find other ways of supplementing my income and did Christmas card designs for Lyons of Glasgow. I was attracted by a design from advertising correspondence courses – "Art, Fame and Fortune" it said and a design, largely a crib from the work of the French designer, Moucha, embellished the advert. I applied to enter the Commercial Studio in which these courses centred, but the pay offered me hardly covered my fares to town and lunches and the system of copying bits and pieces of other folks' designs which largely followed, disgusted me and the unsoundness and pretentiousness of the business convinced me I had taken a wrong step, and with a little new experience I returned to my Art School, which was shortly afterwards taken over from its private board of Governors and came under the County Council Education Authority. Mr Milne left for a new post in Coventry and offered me a post there but I was unwilling to go from the London area, and was offered a part-time assistant teacher's post under the new headmaster, (the assistant of my early days) William Smith, at a salary of £40 a year.

Melville Lambert of the Photochrome Co. was the first to appreciate my work and kept me steadily busy on designs for the title pages of new books, decorative pieces for the Girls' Own Paper and the special designs for his own Christmas cards which were schemed to display the range of his firm's printing cut. He had printed one or two designs for the London "Underground" and at his suggestion I submitted a design for a poster to Frank Pick. It was of Judges' Walk Hampstead, and I made studies for it in the pouring rain in the winter, but it portrayed a summer effect and bore the words "Take your place in the Sun". It was published in 1911. Lettering I had studied as part of my art training and a good grounding in classic Roman proved invaluable.

Following other posters for the Central London – "The Old House, Holborn" and "Marble Arch", I did a series resulting from a bold treatment of Epping Forest in Vermilion, Emerald and Ultramarine – flat colours – a series, the best of which were the ones for Burnham Beeches and Windsor. These established for me some reputation (although I did not realise it then).

> It was at the Art School that "Sprad's" path first crossed that of fellow artist, Haydn Mackey, a Chelsea artist on speaking terms with such writers as H.G. Wells and G.K. Chesterton, among other contemporary figures of the day. He came to take up a teaching appointment at the school, and an enduring friendship came to bear. Spradbery's life in fact embraced a number of unique and enduring friendships which illuminated his life perhaps like few other human beings....
>
> In 1937 Spradbery wrote a brief account of Mackey's life and achievements to the Editor of the Weekly Telegraph in the Hertfordshire village of Waltham Abbey in response to some slur he felt Mackey had been privy to:

"It is impossible to estimate the influence of his stimulating and provocative expression of ideas that has always made him such an inspiring teacher, both in the classes he has conducted at various times and places, and in those chance contacts of life that have caused a circle of the most intelligent folks about to gather around him for the pleasures of discussion and to listen to his widely informed and spirited discourse, everywhere he has moved, but that it has added something of value to a great many folk's vision and experience is certain.

My own friendship with him began at the Walthamstow School of Arts and Crafts to which he came as a teacher about 1906 or 1907, and students from those

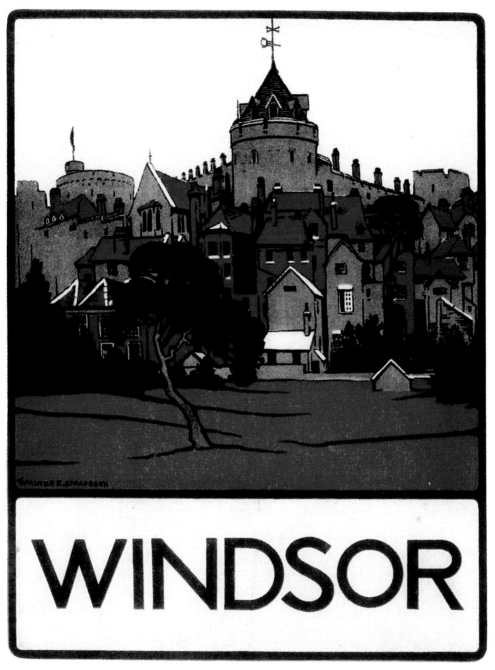

Early poster designs by Walter Spradbery published in 1913

far off days and that defunct institution (it closed during the war) will remember him as the vitalising spirit of the place, and those who have since achieved a measure of success (such as the brilliant young sculptor, H. Wilson Parker A.R.C.A., who designed the most original and delightful of the new coins) still feel gratitude for his early instruction and the clearing and freeing of the mind that his challenging and critical methods begot".

> Walter Spradbery's subsequent years at the Walthamstow Art School and until the outbreak of the First World War – the war to end all wars – appear to be the least documented. His life at that time was dominated by a possessive and in extreme circumstances an hysterical mother; friendships (one imagines) difficult to maintain. It seems that after his father's death, Walter's mother, Emily Spradbery, drove her other sons and daughters to lead lives farther apart from her.
>
> During these crucial years leading up to his volunteering as a medical orderly in 1914 in the R.A.M.C., it is easy to conceive he formed some warm, loyal and powerful friendships. Besides Haydn Mackey, such names as Harold Parker and W.G. Hills must have emerged in those years. W.N. Edwards and his family, and a Schwab and his wife Mary are referred to in later years; he felt a particular attachment to these friends. Subsequently, in the early twenties, one senses it is Mary with whom he had wished for a deeper relationship!
>
> His early professional life – frustrated, tormented and possibly driven at times to despair by both his mother's dependence upon him and the inextricable ties of a mother and son relationship – was beset with the jealousies of her passionate and possessive love, which inhibited his artistic progress. Haydn Mackey always jokingly referred to "Sprad's" one weakness as in the drawing of the human form, because of his mother's insistence that he should never be exposed to the temptation of the thrills and delights of the bodily flesh!
>
> It is conceivable that the passages of "Sprad's" following on from here were some of the last words he ever wrote. I have to imagine that the earlier extracts of his childhood and schooldays were an attempt in his very last months to record something of his mother, father and family before his own life expired under the strains of a debilitating cancer. Spradbery never drank; I had always imagined him to be a teetotaller, but as far as I can remember, he enjoyed the odd cigarette throughout his life.

My home life had become more and more difficult owing to my mother's outbursts of passionate temper – that made her ill and me distracted. We had moved from Acacia Road not long after my father's death, to a similar but rather better situated house at the Wood Street end of Walthamstow (36 Turner Road). My brother (Charlie) had transferred to the Woodford postal district and gone to live there. I chose the house because it was near friends who became very dear to me and help-ful in my troubles. My mother (who distrusted and disliked all my friends) agreed to it because it was more pleasant and near the forest.

The school life and home life should be described, for on the one hand paths unfolded and led out into the world and the possibilities of the creative career of an artist, and on the other held me by a sense of eternal vital responsibilities, which grew rather than lessened with the years – an enthralment that I tried at times to escape but which was too sacred a tie ever to be broken – the inescapable yet often torturing love twixt mother and son. A silver living thread that could only be sev-ered by death....

Dear Harold,

   Enclosed you will find a few poor verses which
I sent to a Woodford Rag. and which they have
been good enough to publish.

    They have left out one verse - the 17th.
It runs

  And we who train at Thetford
  Parade on Barnham Hill
  And prod coarse sacks with bayonets
  To gain the skill to kill
  To disembowel and mutilate
  men, who are brothers still.

Hope you got the photographs safely - and
account of the ending of the whisker do.
I'm too tired to write more now.
I'm looking after another pneumonia
case.

      Yours

       Spratt.

This is the original letter sent to fellow artist, Harold Wilson Parker, somewhere in Egypt in the year 1916, very much confirming authorship of the poem, "The Ballad of Barnham Common" which appears here.

Chapter 2

The Great War

1914–1918

Quoted here is an extraordinary poem written by Private Walter Spradbery possibly in the year 1915 while training as a medical orderly of the Royal Army Medical Corps (RAMC) at Barnham, Thetford, Norfolk. Unpublished and unseen until this day! What is so curious and revelationary to me, his surviving son in the year 2009, is that I am only now aware of this poem's existence. In my mind it has similarities with the First World War's most poignantly remembered poem, "In Flanders Fields", attributed to have been written around the same period of time. "In Flanders Fields" was written by a serving Canadian Military Officer and doctor, John McCrae. It was a poem of just three verses long. "The Ballad of Barnham Common" is somewhat longer, of twenty verses. As far as I can gather, it was written and sent to his fellow artist friend, Harold Wilson Parker, serving somewhere in Egypt. It was written by Spradbery at a time when stationed in the English provincial locality of Thetford, training and treating many wounded soldiers with horrific injuries returning from the frontline in France.

THE BALLAD OF BARNHAM COMMON

"Eyes Have They, But See Not"

The flowers that grow on Barnham's plain
Are beautiful to see;
The bugloss and the speedwell's blue
Fair as a summer's sea,
Blue as a summer's sky are they
As a child's eyes may be:

And the tender little pansy's
Uplifted cherub face,
With golden eye, and purple wings
And unpretentious grace,
Peeps shyly from amid the grass
In every shady place.

But wearily we drag our feet
Over the jewelled sods,
And discipline, it weighs us down
With the curse of an iron rod;
And 'iron rods' we carry
To kill the sons of God.

The cranebill's starry floweret
Is scattered o'er the plain;
Its pale magenta blossoms
We trample in our pain,
And dully long for peace, and love
And our dear homes again.

With iron heels we tread them down,
We tread them in the sand;
We crush their beauty 'neath our feet
Too tired to understand
The ugly ruthless thing we do.
Now war is on the land.

The golden gorse, across the heath
Is a mass of yellow flame;
Its unconsuming fires praise
The Sun God's glorious name.
But war it burns things black and dead,
And fills men's hearts with shame.

And scarlet is the pimpernel
And bright the poppy's red
But brighter still is the blood we'll spill
Ere we ourselves are dead:
No flower so rich, in the deep dug ditch,
As the blood our guns may shed.

The grass is worn with the ceaseless tread
Of our marching to and fro,
And where we drill on the mossy hill
Great bare patches show;
For 'neath the heel of the War God's foot
No fair thing may grow.

But time revenges the patient weak
Whom the Ruthless crush and kill,
And delicate things that droop and die,
Like the flowers on the grassy hill,
Will bloom again on another plain
Fairer and sweeter still.

The barren stretch of Flander's plains
Is desolate and bare,
And the shriek of shell, and stench and smell
Float on the morning air
And splintered stumps are all that speak
Of what once blossomed there.

Yet the flowers our feet have trodden down
Will be born again,
And rich and fine, on Flander's fields,
Will dance in the gentle rain
Will dance on the dead that feed their roots
The countless, ghastly slain.

The little flowers we've trodden down
Will scent each ugly grave,
Will hide the ghastly torn limbs
O the coward and the brave
And gaily smile at the morning sun,
O'er the foolish and the knave.

Oh, the river runs o'er Barnham's plains
This where our horses drink –
And a thousand fair and charming things
Blossom on its brink.
But we have trod them in the mud
Nor paused to praise or think.

The pinkish purple loose-strife
Bows on the river's edge,
Forget-me-not and orchards,
The flowering rush and sedge
While briar rose and bryony
Entangle in the hedge.

And crowsfoot gleams on the river,
Like snowflakes in the sun
And sways in the moving waters
That over the pebbles run.
But we cannot pause for such a thing,
Who're crossing the stream with a gun.

But the rivers which flow in Flanders
Are rivers of blood me thinks
And will, one day, colour the roses
Whose roots from that soil drink,
And a thousand flowers will blossom
Where a corpse now rots and stinks.

And we who train at Thetford
Parade on Barnham Hill
And prod coarse sack with bayonets
To gain the skill to kill
To disembowel and mutilate
Men who are brothers still.

While all around is beauty
And overhead the sky,
Where fleecy clouds in freedom float
Over the men that die;
And nature laughs at our folly
As we pass her treasures by.

With a garland of peaceful beauty
She tempts us to lay down our arms;
With a myriad of fearless blossoms
She mocks at our childish alarms,
With a tangle of wonderful flowerets
She seeks to ensnare us with charms.
Oh, he who sees God in a daisy,
Can see more clearly in man,
The light of the Glorious Eternal
That through all Living Things ran,
When the wheels of time first started,
And the Song of Life began.

W.E. Spradbery

Walter Spradbery's first commanding officer while serving with the R.A.M.C. in World War One was a Lt. Colonel Josiah Oldfield. This first extract of his experiences serving in the R.A.M.C. in World War One is drawn from a tribute he wrote to Oldfield after hearing of his death in the Caribbean in 1952, almost forty years later. It is one of very few instances that he ever felt compelled to recall with his own pen; evidence of his own participation in that most horrendous and devastating episode in our military history. Spradbery and his artist colleague Haydn Mackey both served under Josiah Oldfield as lowly ranked privates. Even so, in later years Spradbery was remembered as a friend. Spradbery's life was filled with a string of remarkable friendships! Many of the friendships survived to these friends' dying days, as a last note from Josiah Oldfield before his death recalls. The epitaph to Oldfield includes vivid memories of serving under his command while billeted in the country's provincial region surrounding the borough of Peterborough. Similar extracts, describing this very period of tour of duty in and around Peterborough, appeared in a booklet published by the Central Library of the city in 1992, a booklet entitled "Posh Folk" edited by a Mary Liquorice, which included a sketch drawn by Spradbery in 1915. Diaries written by "Sprad" at that time were discovered in the library's archives when, miraculously, a copy reached me!

This typical tribute to Josiah Oldfield introduces various extracts from different sources which reveal much of Spradbery's military service in that awesome episode of military history. The whole fabric of Spradbery's subsequent life may have been provoked by reasons of admiration for his fellow comrades or perhaps disdain for others who have doubted his beliefs and perhaps even his honesty....

Private Walter Spradbery RAMC

The Early Years of the Great War

This has to be where the reality of Walter Ernest Spradbery's remarkable life began, shown through his own words – which I have come to realise are as vividly brought to life by his pen, as his paintings by the brushwork and his perception of the landscape and environment around him as an artist.

Walter Spradbery was my father. He brought me into the world via the love of my mother, an artist of equally talented abundance as a singer and musician of extraordinary ingenuity, vivacity and energy. Without his presence and guiding hand I cannot believe, for better or worse, I would have survived as I did. I owe him this story.

It is an amazing tale of paradox, humility, courage and tenacity in every walk of life that Walter Spradbery – "Sprad" – pursued. In some instances I witnessed it. It was also an existence where remarkable friends emerged and deeds transpired that eventually, in my most senior years, inspired this book.

I suppose the impact of life itself and his own future only began to emerge for him from the day he and his artist friend, Hadyn Mackey, voluntarily enlisted in the 3rd East Anglian Field Ambulance Regiment on the 14th September 1914, at the outbreak of the Great War – "the war to end all wars". Walter was always a dedicated pacifist, and Mackey a man very sympathetic to his views. It was the common belief that the vowed pacifist would not take up arms under any circumstances, however Mackey had always maintained if his nearest and dearest were in danger, he would defend them with whatever weapon was available. These unsaid thoughts must have applied to "Sprad" as well, as I do recall in my earliest childhood discovering a heavy hammer under my parents' bed when my father believed my mother was in peril from a gang of unnamed criminals; this threat coming over the telephone in the middle of a fearful night, in our secluded cottage in the heart of Epping Forest!

Spradbery's life from the moment of his enlistment in 1914 remained on a course uninfluenced by any necessity for war or violence, the forces of commercialism or anything else that diverted his life away from peace, honesty and the fellowship of man, as laid down in the teachings of Jesus Christ and the other great prophets and messiahs of history. Highly principled thoughts, words and actions which forever revealed themselves in perhaps the most crucial moments of his life of which there were many!

These early days of his – in uniform and wearing the emblem of the Red Cross are expressed through a unique appraisal of his first commanding officer, Lt Colonel Josiah Oldfield, a man of legendary status, who himself became a fondly-remembered friend. Also through some extraordinary surviving diaries from a tour of duty in Britain, recording the daily experiences of a private serviceman in the English country provinces at that time.

Lt. Colonel Josiah Oldfield

Josiah Oldfield, As I Saw Him

"Happy and grateful memories of Dr Josiah Oldfield clamour in me for expression – lit with the morning light of youth and friendships that have endured since then, and scenes peaceful and lovely through which we passed as a threshold to World War One.

When at Walthamstow in Sept 1914 I enlisted (with, as I have already told, humanitarian intentions and convictions) in the R.A.M.C. I did not know or guess that I was privileged or lucky enough to have as Commanding Officer of the 2/3rd East Anglian Field Ambulance, which I joined, a unique personality who would contrive to give unexpected educational value and fill with memorable episodes the first year of my "training": nor, when I first saw the spritely figure and sparkling eye of the (even then) white-bearded Lt Colonel, did I know the puckish wit and character of the man, or that he was already famous as a vegetarian and advocate of fruitarian diet, nor of his varied high academic distinctions, his originality and provocative intelligence; nor guess what an uproarious time lay ahead in his recruiting campaign and in his handling of men and interpretation of Army Regulations.

But he soon made it plain; for never surely did the army have as commanding officer of a unit one so certain to shock and disturb the habits, convictions and traditions of "old sweats" in the ranks, or "Blimps" among the officers, or, for that matter, in this special field, the orthodox Army doctors: nor one so adroitly able to handle them and transform to surprising use and amusement occasions which regulations designed to be physically exhausting and tedious, to toughen and break us in. He did not hide his light under a bushel; it twinkled, winked and flashed incessantly, radiating, by his intent, "good deeds in a naughty world", and puzzling those without understanding. This was not at first evident, although by the prestige of his name and by advertising the professions of some of the men in his unit he gathered others distinguished in science and the arts, and vegetarians whom he proposed to specially cater for; and so we became a company of mixed views and varied intelligence, always able to make our own entertainment and entertain the officers. Some of my best friends, now even more distinguished, were met thus.

Our first move from the Drill Hall in Walthamstow was to Burghley House, near Stamford, where we encountered bitter winter weather, billeted in the stone-built stables and granary of this famous mansion, seat of the Marquis of Exeter.

Clever as Colonel Oldfield proved on many occasions at getting concessions, privileges and benefits from those in a position to confer them, we did not see much of the inside of Burghley House, although at least once we attended a service in the private chapel there. But to me and my artist friends Stamford itself, with its many fine old churches, picturesque inns and buildings was an unforgettable delight, and we found generous hospitality there and a friend in Mr Traylin, the town architect, who gave us freely from his intimate knowledge of its antiquarian and historic features. When, some months later, we marched to Peterboro' (where we found home-comforts and much fun billetted in other people's homes) Mr Traylin marched with us, and discoursed on the notable places passed on the way – particularly on the fine old sixteen-arched bridge at Wansford – in England and the lovely little Norman church at Castor, I remember.

Colonel Josiah Oldfield continued these informative experiences for us by arranging route marches from Peterboro' (itself of course a city with a splendid cathedral which we had good opportunities to study) to the many outlying towns and villages in which were historic churches and buildings of note. He would write beforehand to each vicar stating the date we should come (so orderly room authority told me) and saying – "A.N. Bulmer F.R.C.O. an organist in my unit will, if it is agreeable to you, give an organ recital in the church; the band will play on the village green while an exhibition of stretcher-drill takes place, if you would tell us something about your fine old church and the surroundings and the ladies care to provide weak, sweet milky tea for my men we shall all be most grateful". In this way, not without protest at being "Fred Karno's circus" and the singing of songs, about "he gave us an apple and an onion to do a route march on" from the more "old soldierly" we saw a great deal of the rich architectural heritage of this countryside – Barnak with its Saxon Tower and "the hills and holes" quarries: from which comes that enduring Barnak rag, of which so many early English cathedrals and churches (and Burghley House itself) are largely built – the great Crowland Abbey rising, a dramatic ruin, in a flat expanse, and the three-way bridge – Stilton and the Bell Inn, Northborough with the great barn with a Gothic entrance arch through it, leading to a fine house in which Cromwell's daughter once lived, we were told – Woodcroft Castle (moated) near Glinton, Thornby Abbey and wonderful Tichencote with its great, richly decorated Norman arch: we got scraps of information and local stories about them all, and I, of course, sketched at every opportunity, and gathered impressions vital to this day.

Once the band, which had been formed before Lt. Colonel Oldfield took command of the unit, rebelled when a visit to Yaxley had been arranged and although its members were on parade for the march they came without their instruments (citing some regulation to support their action) so that the promised playing on the village green could not take place. The instruments having been put in store remained there a week or so at the end of which it was found that Oldfield had enlisted a whole Salvation Army band and their bandmaster, Sgt Sansom, and with this new band we marched again to Yaxley and it played on the village green till dusk. When we started the long march back to Peterboro' the rebellious old band complained bitterly and jeered from the rear ranks. However the new bandsmen were musicians with a more extensive repertoire and they restored the tired spirits and amused the disgruntled by playing with merrily appropriate feeling a popular song of the day – "I'm afraid to go home in the Dark".

On these marches Lt Col Oldfield headed the column mounted on an excellent horse and would often "beat time" to the songs sung during "marching at ease", particularly if they had a derisive intent.

Every morning, at Peterboro', he would ride on to the market square where we were lined up for C.O.'s inspection, with great dash, to the admiration of the lady friends invited to see the parade, and pulling up sharp I recall us all brought smartly to attention. The officers (who were often doctors recently come from mostly medical practice) had to endure conducting the parades under his eye and corrections – "Wrong order Capt. R…" he would cry to the exasperated officer and the amused ranks.

At Peterboro' he established a Vegetarian Officers Mess and Quarters at 2, Deans Court, opposite the cathedral, with a lady as vegetarian cook and housekeeper and squads of men did orderly duties there – a fortnight at a time, living on vegetarian diet the while. It was known familiarly as "The Cabbage Patch" and the housekeeper as "Mrs Wiggs".

There, at the Lt Colonel's suggestion, two exhibitions of my landscapes, and local sketches and my friend Haydn Mackey's portrait and figure studies (including a portrait of Josiah Oldfield in uniform and one of his daughter, then a child) were arranged and many local notabilities attended a private view and I have a note recording that the wife of the Suffrican Bishop of Leicester bought two watercolours and invited me to supper at their fine old house in the precincts where I felt very awkward among a distinguished company of officers and clergy.

These things were accomplished in addition to our R.A.M.C. duties, lectures and parades and he allowed no one to escape humble or dirty jobs. He taught and practised an austerity and economy that to many was somewhat appalling at times, and he put the talents and special abilities of men under his command to uses he conceived as helpful and useful to the unit and its work – and his own. I did designs for programmes, notices, diagrams and decorations of many kinds for him and he took a fatherly pride in the talents of those he so used. He would exclaim at a distinguished botanist cleaning the steps of 2, Dean Court – remarkable. He was imperturbable – but there are too many stories to tell here. I remember when a young ex-carpenter was doing some adjustment of fittings in the Orderly Room, he accidentally struck a nail through a concealed pipe and a spurt of water shot across the room. "Is that arterial or venous bleeding, Private Benson?" the Colonel enquired in the tone of an R.A.M.C. lecturer, and Benson replied as readily, "Arterial Sir – straight from the main". I think he had a Gilbertian desire to make the punishment fit the crime. When after we had spent a field day in Milton Park (he not personally being there) and complaints were received that the place had been left with lunch wrappings etc. he sent the N.C.O.s to clear it, since, he told them it should have been their duty to see the men were not untidy in their behaviour. For those with ambition, promotion was by the way of a long period of "more responsibility, but no extra pay", as a Lance Corporal.

Soon after our arrival in Peterboro' he invited any who had complaints to make about the feeding at our previous station to come to the Office and state them. Our comrades looked to me and my friend Mackey to do so. We did – I being detailed in my comments. He thanked us after a careful hearing at which the criticised Quartermaster was present and put questions.

Within an hour or so I was recalled to the Office and told by Josiah that 14 men (contacts with a "spotted fever" case and under observation) were to go to the Isolation Hospital at North Bank, Peterboro' Common and that I was to undertake the catering and cooking for them and the Corporal in charge, and could demonstrate my idea of good feeding, being allowed the regulation 1 shilling and 9 pence per day per man.

It proved ample in those days and as I was an experienced cook and shopper, having looked after an invalid mother for some years, I made a good job of it and won recommendation from those I fed -and was able to return 16/- to funds, with a record of my menus. Oldfield never forgot overtaking me on my way back to the hospital with a sack full of food I had purchased in town, when he was on his way in

Members of the 36th East Anglian Field Ambulance Regiment

a car to visit us. He inspected when he got there, the boiled rabbits and onion sauce I had cooking – and commended the onions. He recalled the occasion several times in letters to me – for indeed we kept in touch by intermittent correspondence over the years – the last I received being in a slightly shaky hand from Jamaica in the spring of 1952 – he wrote (knowing I couldn't) "Come and join me in the sun or the shade of the mango tree and eat the sweet potato". When Gandhi (with whom he had shared rooms in student days) was in England last, he invited me to a luncheon whereat they both spoke with wit and wisdom. It was a memorable occasion. Josiah Oldfield's personal interest and helpful human regard for conscientiousness and any high endeavour for the general good was evident at every encounter. His whimsicality and friendly yet malicious touches were all stimulating: for kindness was with the mocking laughter in his eyes. It is not, I hope, an unhappy thought that he exasperated a great many commonplace people and bewildered more – intelligence, vision, wit and high endeavour often do that.

It was a strengthening experience to find among men in uniform, so humane and mystical a thinker, one who had taken honours in theology, a Doctor of Civil Law, a Harley Street specialist, a pacifist, a jester with a sense of timing, a spartan who could double round in the early morning outpacing the best of the young men, and who as a health and diet expert in longevity has surpassed so many. Let all who knew him salute the memory".

> In contrast to earlier more whimsical recollections from "Sprad's" days in the Peterborough area some horrific extracts from his original diaries are subsequently included, when days were occupied nursing and tending wounded soldiers at the East Anglian 1st Eastern Hospital, with over 2,000 beds and his R.A.M.C. unit serving under a new commanding officer....

The 1st Eastern Hospital has over 2,000 beds and usually has about 1,500 cases in. Mostly wounded from France. The majority of wounds are shrapnel. Each ward is divided into A and B side – there are 60 beds in a ward, 30-a-side. The wards are open to the air – one side having no wall, only sun and rain blinds to let down in case of severe weather. The patients, considering the frightful nature of most wounds are very cheerful.

The number of men who had lost an arm or leg was appalling. My duties consisted of helping the nurses with dressings, bandaging, applying fomentations, and sanitary duties. Bathing and washing those unable to look after themselves and feeding those unable to feed themselves....

The first dressing at which I assisted was a chap named Wells, who had had his leg amputated at the knee and whose Femoral Artery had become septic. It had therefore been found necessary to make an incision in the thigh about 10in long, to tie off the artery – the wound was very unhealthy and smelt unpleasant. When I first saw the wounds uncovered I thought I should have to leave the bedside and I broke into a cold perspiration but by "sticking it" I eventually came round alright and was able to go all down the ward – lending a hand in dressing wounds even worse without again feeling queer....

The second evening Wells' artery burst again and I, with a nurse directing, applied the tourniquet which stopped the bleeding. After he had been again tied off higher up, he was usually dressed under an anaesthetic. He was improving when I came off duty but had been on the danger list most of the time I was there....

Fizpatrick was another patient who I helped to dress, he was wounded in the left hand, had the greater part of his right shoulder blown away: a wound in the back and slight wounds in the feet. He was unable to feed himself – hardly able to move. Nevertheless he was very jolly and liked as well as any man in the ward. He had been a tramdriver in Walthamstow before the war. He gave me some vivid descriptions of life in France.

After he was wounded he spent about 12 hours in a trench some little distance from the firing trenches. Bombs designed to destroy the trenches were constantly bursting near them. His wounds were undressed – a comrade had merely bandaged his shoulder (which was bleeding profusely) outside his overcoat. When the R.A.M.C. arrived he was told he must walk to the nearest Dressing Station – 2 miles off. It was a frightful walk: part of the time he was blind from loss of blood – however he was likely to die unless he was attended to, so in agony he did the journey. At the Dressing Station he received the scantiest of attention and was put into an ambulance wagon which dashed off under fire, jolting horribly – the journey was the most awful part of his experience, he said. He was taken to a hospital at Boulogne where he was treated for some time – later he was put on a Hospital Ship and sent to England – Cambridge. All spoke of the comfort of the hospital ships with enthusiasm. There was about an inch of bone blown right out of the top of the humerus. A metal plate had been affixed at the Boulogne hospital, but this came away splintering the bone still more – while dressing the wound one day a piece of bone came away with the screw marks on it, where the plate had been attached....

There were several Scotchmen in the ward – one called Jock (as all were) had had his leg amputated near the hip. He used to turn up the stump to gaze at the progress of the end, in a most comical manner. He also had a wounded arm. He was always in excellent spirits....

I worked under Nurse Wilson and Sister Harrison in No. 18B ward, Mackey worked 18A. There were two Voluntary Aid Detachment ladies who washed bandages, arranged flowers and assisted generally with light work....

While we were at Cambridge on Hospital Duty, the 2/3rd East Anglian Ambulance removed to camp at Thetford. Barman Cross Camp. While we were away also some trouble occurred between Lt Colonel J. Oldfield and the A.D.M.S. Col Challis – in connection with the local Red Cross Hospital at Thetford, I believe. Anyway at this time the old boy (J.O.) decided that he would not go on Foreign Service under Challis. No sooner was his decision made known than he was shifted to the Home Service unit at Norwich and Col Rudyard was appointed in his place. When we came back (we were forgotten for some days till our Corporal wrote for cash to carry on, or passes for our return) we found Colonel Rudyard in command....

We slept 8 in a tent as a rule, but at first 12 in a tent had been the order. Being at Cambridge we escaped the muddle of moving and the early crowding in tents.... Soon after Colonel Rudyard took command Sgt. Major Waring became the real manager and director of the corp – only interfered with occasionally by Lts Robins and Linfield.... We first came under our new Colonel's notice when a Brigade Order was issued commanding that all the tents should be disguised from hostile Air Craft by painting the white canvas. We were then called up to disguise the transport tents, which stood apart from the rest, as an experiment. Our efforts were judged to be very successful as the tents were almost invisible at a short distance. However a scheme of bedaubing the tents with red and green in the meantime had been devised by the Brigade Office and we were ordered to treat our tents in the same way. We did the whole of our camp, tents, marquees etc wagon covers too ... later kitchens and latrines were bedaubed also....

In the town of Thetford the V.A.D. ran a little hospital at the "Cannons" and squads of men were sent down to do the greater part (and more unpleasant part) of the work there. These orderlies slept in a great barn, similar to the granary at Burghley. The job was not popular with most of the chaps who resented being under the command of girls with less training in hospital work than themselves....

From this alternating period of provincial tour of duty, of innocent route marches, billeting among civilians and assisting with the appalling wounds of returning casualties from France; accepting military orders without any recourse to disobeying or questioning them, there came what must have seemed from the most unexpected quarter a refusal to comply with the most routine of orders within the traditional framework of military command. To me, upon reflection in subsequent years after "Sprad's" death, it now emerges as something of breathtakingly monumental consequence, an incident at the time hidden from the public arena.

To reveal it – and later its ironic outcome with all its moral implications to the outside world – would or could have been of some embarrassment. It has struck me as something with such reverberations, that I can only conclude it has been almost deliberately hidden from public scrutiny or from public debate. A matter of such embarrassment to our glorious military tradition, its standing and bearing, thereby forcing the military command to reverse a major military order – possibly unprecedented in military history. The subsequent events that later emerged in the field of battle surrounding the figures of Private Walter Spradbery and Private Haydn Mackey amongst others – laid bare some of the myths of both the combatant as well as the noncombatant soldiers of that era.

It is just possible every human being – every living creature – has some defining moment in their lifespan. How that is personally and physically handled is a decision and moment that lives with us and guides us through the rest of our lives; this, within the limitations and capability of our intellect, our philosophic beliefs, our will, our human spirit and the visionary powers imposed upon us by some deeper sense of destiny and a belief in what is right and wrong.

Such a testing and crucial moment came upon "Sprad" in his earliest innocent years as a young voluntary medical orderly serving in Britain's imperialist army as an avowed non-combatant serviceman, proudly displaying his red cross insignia on the arm of his khaki uniform, an emblem symbolising to him everything contrary to the meanness of violence, of killing, destruction, destroying and taking away man's most precious possession, life itself. This was the code of morality his path had chosen from his earliest schooldays.

When the army's military command gave the order to remove the red cross insignia from their uniforms, as straightforwardly as ordering their men to paint their tents red and blue or whatever other colour, they must have assumed nothing more about it. What seemingly transpired from at least 300 men within their section of non-armed forces was a refusal to comply: they objected to a military decision not only to remove the red cross symbol from the international status of the serviceman as a saver of life, a personal symbol, but rather without any further ado to return them to the ranks of the fighting and combatant soldier, opposing the very beliefs which their whole lives were dedicated towards.

The sole account of this extraordinary episode in Private Walter Spradbery's own remarkable stand against a military order at the height of Britain's most nationalistic period of military history is revealed here in his own words (the basis of an article published in the Peace News in 1952). With the prevailing climate of antipathy, harsh treatment and summary retribution handed out to anyone suspected of acting against the country's patriotism or war-like tendencies, it must, on reflection, be imagined that both Spradbery and his great friend Haydn Mackey's lives were in grave danger; possibly saved by the final intervention of David Lloyd George. Inexplicably, the actual dates of this incident, in the accounts revealed by Spradbery himself are not given. However from the dates recorded from "Sprad's" earlier diaries, the incident and the ensuing outcome must have occurred in the earliest days of 1917.

In the widest political context of civil disobedience, from the viewpoint of the military establishment such a rebellion must have proved an unexpected and embarrassing act of disobedience. Something that has probably never before or since happened in His or Her Majesty's forces, culminating in the reversal of a military command of such moral significance at a highly charged period of patriotic jingoism.

The R.A.M.C. and the Red Cross Badge

by Walter Spradbery – As published in the Peace News 1952

Recently, travelling on the Underground, I found myself in a compartment with a group of young men wearing the khaki uniform, hat badge and shoulder flashes of the Royal Army Medical Corps, but noticed with a shock that none of them wore on their sleeves the familiar red cross embroidered on a white ground within a black circle, which, when I served in this corps in the 1914-18 war, was a distinguishing feature: and I wondered why this once essential emblem was not on the uniform now.

I remembered that when an effort was made during the progress of that war to transfer me – and large numbers of others – to combatant regiments (to which I objected on conscientious grounds having volunteered in 1914 for the R.A.M.C., believing its service to be humanitarian to all injured, friend or foe, in the field), the final stage of my contest with Authority had significant reference to that symbol.

While at Newport, Isle of Wight, in the custody of the Warwicks (to which regiment we R.A.M.C. men had been conveyed) I refused to take down the Red Cross symbols (as I was ordered to do by the O.C., Warwicks) on the ground it was an international symbol and a religious one overriding in significance and authority the Royal arms on my buttons: and at that time no one dared or cared to forcibly cut them off it seemed – nor should I have worn the coat if they had.

As a conscientious objector, serving in my own way on the home and battle front I met a great deal of sympathetic understanding and many confessions from officers and men in combatant services that secretly they agreed with my pacifist principles although they had committed themselves to the folly of bloody conflict and war and saw no way for themselves to withdraw from it.

At this Isle of Wight station where many of the objectors to this transference were confined to camp and put to duties such as an R.A.M.C. man might reasonably be ordered to do, the effort to wear down our objections was gentle, although of course it must not be forgotten that we had called attention to ourselves publicly through the kind offices of T. Edmund Harvey MP in the House of Commons and the evangelist Dr Clifford in press and pulpit and even George Bernard Shaw had

33

sent me a reassuring postcard. Moreover an O.C. had been punished for the vicious treatment of an objector, and a promise of "sympathetic consideration" had been extracted in the House from the Minister of War – to which things I called the O.C. Warwick's attention at our first interview. I claimed that we were entitled at least to a Tribunal before any attempt at enforced transference could be given, even an appearance of justice under the existing law (not that I was prepared to accept any judgement other than my own conscience) and something of this sort did ultimately take place after our return to the R.A.M.C. depot months later.

The Isle of Wight is a lovely place and somehow I and other artists with me managed to make quite a number of sketches (some of which I have to this day) while officially confined there. Having refused to clean bayonets or in any way touch arms, there was little for us to do except weed the paths about the camp, and a number of not unpleasant orderly duties which took us with the necessary passes, into the quaint old town of Newport on occasion.

But the O.C. Warwicks went on leave and as a departing manoeuvre put on orders that all men transferred still wearing the red cross badges must take them down forthwith – leaving his younger subordinates to deal with any difficulties that might arise.

Most of the party, assured by the good treatment we had met, complied, but I felt it was a point of honour to keep the international flag flying as it were.

With my friend Haydn Mackey (who protestingly declared with the malice of a friend, that I had always had a flair for advertisement – a reference to my early poster successes – and wanted to make a martyr of myself but that he would not let me do it alone) we kept ours up.

A young officer, wearing a D.C.M. won in the ranks, who ordered our arrest and detention in the Guard Room, took us aside privately into an empty hut to say with emotion, that he wanted to tell us that actually he admired our stand. He had seen war at close quarters and considered it madness, but he had committed himself and could not escape the dilemma. He must carry out orders and regulations and confine us to the Guard Room – but he wished us luck.

In further evidence of my flair for advertisement I feel I should say here that my life-long friend Haydn Mackey was with me a year or so later, with other friends, in an exploit in France on the Somme for which I was awarded the D.C.M. for bringing in (with their help) wounded under machine gun and sniper fire. I have used it often to advertise that one can act as a pacifist and humanitarian even on the field of battle. Mackey got the M.M.

In the Guard Room at Newport, Isle of Wight, we met goodwill too: extra food was piled on our plates and our cigarettes – formally taken away – were informally returned; and the Adjutant Quartermaster of the camp, an elderly officer of fatherly geniality came to see us, saying that he disliked knowing intelligent men were in such a place and would we dig potatoes for the Regimental Store, under the eye of an old corporal gardener who "had seen long service in India" and was "a charming fellow".

Well, we felt it harmless enough and spent some agreeable sunny days on this, until a week or so later we were called to the orderly room and shown a huge pile of papers relating to our case, including we were told, one from Lloyd George himself. The sum total was that Mackey and myself were officially returned to the R.A.M.C. depot in Blackpool.

Our arrival affected the depot Sergeant Major so as to give him an appearance of threatened apoplexy. But he was still further surprised when some 300 more men who had been transferred under protest and some who had not protested came back a month or so later.

The point of all these (to me) delightful reminiscences is that the Red Cross badge had significance and effect then. It was recognised, it seemed as a symbol above national sovereignty and patriotism – to which one might appeal.

Is that why it is no longer on every R.A.M.C. man's arm, I wonder!

"Sprad" and "Mac" spent a period of military confinement when it seems questions were asked in the "House" and support was forthcoming from such a figure as George Bernard Shaw (Spradbery himself mentions a personal telegram from him) and he also comments on the batch of official documentation and correspondence shown him; all this evidence has seemingly disappeared. One wonders perhaps what influential friends or acquaintances Mackey himself had? He was known to and mixed with such eminent literary figures as H.G. Wells and G.K Chesterton. Whether such influences and contact helped in their release from detention on the Isle of Wight is certainly a point of conjecture. However, what one must be aware of was, at that time of imperial military history, young men serving under the British military command were shot for less.

The Distinguished Conduct Medal

Private Walter Spradbery mentions being returned to a service depot in Blackpool after he and Mackey's sojourn in Newport, IOW. Subsequently in an extraordinary letter "Sprad" felt compelled to write to a mysterious correspondent, an A.L. Barker or Barber, who lived in some close proximity to Westminster at 66 Victoria Street, London, S.W.1. (was this a nom de plume for some well-known parliamentary figure of the day?). Spradbery revealed perhaps as never before or since certain instances in his frontline service on the Somme to defend whatever aspersions this correspondent had previously alluded to.

This draft account of certain instances of his frontline experience in France is all I am aware he ever personally revealed to anybody. This is the citation from the London Gazette dated 16th January 1919: "For conspicuous gallantry and devotion to duty near the village of Mametz on 26th August, 1918. He accompanied an officer when rescuing one officer and three men of an infantry battalion under very heavy machine gun fire. One of the party was killed, two were wounded and two other men got bullets through their clothing. Notwithstanding this he, with his squad, after bringing in the first party of wounded, returned under heavy machine gun fire and brought in a N.C.O., who was wounded."

These are Spradbery's words from the original draft of a letter to a so-called A.L. Barker or Barber. The letter is undated and somewhat more detailed and revealing than the actual citation!

"When you tell me that you were unaware that I had served overseas during the War you make it almost impossible for me to resist the temptation to start yarning to you. One can hope for no other adventures to compare with those that were crowded into that time, nor to see humanity more intimately with all the humour, pathos and camaraderie that such conditions bring out. I think the gods must walk abroad in such scenes of desolation and bear rare gifts to those who retain their spirit and love their kind in the face of death. Certainly the emotions are lifted above their ordinary level, and the friends and comrades of those days have the glamour of unforgettable characters, rich in their variety, quality and flavour as it were, yet unmistakably brothers, other selves: for when fate is in such uproarious mood our kinship, our mutual likeness, weakness, hopefulness is very evident. I wish the spirit, mutual support, helpfulness and willing self-sacrifice of those days could have continued into peace times: but I suppose all men conceived themselves as playing something of a hero's part then and were, in consequence, lifted above the level of their ordinary behaviour. They forget their capacity and strength now too often – they're not so keen on the fair sharing of rations even. But one forgets they did not all learn the lessons of the field. Doubtless it was only the most gener-ous who were there.

Of course I served with the R.A.M.C. and was engaged with men on humani-tarian labours. Perhaps for us it was a little different to others: the consciousness that we were fighting no one but circumstances that had embroiled masses of men in wild carnage, with powers of destruction beyond their own comprehension, and amid the general madness were arresting and lessening the results of the folly, was sustaining; and the gladness of easing and comforting good fellows who were the victims of chance and their sense of duty, and packing them off home or to the base was intensely satisfying.

Although I joined the R.A.M.C. in 1914 as the only civilised thing one could do in such a catastrophe (and to my mind a service much more likely to preserve some remnant of what in essence is civilisation than any organised violence was likely to do) I had conscientious objections to combatant service – not to mention conscientious objections to inoculation, vaccination and other scientific superstitions – and so fought one or two little wars on my own or with a small group of friends, with authorities who had some idea that they had men's bodies and souls entirely in their control. They were victorious wars for me and those who stood with me and full of humorous situations that are sheer delight to recall.

Eventually we got to France (as we wanted to do when we enlisted) after three years on a variety of duties in home hospitals and training camps, and a period of some months spent very merrily at the Isle of Wight when futile efforts were made to force us into combatant service, and in the R.A.M.C. well in the line with the 13th Division and the 36th Field Ambulance from the later end of 1917 till the Armistice.

At Mametz for bringing in wounded and taking out a party of my friends to bring in wounded from No-mans land (in a spot where Mametz had once stood) I was awarded the D.C.M. and my pals M.M.s – it was a second journey....

> The handwriting of "Sprad's" at this crucial point in his story is ironically difficult to decipher, however it goes on...

It was a second journey out into the vacated remnants of old trenches for some of us – the first journey being with an officer who lost his bearings on the way back, when our sergeant was seriously wounded and a friend named Jeremiah Higginbottom killed as he (already wounded) was indicating that he would not go on ahead to safety till we got our stretcher case down. Having an eye for tree shapes, I knew where we had to make for by four grotesque stumps of trees that were some distance behind our Aid Post, and so instead of wandering back into the German lines as the officer was about to do, I was able to indicate the way we had to go. The officer asked me if I'd go out again with a party to bring in our own sergeant and any other wounded officers and of course we readily did. Among the squad of bearers was another artist who enlisted with me and was with me throughout my army career. We were a well known pair, familiarly known as "Mac and Sprad". His name was Haydn R. Mackey. My other friends were Jim Berry, a man of splendid worth in any situation, and young Hedges....

> Hedges is a comrade of that time whose name is all I have any record of (mentioned in that particular incident). However the comrade, Jim Berry, and Walter Spradbery's subsequent correspondence to him over the next fifty years of his life is the inspiration and driving force behind this documented account of

Numb. 31128.

FIFTH SUPPLEMENT
TO
The London Gazette.

Of TUESDAY, the 14th of JANUARY, 1919.

Published by Authority.

The Gazette is registered at the General Post Office for transmission by Inland Post as a newspaper. The postage rate to places within the United Kingdom, for each copy, is one halfpenny for the first 6 ozs., and an additional halfpenny for each subsequent 6 ozs. or part thereof. For places abroad the rate is a halfpenny for every 2 ounces, except in the case of Canada, to which the Canadian Magazine Postage rate applies.

THURSDAY, 16 JANUARY, 1919.

War Office,
16th January, 1919.

His Majesty the KING has been graciously pleased to approve of the award of the Distinguished Conduct Medal to the undermentioned Warrant Officers, Non-Commissioned Officers, and Men for gallantry and distinguished service in the Field :—

120082 Pte. W. E. Spradbery 36th Fd. Amb., R.A.M.C. (Walthamstow).

For conspicuous gallantry and devotion to duty near Mametz on 26th August, 1918. He accompanied an officer when rescuing one officer and three men of an infantry battalion under very heavy machine-gun fire. One of the party was killed, two were wounded and two other men got bullets through their clothing. Notwithstanding this he, with his squad, after bringing in the first party of wounded, returned under heavy machine-gun fire and brought in a N.C.O., who was wounded.

The London Gazette notice of Distinguished Conduct Medal awarded to Walter Spradbery, 16 January 1919.

David Berry, Jim Berry's son, took this photo of Jeremiah Higginbottom's official war grave in France on a journey of discovery with his wife, Elaine. David Berry has since passed away. Jeremiah Higginbottom's body might very well have been lost with the millions of victims needlessly slaughtered in a war drawn out to a meaningless conclusion. That his fellow comrades brought his body back to be buried in a recognizable grave, under the most dire and desperate of circumstances, has meant that he now lies in a hallowed burial ground, as an acknowledged hero. Today - recalling this incident - I have heard of plans to locate the missing bodies of millions of fallen soldiers of that futile war nearly a century onwards and relocate them to new official war graves. It would seem something both impossible and ridiculous to undertake and even to comprehend after such a long period of time. I suspect that Privates James Berry, Haydn Mackey and Water Spradbery were very much responsible for bringing their dead comrade back to behind the comparative security of their own lines, rather than leave his corpse to be another of the estimated twenty million dead, whose bodies have never been located, remembered and mourned by the masses of the bereaved, right up to this very day.

my father's life which I have tried to put together (not only to enlighten posterity about someone who all his life carried a torch for humanity and his fellowmen, but for my own personal satisfaction and belief in someone I should have supported more assiduously in his lifetime).

James Berry when "Sprad" first met him on the Somme in France was just three years younger than himself. Walter Spradbery was 28 years old then. Berry must have appeared to "Sprad" a deeply motivated young man from humble Yorkshire stock; and he was to have the most profound intellectual and spiritual effect on Spradbery's whole being after meeting up with him under those atrocious circumstances of war. Notwithstanding his long friendship with Haydn Mackey and other such friends, he must have felt a companionship and kinship as never before. Their similar beliefs and socialist ideals were such strong binding factors which must have embraced Spradbery in thoughts of brotherly love and friendship like something he had not previously experienced.

One has to imagine that it was through the impact and consequences of the war, supposedly to end all wars, that "Sprad's" ensuing life unfolded in the inevitable way it did. James Berry himself became "Sprad's" most cherished post-war friend and it is in the ensuing pages through his own written thoughts and words that perhaps the relevance and persistence of Spradbery's life is truly revealed.

Higginbottom's tragic death beside both Spradbery and Berry, has recently emerged in the most poignant manner. In the course of assembling this chronicle of "Sprad's" existence at that time, remarkably, a letter has been passed on to me, almost a century onwards! Strangely or not, it is the only letter written by Jim Berry himself that I quote from in this odyssey of my father's life!

It provides further evidence of a life-saving mission which possibly caused as much controversy in its awards for bravery as the mission itself. There is no doubt that "Sprad" was awarded the Distinguished Conduct Medal and Mackey the Military Medal, but according to accounts recorded and exhibited some years ago in Walthamstow's Vestry House Museum, this particular mission resulted in as many as ten separate awards and recommendations for bravery. "Sprad" always thought Jim Berry should have received some recognition himself.

This is the letter James Berry wrote at the time to the brother of Jerry Higginbottom killed by their side on the day of 26th August 1918.

Dear Mr Higginbottom (August 1918)

No doubt by the time you receive this letter you will have heard officially the sad news regarding your brother Jerry.

I take this privilege of writing to you to express the deepest sympathy of his comrades and to give you some details of the affair.

Jerry was a good comrade and well respected by all of us. We were very sorry indeed to lose him. He met his death while performing one of the bravest acts and he died bravely. The wounded were lying out within a short distance of enemy machine guns and Jerry and seven other men lead by our colonel and bearer sergeant went out to bring them in. It was when returning with the wounded men that he was wounded in the cheek but in spite of this he remained with the squad he was working with. Shortly afterwards he was struck by a second bullet and was killed instantly. We brought him away and he was buried behind the lines. His valuables we sent to our headquarters to be forwarded to you.

Jerry received a parcel of cigarettes a few days before and ten packets of them were left. We thought it was hardly worth sending them to you so we shared them amongst the squads he was working with.

I found a photograph in his haversack and with your kind permission I should like to keep it so that we can get a reproduction of it so that each of us can have one. If you desire the photograph to be returned I shall be pleased to send it.

In conclusion let me express our deepest sympathy once again.

I remain yours truly…

James Berry

The letter was read out to a congregation of people in Nantwich on the 11th November 2008, 90 years afterwards, by Jim Berry's daughter-in-law, to an audience which listened in deep silence. As already mentioned, Jim Berry was a young man in his early twenties when he wrote that poignant letter.

This correspondence to a disbeliever of my father's military service includes the only descriptive words I have ever seen or heard from my father regarding this frontline incident – mission – escapade which resulted in his award for valour. It was someone, Mackey or Jim Berry, who mentioned to me at some time after Spradbery's death that his award was late in being announced through the channels that such awards do come through. They themselves believed he was to be awarded the highest possible medal, the Victoria Cross. Whether he was to be considered for such a higher award or not, it must be remembered he was known as a pacifist, and months previously had hugely embarrassed the military authorities with his stand against the removal of his red cross insignia.

Australians have always figured prominently in my own life, and one of the finest, who gave me my earliest encouragement in life was a great post-war boys' club leader, Bernard Faithfull Davies who befriended "Sprad" in later years when both were well known figures within the country's National Association of Boys' Clubs. At my father's funeral wake F.D., as he was commonly known, came up to me and whispered: "John, your father was the bravest man I ever knew – I never knew of any other man who went 'over the top' willingly a second time". I don't think I had ever wept tears of sadness before, other than when my mother died almost 20 years previously. In the conventional look or sense of a hero, my father never conveyed such an impression to me, although I was forever aware of his strength of character and altruistic nature. What astonished me at the time was how F.D. knew anything at all of my father's service in those extraordinary years....

Spradbery's letter continues:

I should like – if your time and mine allow – to tell you how, when in training, an adjutant who was training himself to be a disciplinarian (and making the unit most miserable) insisted on us all growing moustaches under Kings Regulation No 1696. We found that there was a clause in the regulation (since it dated from old volunteer days I suppose) allowing the growth of side whiskers, and how by growing them we led him to exceed his powers and made a great joke of him to the delight of a whole camp and many of his fellow officers. Eventually the order enforcing moustaches was out of Kings Regulation – and good soldiers may now be quite clean shaved.

Perhaps the most delightful evidence of the mentality of a certain type of staff officer is this. Five years of soldiering never taught me to salute correctly, with every will to be polite; and to the end I was as likely to salute a Warrant Officer in mistake for the higher ranks as not. More often I forgot to salute at all, and was advised "to keep my eyes skinned".

While at the depot at Blackpool a very important staff officer entered the vestibule of the Winter Gardens accompanied by a suite of lesser brass hats, just as I was coming out. I had some idea the vestibule might be considered a place of entertainment and therefore not one in which one need click the heels and swing the right hand to the level of the top of the ear, an inch from the right eye. So, I looked at the group with interest and a pleasant smile (I hope) but nothing more. Swiftly a dapper little officer, in plaid trousers, sprang towards me: my impression was that he was quivering with suppressed emotion all down the legs of these plaids: they vibrated as did his voice, when in a shrill crescendo he cried, "Hasn't GOD GIVEN YOU HANDS". This unexpected question left me looking flabbergasted at the end of my wrists to make sure I suppose and I said, "Yes it seems so" – "THEN WHY DON'T YOU SALUTE!" he screamed.

The idea of God giving an artist hands to salute with, struck me as the best blasphemy I'd heard in the army, but suppressing, until I got outside, my uproarious laughter, I managed to explain what my impression was as to the regulations in the matter of places of entertainment. I did the action more or less in the approved manner. Fortunately no Red-cap (Military Policeman) was standing by, or, in view of the importance of the old dodderer I'd failed to honour I should have been on the carpet at my Company orderly room. No doubt I assure you the officer was very serious and had no glimmer of humour about him: he meant it.

I am enclosing in the hope that they may interest you a few photographs of the watercolours painted for the Imperial War Museum from notes made while serving in France (got arrested in mistake for a spy when sketching once!) perhaps you'll let me have them back later – and forgive me playing the old soldier.

The letter continued – on a fragmented page:

But I cannot outline a fraction of our field adventures which were after all much the same as those experienced by thousands of others. I was a victim of mustard gas at Senlis (in France) and had my eyes under a shade and lost my voice for a fortnight but, on my request, did not leave my unit as I felt very sure the effects were going to prove very temporary as they did.

It often seemed strange after a nightmare night of bombardment that the sun rose in glory, that exquisite wild flowers still bloomed in the broken ground and swallows wheeled under the eaves of ruined cottages – nature persisted in being lovely wherever she had a chance – and only ambitious man seemed too damned silly to deserve her forgiveness and persistence. What lovely villages they were where we went out on rest, and how unbelievably complete and hell-like was the devastation of the Somme district when we crossed it for the last time following up the German retreat – and then into the long occupied area where things were a little more comfortable again and we billetted in deserted cottages in which were the remains of civilised comforts hastily left. I remember finding a copy of the Yellow Book in one partly demolished house, and lying on a mattress reading a Max Beerbohm essay and trying to explain to some scandalised Tommies the true beauty and appeal of the nude in art when they found in the same place a number of art journals. But hospital experience in the early days was full of strange satisfactions too and days of training were not all boredom and waste of time but had some merry episodes....

Although as one of Walter Spradbery's two children, in my case, reaching almost his own length of life, it seems that the breadth of life and the experience it brings passes so rapidly. In earlier years I really had no notion or thoughts of writing or compiling anything of Walter Spradbery's past existence; so I suppose there must have been some intuitive foresight on my own part (essentially living a nomadic life in the precarious career of a thespian) that brought me to hang on to remnants of my father's past: that I can pull out old suitcases from under beds crammed with "Sprad's" written words reaching back to almost a 100 years ago.

After all to the outside world today (apart from a minority of surviving local folk in the Epping Forest and surrounding areas) he seemingly remains a generally forgotten and enigmatic figure. Although surprisingly perhaps, in such a conservative parish of Buckhurst Hill where the local community association still magnificently flourishes in a local pre-war manorlike building of imposing presence – and a present-day community spirit still exists – Walter Spradbery's name is still remembered; along with (allowing for some prejudice) that of another local man, Eric Southwell, a dedicated member of the Communist Party who co- founded the association with him.

Returning to "The Great War": much of Spradbery's later thoughts and revelations are coloured and influenced by the horrors and incidents which confronted him as a working class young man, an artist and certainly someone of a visionary perception in those gruesomely remembered years of 1914 to 1918.

The story of the Red Cross in the pacifist newspaper "Peace News" in the fifties and the letter "Sprad" felt compelled to write to an unknown fellow to justify his honesty, integrity and the genuineness of his thoughts and beliefs are, as far as I am aware, the only words he ever outwardly expressed graphically on his war service in France to anyone, in what has been acknowledged as one of the most futile, wasteful and horrendous of sustained military campaigns ever experienced by the human body and human spirit. Millions of young men (mostly working class) tragically never survived. Walter Spradbery and such friends as Haydn Mackey were, perhaps by some godlike will, fortunate to come through such an ordeal and pursue their careers with some distinction as artists and teachers – "Sprad" himself forever seeking a quest for a more peaceful and sane world.

The only other direct source I ever discovered that really related back to those extraordinary and shocking years is a tribute in later years: "Sprad" felt impelled to write to a local newspaper in the outlying township of Waltham Abbey, in the process pointing out his friend Mackey's standing as an artist and a human being! This was something 'Mac" deserved, after Spradbery felt his friend had suffered some ignominy in his local press.

However it is sufficient, perhaps, to say that we enlisted in the R.A.M.C. for humanitarian reasons, in September 1914; by good luck and ingenuity remained together throughout the war; maintained our principles and kept our sanity through that dangerous and difficult time, emerged safely at the end, and, after the armistice was signed, made many pictorial records of what we had seen for the Medical History of the War, and the Imperial War Museum.

In moments of respite from stretcher-bearing and amid the discomforts, dirt and "danger of the line" and in the "rest stations" not far behind it, Haydn Mackey made many remarkable portraits and pictures, some of which were unfortunately soon after destroyed by shell fire, but those that survived are now in the Imperial War Museum, to which he presented them.

> In some other source somewhere, I discovered "Mac and Sprad" were forever trundling an old handcart around which carried their sketches, paints and brushes. This was at one time hit by an enemy shell. I briefly continue Spradbery's own words on his pal written some 20 years later....

At the time these (paintings) were made he was not an official war artist holding special rank and privileges, but serving as a private in the 36th Field Ambulance and taking part in their work in the last great offensive of the War.

He was awarded the Military Medal for his part in rescuing wounded under machine gun and sniper's fire and I had the honour to be with him then and in other situations of extreme danger when his humour and philosophy were as inspiriting as his courage and unselfishness.

And amid the mud, the horrors and all the weariness of trench and dug-out life, joyous interminable arguments went on, the circle was as certain to form at every opportunity, there as elsewhere.

> As armistice was declared "Sprad's" immediate thoughts were towards his mother. I can imagine him instantly composing the actual letter which somehow has remained in my possession from 90 years ago. A letter of such poignancy – of such feeling for the living and for those dead....
>
> Reproduced here is the very letter Private Walter Spradbery wrote home and posted hastily to his mother. Obviously in such haste and joy, that he mistakenly dated the letter (a date to be one of the most memorable in history) a month earlier – a month lost in the melee of war. ...
>
> Such true and heartfelt words, worthy of Shakespeare, Tennyson or Wordsworth.

France,
11th Oct. 1918.

Dear Mater,

Hostilies ceased on all fronts
at 11 a.m. today.

Oh happy mothers. happy.
sweethearts, happy wives, whose
loved ones will come safely back. —
I see you all laughter and tears,
all joy and inexpressable relief — all
hope all eager with anticipation
and emotion — and those lone
souls who have lost their very own;
to-day is too unkind to them — how
can they face our joy?

Thoughts that lie too deep
for tears, thankfulness that is
inarticulate fill all hearts — "Peace
on Earth, Goodwill towards men"
— an unseen choir sings it in our
breasts — prompting men to
evolve a better world more
worthy of our ideals and
aspirations. Let us begin.

Your loving Son
Walter

Original letter written by Walter Spradbery on Armistice Day 1918

Chapter 3

Post World War One

The Imperial War Museum and a Medical History of World War One

After armistice was declared, both Walter Spradbery and Haydn Mackey were seemingly drafted into duties in setting up an Army Medical Section for the Imperial War Museum. A year before leaving the army, they jointly committed themselves to helping towards establishing the first Army Medical Section of the country's Imperial War Museum situated then at Crystal Palace.

Still in uniform, Privates Mackey and Spradbery were the leading and crucial working figures of a team of artists assembling their own graphic experiences for the original painted records of Britain's first museum of war! This, possibly before the corpses of the Great War had been respectfully and properly buried. Never could the Ministry of War or the powers administrating the Imperial War Museum have been so blesssed with artists such as these – straight from the front of war – serving their interests in developing a new section to their museum. Serving stretcher-bearers who had woken up in the trenches in France to hear with unimaginable relief of an armistice to all living men on the 11th November 1918.

As ordinary serving working class men escaping from the immediate horror of their particular locality of war, the bigger picture of war all over Europe and the disastrous loss of life and unimaginable destruction may not have immediately struck home to them. Nevertheless, as artists, their vocation and situation in the immediate aftermath of such a war must have been unique. In the eyes of the authorities, military or otherwise, they lived its reality and had applied their hand and eye to expressing its terrible consequences with their art. A war that tragically has been repeated a number of times since with few if any lessons having been learnt.

It is in fact not difficult to conjecture, some huge part of a century later, inspired by "Mac and Sprad's" very antics with brush and canvas in the fields of France – that this might conceivably have provoked the Museum's whole original concept of such an art section!! In fact, whenever did the post of "War Commis-sioned Artists" ever officially exist? A point we might just think about.

These are "Sprad's" further words from his letter to The Editor of Waltham Abbey's local Telegraph:

Haydn Mackey spent a year before demobilisation executing several large pictures from the sketches and notes he had made in France, and these formed a very notable part of the R.A.M.C. section of the Imperial War Museum, and when that was first opened to the public at the Crystal Palace, the "Manchester Guardian" singled his work out as "being a most powerful and truthful portrayal of the conditions of modern war, eloquent in persuasion against a recurrence of such things."

Spradbery himself contributed over 90 watercolours to the Museum's original collection; a number are still retained today. How many of Haydn Mackey's colossal oil paintings remain in the Museum's archives I do not know.

Here a letter of recommendation only recently discovered, hidden amongst other endless papers left to me some time after my father's death. It was written by the artist, Gilbert Rogers, who was appointed to be the first Officer in Charge of the Imperial War Museum's Army Medical Section.

Recently I was shown around the archives of the remarkable Wellcome Institute beneath the rumbling traffic of London's Euston Road, where the huge archives collected by Henry Wellcome are held. Some of both Mackey and Spradbery's sketches from the First World War frontline can be found there. Also those of fellow artist and subsequent colleague and friend who served in the R.A.M.C at the same time – Austin Osman Spare – a trio of artists to breathe fire and brimstone into the fullest debate of every conceivable eruption and matter of art that was then setting out to transform the whole perspective and shape of art, perhaps like at no other time.

Spradbery's glowing praise of Haydn Mackey's stature as an artist foreshadows many of "Sprad's" other worthy acclamations throughout his life: of such artist figures as one of his earliest students, the unassuming Edith Lister (one of Joseph Lister's nieces), the post-second world war water colourist Dennis Flanders who also emerged from Spradbery's own art classes, Eddy Rix – a young flyer killed in the early days of World War II – to the monumental figures in his life of Sir Frank Brangwyn, a decorative artist whose great gift of art in 1935 to the Borough of Walthamstow was so remarkable at the time, but has since been treated with utter contempt. He also savoured his friendship with the great art nouveau figure of Arthur Heygate Mackmurdo. Throughout his life Spradbery lectured on William Morris, Brangwyn, William Blake and others. Even on the suffragette Sylvia Pankhurst who was not unknown to him.

Morris's great motto "Fellowship is life" was part of his own philosophy. Friendship, love of fellow man, and loyalty to concepts and ideas of creative

IMPERIAL WAR MUSEUM,
Crystal Palace,
S.E.,19.

1st June 1920.

Mr. WALTER E. SPRADBERY, D.C.M.

Mr Spradbery has worked under me for the past two years in preparing the Artistic side of the Medical Section of this Museum and I have the greatest pleasure in testifying to his high artistic ability and enthusiasm.

Mr. Spradbery's work can be seen at any time in the Museum, but is due to him that a tribute should be paid to him for the conditions under which it was produced. Almost the whole of his exhibit, consisting of nearly one hundred pictures of historical importance, was done after the Armistice was signed but before demobilisation, Mr Spradbery willingly deferring his demobilisation to put the whole of his ability and keeness at the disposal of the Museum.

I am unable to speak directly of Mr. Spradbery's abilities as a Teacher of Art subjects, but, as a Teacher of fifteen years experience, I may be permitted to remark that he possesses in no small degree those qualities of patience, perseverence, enthusiasm and the ability to create enthusiasm in others which I consider the most essential characteristics a Teacher can have.

Should Mr. Spradbery at any time desire to apply for a post as executive Artist or Teacher of Art I have the very greatest pleasure in saying that whoever shall receive his services may rely absolutely on faithful and loyal performance of all duties which may be entrusted to him

Gilbert Rogers

Officer in Charge,
Army Medical Section,
Imperial War Museum.

Walter Spradbery watercolours – Buire-sur-Corbie, August 1918

This is a photograph of James Berry taken in 1931, aged 38 years. From 1929 until
1931 he was Chairman of Earby Council in Yorkshire

issues were the essential ingredients of his life. His subsequent remarkable and enduring friendship with a James Berry whom he met while serving on the battlefields in France is the prime focus of this literary journey through Spradbery's truly moving and remarkable life. It is here that Walter Spradbery's actual correspondence to James Berry now becomes the essence of such a journal as this sets out to be. This original correspondence, placed in my hands only a few years ago by Berry's daughter-in-law, Elaine Berry, is to my mind the pivotal force of what is intended to be as full and as accurate an account of Walter Spradbery's life as possible. A man whose ambitions and motivation for living were never more than providing himself with a means to live creatively and happily and certainly with a woman he loved with a passion of joyfulness above all else. In the very existence of this unimaginable happiness he also built up a devoted following of friends, who were themselves exceptional human beings from many exceptional walks of life. This has to be something of an extraordinary odyssey – particularly as penniless hardship was never far away.

Jim Berry made the most profound impression upon "Sprad" as becomes, only too apparent in a correspondence which went on for a lifetime, despite deep personal tragedies in James Berry's own subsequent family life in the north of England. Talk of man's friendship for man and this surely epitomises that ideal.

Berry himself was a deeply moral man and a socialist with possible political ambitions. I have understood that as a young man he met James Keir Hardie and was deeply affected by him. Walter undoubtedly saw him as a future political figure. That Berry never realised his political objectives and ambitions was because of the personal tragedies in his own home.

"Sprad", by his own beliefs and moral sense of duty, lived his life simply and honestly to the end. He possessed a moral conscience beyond the normal reach of other men; he walked and lived on a plateau unobtainable to such average human souls as myself who perhaps look for more selfish and tempting solutions.

My Dear Jim . . .

Walter Spradbery's earliest letters to James Berry are the prelude to a remarkable correspondence he might have subconsciously imagined could well be
saved for posterity! Berry obviously made the profoundest impression upon my
father as a fellow comrade. A romantic attachment of minds, a sense of extraordinary masculine brotherhood. They met under the most arduous and trying
of conditions imposed upon young men – and held together, through their
corresponding pens, a bond of deep spirited friendship of never-ending faith,
loyalty and brotherly love verging upon the depths of romantic fiction. Up until
this point and later, women seemingly had little substance in his life, although they
were not without presence, notably his own mater! Reading this mass of letters,
held on to by Berry, and miraculously ending up in my hands three quarters of a
century later, I cannot help but feel there was a subconscious deliberation that
one day they might be revealed to a wider readership!

Not only does ''Sprad'' reveal the passions of friendship, but shows himself in
no small measure as a chronicler of his time. His talented dedication as an artist
was only one abiding aspect of his life; his cause to peace and fellowship among
his fellow human beings was another abiding part of his existence.

Today in the utter corruptness of our present society, the unforgiveable selfish
intent, global poverty and violence prevalent everywhere, as Walter Spradbery's
one remaining progeny, I look back upon him as some shining martyr and spiritual
figure from a bygone age. A man not without a sense of devastating humour and
inner mischievous who made his way through life as generously as any human
being possibly could, despite constant financial hardship. Nevertheless he never
wavered in his moral beliefs. A standard-bearer for Godly instruction and
evolvement in those principles, though never did he step inside a holy building
other than to paint its portals with brush and palette! Or to attend some dear
friend's funeral or to celebrate a friend's wedding.

The following words are the main extracts from what is almost certainly
Spradbery's first written letter to his friend, Jim Berry, as true a breed of man of
the county of Yorkshire as there could be, a locality of Britain where the unique grit
and character of the country's working class masses revealed themselves like no
other part of Britain in those extraordinary years. These passages are the main
contents taken from three letters written through the month of December 1918,
less than a month after armistice and the year Britain's women first got the vote!…

36 Turner Road,
Walthamstow E.17
3rd December 1918

Dear Jim,

Thanks for your cards. It is really very good of you to find time on leave to write to me. I am glad to know your journey to Yorkshire was not too bad – that you got a sleep and a pleasant breakfast with your cousins – but sorry to hear of your mater's ill-health. Give her my best wishes for a speedy recovery. I expect your return will brighten her up considerably. As to Miss Edith's smiles, I have no doubt of their radiance. Lucky Jim! Lucky Edith! I drink your health and continued happiness.

I hope you are not neglecting to tell your people of your gallantry in France; what a good pal you have been to us all; how cheerful, how helpful, and coura-geous. I should like Earby to know that even though you have come back without a decoration you have richly deserved one – I'd like Earby folks to know you are respected in the Unit for your many excellent qualities – your manhood, your intelligence, your good heartedness – to know how fearless you have been, how independent....

On the election! What a flutter among the womenfolk! What hysterical dis-putes! I gloat, I laugh, but I wonder what will come of it all. I don't believe half the soldiers will get a chance to vote, much less receive all the election addresses of their various candidates. There will probably be an awful riot after the election because of this and I should not be surprised if the election has to take place a sec-ond time under different conditions.

But really the dear overwrought ladies are amusing – the intelligent district-vis-itor type – who are out to inform and capture the vote of their bewildered and ignorant sisters – (good homely souls who never wanted a vote and who feel embarrassed with one, who appeal to husbands and brothers for advice, and then get into the most incomprehensible muddles with the information they receive).

The lack of ideas on matters of government and citizenship is appalling in our menfolk, but the complete innocence of a notion among the mass of women is even worse. They are more easily led – with the exception of the vixens – especially by folk who appear to talk with authority. These they will believe before their hus-bands who are usually regarded as dear stupid fellows, too cocksure and wilful. Where will they be led? That's the question.

We live in an age when necessity and wild conditions are forcing folks to realise the vagueness of their ideas and eventually they are being brought to think – to try to think: clear, hard, practical thoughts. We shall progress presently – after a few chaotic years. But meanwhile – what a spectacle!

In my district – Walthamstow (East) – we are faced with the alternative of a coalition candidate or Sir John Simon. No Labour or Socialist is putting up. If he did I fear he'd only put the coalition man in by splitting the Lib-Lab vote, whereas now at least I think we can be sure the coalition man won't get in for our district. I shall give the rascal (Sir J.S.) my vote – after all he did oppose conscription.

If I get a chance I'll put him a few questions about the revision of Army Regulations on Democratic lines – about the soldier's right of political freedom – and as to whether he is in favour of Ireland being represented at the Peace Conference – which is to come off before the new Parliament sit, after all, it seems....

I am sorry to say that, although mater looks very well, yet it is apparent that her age is beginning to tell upon her. She soon tires, and the excitement of my home-coming has been a bit of a strain....

I have seen few familiar faces yet – I feel almost forgotten. However I am launching out to visit various friends tomorrow and have given today to the "Beaucoup piccaninnies" of my sister and sister-in-law. Bless 'em....

8th December 1918

My Dear Jim

Things are moving – almost too quickly unless they are moving as speedily for you.

It is quite likely that I shall not be going back to France with you, and possible that Mackey will soon be joining me here, and that we shall both be established in studios in Fulham Road working on illustrations for the Medical History of the War, before the end of this month.

This may not be, but is very likely: the machinery to effect it is in motion.

It is with drastic feelings that I contemplate this change in affairs.

I realise the great advantages of being in London now for the purposes of for-warding my interests and work, the splendid opportunity of contributing to an international memorial in company with men of undoubted talent, the pleasure and freedom of the actual work practically released from Army discipline, though not actually discharged from the Army, and the possibilities that may result from the notice such work is bound to attract when it is eventually made public.

But I am attached by all sorts of ties of affection and mutual goodwill to the old 36th Field Ambulance and to leave it so suddenly seems almost like deserting, without the courtesy of farewell or the sincere expression of regret.

And strongest tie of all, there's you. Although our friendship does not date back a year yet, to me it is a remote time when I did not know you. When was it? I have almost always known you – and never quite – nor shall I – nor you, I.

Surely I have known of your coming down the ages; our friendship is a greeting in Eternity – a passing passion and pain; passing in one sense but enduring in another.

Of what friendship consists is hard to say – it seems like a recognition of oneself in another, a glimpse of the inseparable brotherhood of man, a realisation of the unity of life – perhaps a momentary vision of God. Yet always is it plain that complete understanding is impossible: that everyman's inmost motions and thoughts are his only. Friendship is sympathy and partial understanding – a yearning, an appreciation of the mutual pathos of life (of little man struggling in a brave fight with the gigantic forces of circumstance) – a desire for peace, security, affection – nirvana.

And this great effort at spiritual union and recognition which we call friendship, finds its expression inevitably through material ways – has no other way – is evident only by material senses – so that to be near a friend is a consolation, an enjoyment, and to render a service a sweet significant pleasure, to make a sacrifice a joy-offering at the very altar of the universal. And little things and acts become charged with great symbolism and meaning, and the common places of life become full of promises and burning goodwill.

Yet I have accepted the opportunities with regard to my work and its advancement and allowed myself to be separated from you a few months earlier than would otherwise have happened. I hope you won't be hurt. I know you'll miss my company and I shall miss yours: you will be constantly in my thoughts till we meet again. Parting for a time is inevitable, and might have worn a worse aspect. If for a while we have to take paths a little apart we will call across the space between like separated companions in a wood, and sooner or later the trees will open and we shall see each other again....

But I have not told you yet exactly what happened.

Well, I visited Baxter – of whom you have heard me speak, and found him working in very good conditions, with excellent opportunities of turning out good stuff. I had my sketches with me to show him. Lieut. Gilbert Rogers was painting a huge canvas in the same studio. He saw my work and immediately offered to try to get me employed upon the Med. His. of the War, pointing out the advantages of the work. He showed me around the studios and we saw the immense supply of material and picture making – artists materials and what might be called "properties" – Jerry helmets, clothing, shell cases etc etc. Models are provided, orderlies keep the place clean, wash brushes etc. an excellent cook provides meals on the Army allowance. It was explained that in undertaking the work I should not delay my demobilisation and complete discharge. Visits to France, with an orderly to help, a car at my disposal, and with a friendly Colonel to watch my interests and smooth my way for work, were likely to occur from time to time. What I have to produce is large pictures of places and subjects in connection with the Medical Service during the War.

These pictures will be hung in a permanent exhibition – the Medical History of

War Museum – together with Austin Spare's work – Rogers himself etc. The pay will, at present only be army pay – though all materials are provided, but the work may not be complete when demobilisation takes place in which case pictures will be commissioned.

However, apart from living in the heart of London, having weekends free, and working only from 9 a.m. to 5 p.m. at my civil employment, are other advantages. One could personally superintend the submitting of one's other works to exhibitions – keep in personal touch with old clients and watch for opportunities which would slip by were one in some out-of-the-way village in France.

I saw at once the job was more suitable to Mac – just what he's declared he wants in the way of conditions – so put in a word on the matter. As a result, if he's agreeable he will probably be employed over here also.

Gilbert Rogers said if I would make up my mind at once he'd probably be able to get the matter fixed up before the expiration of my leave and so save much inconvenience. I gave the matter a day's thought and then agreed. Had I thought that beyond hastening our temporary parting a little, accepting his offer would make the separation longer or wider, I would have rejected it. I don't think it will.

I have not heard definitely from the War Office yet. Nevertheless in case I don't go back with you, if the little girl and your mother can spare you a bit earlier, I should be so glad to see you for a while on Saturday; we'd put you up for the night and I'd see you off on Sunday morning. Try to arrange it. In any case write and I will see you somehow before you depart, if it's only on the station.

I must end – though I've a lot more to tell you – I know if Mac and I are not with you things will be duller than ever. I know you'll miss us more than anyone will. I'll write at least weekly. Don't go on the Vin Blanc.

Dear old boy don't be upset about it – it's a bit sudden I know. Au revoir. Your affectionate friend.

Walt.

14th December 1918

My Dear Chum

Cheerio! Am so sorry to hear that your mother has been so ill, and that you have had such a quiet time in consequence. What a brick you are – you reduce grumbling to a minimum. Dear lad, things all work together for some good purpose and out of apparent ills great goods often take form.

Keep cheerful – keep confident.

Time's a whirlgig – I'm almost giddy with the twisting the last few days has given me.

Until a moment or two ago I was packing up preparatory to returning to France, as I had heard nothing definite from the War Office. The situation had been complicated by the discovery that there were no early morning trains up to town on Sunday and it was therefore necessary to leave home over night and fix up a bed in the city.

Your letter then arrived with the news of your probable extension of leave, and the possibility of making a futile return journey without the pleasure of your company did not improve the prospect. However, I laughed – fate is so surprising – and tried to reassure mater, who looked very blank. I felt confident things would straighten out – indeed I believe they are going to absolutely blossom, old man.

The thought-power stunt! Well, just before I started this letter, which otherwise would have been short and different, a telegram arrived – "You will be required for Home Service, do not return to France, letter follows." Good luck!

But that is not all – more thought-power yet!

I wrote to old Mac, pressing him to accept this splendid opportunity and concluded with – "I wish I could fix up old Jim to be over here with us – as a model or something." Well, don't get excited or "count your chickens before they are hatched".

Yesterday I took mater to town to see a matinee, and after determined to call on Lt. Gilbert Rogers to see how matters had progressed over this Med. His. of the War business. He had heard nothing, but telephoned through to expedite matters. While chatting he complained that they needed a really capable chap who would take an interest in the work to do little out-of-the-way jobs – improvise for general comfort and also to make things for model groups – you know what I mean – miniature representations of incinerators etc., to show in cases, illustrating on a small scale the way these things are made in France and elsewhere – a man who could use intelligence and tools – who'd be able to attack the difficulties that are too much for a mere artist.

Well, I immediately burst into an absolute song of praise, about a certain chap I knew, who was so capable and workmanlike in dealing with metal stoves that we'd thought of inducing him to take up repousse metalwork, who had a great interest in drawing and artists, who'd seen things as they really were in France, was intelligent, of extraordinary energy – and incidentally a chap who'd make a perfect model for physical manhood – and so on.

I excited his interest – I've yet to bring him to the point of applying for you if you'd care to join in such work.

He went so far as to ask if you were in the 36th Field Ambulance.

Now, nothing may result from this, and it is even poss that you wouldn't care for the job, but if you would let me know your reg number by return post and we'll see what can be done to reunite Mac you and I in Fulham Road.

Even your mother's illness and the extension of leave may facilitate matters –

make it possible for you to put in a personal appearance at the psychological moment – if you think there is any pleasure or advantage in the job.

If we bring the matter off it will not interfere with your speedy demobilisation any more than my accepting the job will with mine. You'd be in England and I'd not lose your good company. Shall I work the stunt if I can? It's a vague hope perhaps – but I'm confident – if you are too – it's sure to come off – you know the theory.

And now, dear old Jimmy, you rascal, not so many compliments and all this rot about the "radiation of character which emanates from my being." It's great to have the assurance of your affection and goodwill – but I've always believed in it – except at such depressed moments as when one does not believe in anything or oneself. Perhaps when one is full of doubt and suspicion – when one fears most for what one loves most. If there's any "radiation of character" to be mentioned – I'm very conscious of it when with you – you seem to have a vast store of energy and vitality which emanates from your being in a comforting and sustaining atmosphere of helplessness, which makes it so damned good to be near you.

Well, I got the inevitable suggestion for the removal of my depression, that I expected – a dear girl – they are all so damned dear though – and such change upon one's personal liberty, and finances too.

Still, Fate, or Time, or Chance, or my own will, may have got some good thing in store for me – and someone may come along one day in answer to the unending call of my being, someone not afraid to face the future with me and in my way – and all the secret agony of longing be rewarded....

Perhaps – P'r'aps not – Who cares. Life's very much of an illusion – what you choose to see in it – what you make it – an adventure upon a sea of powerful currents, a journey across a desert full of mirages, a struggle through a wood of entangled circumstances – full of wild possibilities and unexpected things – things that one half knew of, yet never expected to have in reality – things rejected as too good or too bad by one's own imagination.

But I run to incoherence again – you're getting a fair share of letters I guess your people think. I'm neglecting all sorts of little duties to write to you. So au revoir. Don't forget to send your number and say what you think about the idea of joining us if it can be worked.

Don't count too much on it – it's a hairsbreadth chance – the most exciting type.

Your affectionate friend.

Walt.

One must remember that Spradbery, since his father's death in a London fog, had lived supporting his mother on the meagre earnings from odd design commissions that came his way in both the pre- and post-first world war years sharing a tiny house in Turner Road in London's east end borough of Walthamstow, except for the intervening war years. His other siblings had left home, married and begun to raise their own families. His two closest siblings, Charlie and Flo, though, lived in close proximity to him and his mother, Emily, perhaps ready to step in and help out if occasion demanded it with their mother's frequent outbursts of irrationality! A strangely frightening cloistered domesticity in a nondescript working class part of Walthamstow, that divorced his home life from other more worldly activities that he began to become engaged in....

In "Sprad's" ensuing correspondence to James Berry, there is forever reference to his mother's reliance on her son and her possessiveness of heart and mind towards him, as well as certain psychological traits towards him, and an incessant vindictiveness towards his friends which began to emerge. An antagonism towards anybody she felt was taking him away from her or seemingly drawing too much on his affection. As her grandson, who remembers her so faintly, and knowing the very nature of Walter Spradbery, it is an almost impossible relationship for me to comprehend today.

Only in this close and intimate correspondence with Jim Berry over those immediate post-war years, has Spradbery revealed the worrying traits that existed in his mother's latter-day life. Despite being on her own and dependent upon her youngest son's overwhelming love and support for her, he was forced to suffer his mother's haranguing and outbreaks of hysteria which peppered his frequently-penned letters right up until Emily Spradbery's death at "The Wilderness" in the early thirties, not long after Spradbery's marriage to my own mother, Dorothy and my subsequent birth. Within the family circle it is inconceivable to imagine that his mother's outbursts and traits of irrationality may have ever been openly discussed. Despite these humiliating instances, he undoubtedly loved his mother intently with a bond of deeply-rooted affection. By all accounts, from his earlier recollections and letters to her from the frontline in France, a not unremarkable woman!

"Sprad's" Immediate Post War Years

From the concluding moments of surviving the trenches and desolation of the Somme, Spradbery's place in the unravelling of life must surely have taken on a new dimension. Before the introduction of his service in the R.A.M.C., he was a human being without airs or graces, his essence of life and height of ambition were what directly confronted him in his own restricted working class existence. The life he was born into was what was before him; his friends, his respected companions, his talent as an artist and painter, his vocational destiny.

Spradbery's correspondence to Jim Berry over successive decades is a key and grand entrée to the visionary intellect, imagination and fortitude of a young spirited soul, the heart of a young man who rose from the doldrums of a colourless working class existence in the humblest of circumstances.

Progression from Spradbery's first letter to Jim Berry, directly after the return to their home country after Armistice had been declared is not picked up again until some years later, simply because unfortunately such earlier correspondence has disappeared, been lost or was never retained by the recipient until later years as recorded in these subsequent passages and extracts; passages and extracts of correspondence that took on an extraordinary range of topics, anecdotes and philosophising, besides literally painting a unique picture of a working class background of that particular era and locality.

Walter Spradbery's years directly after the Armistice remain largely undocumented in correspondence to James Berry. Undoubtedly there were letters but the letters of that particular period never came back into my hands! These years must have been early formulative years for the evolving Essex Art Club, a club with some local standing to this very day.

Again, constantly in harness with Haydn Mackey, these two artists' art classes at Walthamstow's Greenleaf Road took on a certain celebratory status in local circles where other young artist students began to move into the professional ranks. Indeed in later years the Greenleaf Road institution became the borough's Adult Educational Centre and held such a unique and elevated place of adult education within the borough for over half a century – until its most recent years. Within the borough, one can imagine it had a certain continuing and sustaining presence and influence from the earlier demise and closing of the borough's art school.

How life shaped up for him at that time reaching his thirtieth year cannot be too difficult to visualise. Writing articles on art and design and giving lectures on Ruskin, William Morris and various movements and attitudes to art – and sustained by a stimulating fellowship of friends – embraced an active existence. Spradbery seemingly trod an exalted path in those inauspicious worrying loss-laden years of the country's younger generation of manhood, especially so in the prominent working class east end borough of London's E.17. This, with the added responsibility of a mother showing signs of stressful behaviour, irrationality and possessiveness beyond a normal parental relationship. Within these early not unaffected post-war years, Spradbery's ageing mother was of some concern and personal responsibility for him, a devoted son; also being the surviving sole progeny still living under the same roof.

Here, through the revelationary extracts of correspondence preserved in a distant attic in the Yorkshire Dales, I hope to reveal the remarkable vicissitudes and wondrous schemes, episodes and spiritual motivations that drove Walter Spradbery's life on – perhaps to a level of sacrifice and martyrdom for his fellow man and nature itself – that was the driving force of his life and was in the wider sense of his times, unheeded, unappraised and derided....

Before this fully-quoted letter to James Berry on the 18th August 1924 it is apparent a ceaseless amount of missing correspondence flowed between them forming an extraordinarily strong and intimate bond. This particular letter encapsulates the whole meaning and tenure of such a friendship; an affirmation of a deep and brotherly enduring devotion and loyalty to a kindred spirit.

This letter unusually written on tiny sheets of paper is a disconcertingly homely communication commenting and philosophising on Berry's apparent state of mind and low morale at that time, a need for a break to meet up with a friend.

Travel, even in 1924 from north to south was not compensated with allowances, even for people in local politics and artists certainly had to dig deep in constantly empty pockets!

18th August 1924

My Dear Jim,

I must confess your letter is rather disappointing in several ways – (I'll give you the good hiding you deserve in a few minutes) – and anyway demands an immediate answer.

First, I had no idea that your holiday was so early in September – or rather between August and Sept. – and I shall certainly not have done what I want to do by then nor have received the cash I hope for. Moreover I should be sorry to cause your brother any inconvenience or make him feel that your hospitality to him was not all it might have been had you not had a friend with you. You fix up immediately for him to come to you if you can. I am sure your mother would like it and probably he is expecting it. Your mother will have received all sorts of attention during her own stay at Birmingham and will be anxious to show her appreciation and extend the warmest welcome in return.

Added to which if Edith (by then, Berry's wife) has been making plans and cal-culating on having some good times with you on this holiday I should be sorry to interfere with the arrangements. I thought perhaps you would just mess away the time with no particular plans, and that if my suggestion for a little walking tour appealed to you, that Edith would be able to enjoy herself among her own friends in some ways of her own, quite happily and delighted to think you were having a change and agreeable (more or less) society.

But what I will not listen to with patience (or read with patience if you demand exactness of statement) is all this talk about the "carefree, happy" days that have been, as if they were gone for ever – all this "Such a spirit as we possessed then, once gone, can never be regained". For my own part the spirit has not gone – its quality is temperamental; it can exist with ignorance, but philosophy is a surer foundation for it – and "consciousness of security", "knowledge of economic facts" but make ·the way more adventurous. If you were willing to risk your last pound on a holiday, a charity, or a sport, before you knew the whole structure of society was insecure, you have less reason for saving it now you know it will be of no avail in this world of infinite possibilities, but courage – the will to go on, – to deal with difficulties as they arise and snatch what enjoyment and satisfaction the experi-ences bring you.

In these adventures the insecurity added zest, had you wanted security you'd have stayed at home in bed and prayed that the roof might not fall in.

"Added responsibilities" need more courage, more buoyancy of spirit, and, as these added responsibilities are also in some ways added comforts and satisfactions; in fact, inexpressible joys – there should be a gleam of triumph in your eyes at hav-ing attained them. I refuse to accept this temporary loss of buoyancy as a prelude to more loss. The best is yet to be for you. Your greatest fights and glories have yet to come. This loss of buoyancy is a tiredness due to overtaxed nerves, a need of change. You have surveyed the road and a great weariness has come upon you – your progress seems so little when you see what yet lies ahead.

Let me refer you once again to that excellent source of inspiration for you, William Cobbett – who retained his buoyancy through a very agreeable married life, with a family on his hands. His love of domesticity and severe views on the duties of a husband, I might mention, did not prevent him from going on those delightful rural rides which did so much, no doubt to keep his mind sweet and healthy and on which he learnt so much besides refreshing himself and composing some profitable essays. You have many rural rides ahead of you. If not before, then when that son of yours finds pleasure in such things and has grown up a companion to his father – I can imagine you striding over the hills together – you enjoying his young enthusiasms, he gratified by your experienced comments.

For heavens sake put off this tendency to settle down and this nervousness about things being "extremely uncertain in cotton-land". You are better equipped than most, to turn with hope of success in other directions. You are only tied up in the cotton trade through early associations – perhaps you would be better if you broke these many threads. Anyway you are a man of capacity, with ability not only to help yourself and those who are dear to you, but in some ways humanity at large I believe.

I think a jolly walking tour would do your spirits a lot of good. Your business rarely takes you from your wife and it would do her good to have you away too – if only to have the joy of your return! Your affectionate relations will grow humdrum and stolid if they are not agitated a little by occasional partings. Your studies proba-bly give her more uneasiness and "secret hurts" than your taking a holiday in the way I indicated would do, and the time they steal, does not occasion the same pleasures of reunion. In fact you are there but obviously indifferent to her – 'tis awful. I could develop this into quite a tragedy if I'd a mind – but you wouldn't believe it.

Of course I warned you that Determinism inevitably led to despondency and often to despair, and if you examined the matter deeply enough you might find that this philosophy was the thing that sapped your buoyancy at root – that a conviction that circumstances, environment etc. were proving too much for you – that the things you dreamed, the destiny you felt within you could never be realised because you were imprisoned by these things, took the strength from your spirit.

Predestination is better than Determinism in that at least a man may believe he has a destiny and is not the sport of blind circumstances – he fulfils an end then – Predestination allows a faith – "He knows about it all, He knows, He knows" says Omar. The voices within one are not then, entirely mocking voices – one's inspira-tions have a justification then. One's petty Will may be circumscribed but the Will of God within one is not.

Determinism in its effort to be scientific remains materialistic, and enmeshes life into a chemical action – unmeaning – the soul rebels – or sinks in time if this negative belief is forced upon it. You must change your philosophy. Try Shaw's. Among the evidences of your state of mind that I noticed was your choice of the verse you put in Miss Ison's autograph album. It revealed something of your thought and feeling – "The Worldly Hopes men set their Hearts upon etc". Perfectly true no doubt, beautifully expressed, but hardly buoyant. "Pack up your troubles in your old kit-bag, and let us away over the hills to an Inn where, opening our Omar, we will quote a more cheerful verse.

"Ah fill the Cup what boots it to repeat
How Time is slipping underneath our feet:
Unborn Tomorrow and dead Yesterday
Why fret about them if today be sweet."

It is in the year of 1925 that "Sprad's" correspondence to James Berry takes on a seemingly endless momentum – taking ideas from the mysterious subject of the "Scroll of Fate" and on to higher matters of a scientific nature and political debate and thoughts of a calibre beyond my own frail and limited comprehension. Within this early letter in 1925 are also the suspicions of a deep attraction for the wife of one of his good friends! Also interspersed in all these literary wonderings on a less high plain are everyday domestic matters – such as trips to Blackpool and Scarborough – and a description of a niece's wedding – and mention of an Ernest Jackson who at some time disappears off to the distant continent of Australia – never to reappear again; which presumably in the twenties was the ultimate intention of any human being considering such a faraway trip!

Here perhaps unnecessarily, I feel compelled to quote Spradbery's digressions to James Berry on matters above my own intellectual powers, and to illustrate the range of his own intellectual capacity....

An opening page of a letter dated May 18th 1925, a letter running to twenty-one pages:

Thanks for your letter and for returning the "Scroll of Fate" and Jackson's letters with my replies riding on their backs.

You ask, in the course of expressing some opinions on the Scroll, "do you think it is wise to introduce so many mighty big subjects into a controversy, when the discussion of one subject or a part of it might lead to a better result?"

I think it is almost inevitable in an attempt to establish the idea that Will is, in essence, the energy that gives and holds all phenomena to its form and changes it to new form by its self-conflict, and that in man touches, so far as we can judge, its most organised and conscious form, i.e. known purpose – (whereby man appears to be able to create, from a human point of view, order out of chaos). I think it is almost inevitable in expounding this idea, that the nature of existence, consciousness and experiences innumerable but vital should pass under the review of the contemplating intelligence.

The scientific Determinist (Prof Soddy says it should be called the ultra-materialistic philosophy) – the Scientific Determinist, in his attempt to establish his case has to include the whole Cosmos in his effort: labelling this "Heredity-Cause" and that "Environmental Cause" enclosing all in order to hold his position.

To meet it one must do the same and find evidence of Will in everything – demonstrating man to be its most conscious form....

This philosophising and debate goes on for seventeen further hand-written pages, before "Sprad" describes a visit to the theatre accompanied by another close friend, the sculptor, Harold Parker and two ladies from Kensington!

I sold my picture at the Royal Academy on the Private View Day and before 12 noon. It was bought by a Mr Grange of Gray's Inn for 12 Guineas. He went to the R.A. with a Miss Phyllis Abbott, a young lady I once met, and who is a friend of Miss Birch (of whom I have spoken once or twice I think – she keeps an Art Jewellers Shop in Kensington) and who called his attention to my work. He had gone with the intention of buying something so bought it then and wrote to me saying he thought it very cheap – with a compliment or two. In view of the fact it had been shown for three years at various other exhibitions at prices varying from three guineas to ten I was glad he thought he'd got a bargain.

Miss Birch did not neglect to write to tell me how the sale occurred (delighted she said to have a hand in it) and invited Harold Parker (who I hope I told you has a modelled head in the academy too) and me up to dinner one evening. To this the only possible reply was to offer to take her and her friend Miss Abbott to the theatre after, by way of thanks. And on Wednesday last we all went to see "Caesar and Cleopatra" by Bernard Shaw at the Kingsway, where I'd booked seats. As the ladies got themselves up in West-end style, well powdered and very "modern Chelsea" I stood a taxi too – and as Harold arrived rather late for dinner there was need for hurry also. We all enjoyed ourselves very much; it was a most excellent performance, and is the play that first firmly established Shaw's reputation – according to G.K. Chesterton. It is very witty and the youthful Cleopatra was played delightfully by Gwen Francon Davies. We all chortled with delight.

Friends and a love lost ...

On Sunday I went down to see Alfred Schwab and Mary and I took them over to the Parkers (who are now their near neighbours in their fine new house at Ewell – which I may have described already to you) – in order to introduce Mary to them.

Jim, she looked absolutely lovely. A splendid English girl, like a beautiful pink rose just open, fragrant – Oh how so glorious and consoling natural beauty is, how rare, how passing. Mrs Parker was overwhelmed by her. She said "Sprad, she is delightful and Alfred is a very very lucky chap": you know I agreed. Walking through the meadows after tea, when we all went for a long stroll, it was a pleasure to me to watch her peaceful movement. I liked her simple tasteful clothes – all in cream she was with a white hat with a brim that threw a light shadow on to the clear complexion of her kind face beneath it – rippling with smiles. She was at ease and happy yet just touched by that responsive nervousness that moving among even the most homely and agreeable strangers (such as Parkers) gives to a nature naturally a little modest – though capable. They all liked her. Harold's uncle devoted himself to her. He a rather sour cynical chap as a rule with some malicious humour, but he talked merrily to her told her stories of his youth (he's only middle aged) in a way alto-gether surprising. Dad Parker beamed on her and did his best to make the wireless extra fine in the evening.

Alfred looked the picture of health too: and oh my dear lad, he tells me that a "little stranger" has recently started on the way. Lucky, lucky, Alfred. She will be more lovely still as a mother. I wish you could have seen her – I'd like you to see her at her best to hear you justify my praise with your own – perhaps she may lose the bloom that seems to rest upon her now, ere long....

In the year 1925 "Sprad" was not short of a friend or two. Besides his unique loyal friendship from the art school days with Haydn Mackey, there was a local fellow Higgins whose name crops up from time to time, a Reverend Dunning from Kendal, the Schwabs whose Mary had such an emotional effect on him and the Parkers (Harold, the sculptor who designed the original wren on the pennyfarthing); other influential friends were the Edwards who are mentioned in a shorter note to James Berry in June 1925. Was this early nucleus of friends part of his coterie of life-long friends and correspondents from his RAMC days or from some other source?

12th June 1925

My dear Jim

... Last weekend I saw Edwards and his wife at their home in Welwyn Garden City and heard their account of their travels in Northern Africa and the wonderful things they saw – the ancient city of Carthage; the ruin of one of Rome's largest colonial cities, Timgad; and Constantine, a wonderful city bounded on three sides by a natural gorge of fearful depth, a place of romantic appearance and strange his-tory – full of subject matter for an artist – should like to visit it myself – and much more....

"Sprad's" letter to Jim Berry following on some little time later recalls his recent visit to the Yorkshire Dales with him and their overnight stay in a rather strange and foreboding lodging house, surmising something of the life of the incumbents encountered there!

14th July 1925

My dear Jim

...When I succeed in getting into your district again I will remind you of your sug-gestion to take me to this place. The very fine day we had together at Wycollar stands in my memory very clearly – I recall the lines of the undulating hills; the brown grass, sun dried, the deep shadows, their blueness, and the changing sky: the descent to the old deserted mansion, in ruins beside the stream; the broken bridge; the half-deserted village with grey moss-grown stones; the air of mystery and melancholy, the brooding tragedy and half-guessed associations of the place. And then that most excellent tea with all its well-made, home-made dainties so lavishly spread before us in the rather dark room, and the fine, steady-eyed motherly woman who provided it – and then the rather seedy, worn and wretched looking husband whom we saw after, who had all the character of the place afflicting him – a man who seemed a victim to sinister influences, decadent perhaps, while his wife seemed to stand calm, dignified and good – a tower of strength keeping away evil influences – the uncanny terrors the place might hold. I remember the glowing colour of the fading sunlight that fell upon a fine group of trees, ash I think, that we saw from the cottage window, lighting their topmost branches – the autumnal tinting that was on everything – the sense of farewell and passing, in the place, the season and the day – the poignant beauty, romantic, dramatic, haunting.

We saw it at the perfect moment – free from too-jolly noisy trippers (even Labourites) at the season and hour that intensified its particular character.

I often think of that fine woman, alone, it seems to me, in that sinister haunted valley, which in the evenings and nights of winter must be isolated, a graveyard-world of its own. I imagine the man, a creature more of temperament than character, unable to stand the imaginative appeal the desolation of the place has, drinking and growing wild and desperate; I imagine the woman protecting the children from his madness – they frightened and whimpering in a room behind her. I imagine that about him circle the dreadful passionate spirits that dwell in such a place, inspiring him with wild-beast-hatred of the very woman who by her industry keeps home together and children healthy – I can see his eyes gleaming with treachery – possessed – picking up the lamp, perhaps to hurl.

I can imagine her calm and resolute still – I can imagine her with dreadful deliberation doing some terrible thing to protect and save herself and home – but such a scene would be but a climax.

Their characters have been slowly built up; her resolute look, her very strength has grown as he yielded to the desolating spirit of the place. Temperamentally sensitive he is a subject for pity rather than contempt. Their fate like that of characters in a Hardy story looms over them. His type of intelligence would be against him. Probably she has some simple faith to him unintelligible, but to her a support in those moments when unknown evil influences seem to assail. I can imagine that when they were married it amused him, but how her calmness, and the superiority it gives her, maddens him in a drunken frenzy driving him to a wild blasphemy.

And then from those early days to the winter of despondency when, to relieve his terribly afflicting gloom, he first drank recklessly and went home a creature half-demented. Her sudden coldness and yet helpfulness – her realisation that she must master the situation and keep up the fight alone against the demons that now no longer howled only about the door on dreadful nights, but had entered the very being of her beloved and changed him to a menace to himself and his own, facing her with glowing eyes in her own home.

I can picture scenes where he wildly weeps his repentance for his unnatural violence, for his waste of hard earned cash, for stealing hers to satisfy his craving – the decline, the moments of abasement and the moments of desperate urgency when her resolve to keep him from his vice and weakness darkened his mind and inflamed him.

And then this climax – the snatched lamp – you know the one – incandescent paraffin gas – the leaping flame – the devils change sides – all is red – he lies on the floor and she is smothering the flames about the fallen lamp with a rug – subconsciously – in a wild nightmare – and pushing a frightened child, before it shall see the heap on the floor, into the bedroom again – bidding it be quiet – go to bed go to sleep – 'tis nothing – don't wake the others. What shall she do now – think, think – gone is the calmness, gone the resolute eye; the heart palpitates, she wants to weep, to cry out, to fling herself down, to drown herself, to recall the youth that flashes across her memory – to omit the latter years – a dream – and then this act. Oh god! It was not he she killed, no, but some devil that had possessed his frame and ruined it – made it the dreadful thing that threatened and fought against her. Oh calm come, she must think, return resolution! Oh babes to wake such dreadful orphans, what's to become of you! Act, act, hide, hide, away with that rag of a thing upon the floor.

Have none heard, none seen? Take that dreadful burden to the stream, now in its wintry flood; by the broken bridge there, fling it in – 'twill seem so natural that he should stumble there and drown with his head gashed on the rocks – the stumble of a returning drunkard – 'twould surely not be enquired into overmuch. Oh quick, quick; yes that must be done – the babes, the helpless babes. Had she protected, nurtured them so long for this – to feel a rope about her throat, and to leave them.

Oh terrible place, oh haunting demons, would you triumph now? Why had she given up the fight before, left all, faced any difficulties rather than the terrors of that place. Had she not felt its influence, like him; but the pride in her had sworn to overcome it – she had stood till she dare not move – till she made that awful movement that left a one-time sweetheart a dead thing upon the floor: he had been an easy victim.

Oh, no thinking of that – no looking at the terrible face with staring glassy eyes above the matted hair, to see the faint resemblance to the laughing youth who bore her here so happily, and she so gay, so many years ago – no thinking of that. Open the door – the awkward blowing door – the willful, banging door, with laughing demons pushing and shaking and banging it – Oh that fierce wet wind, that howling, powerful, pushing wind that takes the breath already panting from the lung of one with a heavy ragged burden – that wind that stirs the white tablecloth and the curtains – grinning faces, mocking faces are behind them all. Oh black night, desolation, rain – noise! Pour down rain, shriek wind, obscure all sight black night! – none must see, oh none must see – would we could not see ourselves. The stony yard – drag on, even though its stones seem to speak, to mock as the burden passes over them; drag on in the dark – hear the rushing water – hear it above the noise of rain and wind; swirling little flood, gurgling, greedy, but not strong enough to carry him away – and a yard or two perhaps; no more, alas. Horror to see him in the morning, to pretend surprise – it cannot be! The bridge – its uneven mossy stones beneath our feet – it must be, 'tis done. "Mother what are you doing" a white clad figure, trembling in the rain, crying. Oh terror, fresh blinding horror of it – the child – poor child – so wet, so frightened. Oh crave resolution oh calm eyes, oh strong spirit, return, return.

'Tis here – or some awful resemblance of it. Some voice, surely not her own, issues from her mouth bidding the child to bed again, chiding it for coming out in the rain, to mother who had but gone out to let the dog loose from his kennel into the house on such a bad night. See here he is – sniffing round on the floor oh God – by the dark small stain on the floor!

But enough – I'll spare you the discovery, the insanity of the child (complicated by a chill) the police, the "News of the World" treatment of the subject – and well, we better go and have another tea there to reassure ourselves that it has not all happened – but that she's as calm and resolute and makes as good teas as ever. Perhaps the little husband has cheered up!

How these things roll off the pen – and I'm so busy too – or ought to be.

And it occurs to me that I may have written something similar before!…

Was this just an extravagant imagining of the mind on "Sprad's" part? Or is it a parable of the tragedy of life that can afflict an unfortunate few? Another letter of 15 pages in length. Further correspondence ensues, surmising to Berry and his wife basking in the Blackpool sun and references made to this mysterious Jackson figure luxuriating in the privileged atmosphere of Oxford – hoping he would not come back with an Oxford drawl and an exclusive air of learning:

Talking of exclusive airs and such things – it was the Royal Academy Social function a few days ago, to which exhibitors are invited for the purpose of meeting the President, the R.A.s and other notabilities. I received an invite but I did not go as it is an evening dress affair, when decorations are worn and all that.

I haven't an evening suit to commence with – they cost about 11 guineas and then there's hat, and gloves, and socks and shoes, and shirt, and tie, and (in that get up) a taxi to go in – altogether a good bite out of £20 I reckon – so, as I say, I didn't go although I could have sported a decoration no other artist I know of has, and although I realise there is value in showing yourself at these affairs and becoming acquainted with important folk in the art world….

Some words of Spradbery's on Blackpool:

4th August 1925

My dear Jim,

… I am very glad to know you had a good time at Blackpool. Of course sensible people who determine to enjoy themselves ought to be able to have a merry time at a place designed especially for holiday making.

I have seen the Tower Circus and remember it as an excellent show – certainly just the thing to appeal to a lad of Norman's age. He would be thrilled – and I expect his athletic father found much to entertain him. The sands are undoubtedly a good playground, I have also seen the menagerie and visited the Aquarium also.

However Blackpool is a place with no atmosphere except one of vulgarity. Tawdriness is the note of its decoration – and as to manners it hasn't any – anyone with a love of beauty or an appreciation of fitness is a lost soul there. There are many places with entertainments as good and better than Blackpool, with as excellent sands, graced with natural beauties, architectural taste, not so crowded, with some historic associations, and some honest pursuits belonging to the place other than fleecing visitors.

Scarboro' where you are going in Sept ought to be better – from photographs its natural setting seems delightful – it has an interesting and historic harbour and generally appears to me to be an altogether more attractive place. Of course you will visit it at a rather poor season when most of the entertainments will have closed down or have been curtailed, when the weather on the East Coast is likely to be very cold – but with luck its superiority to Blackpool ought to be apparent even then. I hope you get nice apartments.

The letter goes on to describe the people who go to Blackpool!

Such dreadful people go to Blackpool – I seem to remember its streets filled with the gross leering faces of the overfed – greasy – folk, loud-voiced, ill-dressed and over-dressed – ugly, sweaty, sensual-looking – but no doubt there are charming people there. I know two at least. One is a Mr Maxwell a printer and publisher whose acquaintance I made during the War and who not only showed me much consideration and courtesy in all my business associations with him, but who took some personal interest in me and sent me boxes of "Abdullas" (100 at a time) during the first part of my overseas service. The other was a young lady at the library, who took the trouble to show me where in the Town-Hall I might find the arms of the principal towns in Lancashire for a design I was doing.

> Again in this particular letter amounting to eight closely hand-written pages "Sprad" goes on to refer to Berry's young son Norman whom he describes as a bonny fellow from a photograph James Berry sent to him. He goes on to hope he digs some really fine castles in the sand at Blackpool There is also deep concern for Jim Berry's sister who at the time had undergone a serious operation. . . . Berry's life it seems at that time suffered a number of domestic and personal family set-backs. . . .

3rd Sept 1925

My dear Jim

Your pal Ernest Jackson is, to put it mildly, a nuisance, with all allowance for his ability and earnestness! No doubt he has induced me to formulate some ingenious ideas to toil through the depths of my own consciousness and the like and something may or may not come of it – But for the present he has induced me to give days to thought and devising answers to ingenious questions, robbed me of time that might have been given to my friends, of the prospect of a holiday, imperiled the production of my booklet, made demands on my energy which ought to have gone to earning my living – and I have not done with him yet.

A fortnight ago I took my mother down to Dovercourt for a holiday, left her there and returned immediately. On the morning that I took her 45 pages arrived from Jackson. I put it aside and got on with the decorating of the living room that I'd planned. I have transformed the place (with some manual assistance). I hope and think my mother will be delighted.

But you can't ignore a man who sends 45 pages analysing, according to his light, what was thrown out to be "apprehended rather than dissected", nor can you equal all the ideas that come crowding to the mind when vital questions are posed. They must be expressed, the riddle of the Sphinx must be answered or we die. So ever since the room was finished – ceiling lines, whitewashed, picture rail affixed; paint repainted – (one foundation, two coats) – walls repapered, pictures rehung or new cord and cleaned, curtain pole put up, sofa mended, table mended, windows cleaned floors scrubbed – God bless my soul the jobs! – ever since they have been brought to an end I have been scribbling away for dear life, every day hoping to end my reply to his reply. He has made some amusing bloomers, puts some good queries, supplied some interesting matter in the way of cuttings and quotations and deserves less good treatment than I shall give him – for I shall turn him inside out.

The notes are all drawn up, 29 pages are written – there will be at least a dozen more – but I shall have mother home before I have finished, go bankrupt, develop brain-fever, and let you think I have forgotten you – most worthy friend....

... Did I tell you that I am requested to be best man at my niece's wedding on the 12th. Heaven help me – and the bridegroom – I'll see he's there! Oh these ceremonies that no one enjoys and everybody pretends to take so seriously – they go through them, spend money on folks who criticize every detail of the arrangements – have a crowded uncomfortable expensive day, when sense and decency would be better served by a visit to the Registrar and done with it....

... Well – send me a view-card. You needn't trouble about the Scarboro' rock (the pink sort in sticks I mean).

In regard to my last letter to you I hope nothing I wrote hurt your feeling seriously. My running criticism is meant to be no more than a dig in the ribs, a sly tickle – I am frank because I think you understand me, can stand it – prefer it....

8th Sept 1925

My dear Jim

Thanks very much for your little note. I hope you got mine, written in haste, wishing you a good time while about the business of a delegate to the Congress at Scarborough. I note that it is one (the Congress), at which some vital points of policy are being discussed; and the separation of the Headquarters of the Trades Union movement from that of the Labour Party is a significant thing. If it does not represent a real division but only a sort of development of organs with different functions to serve the whole – that is the working masses, then it is an excellent thing. But if it becomes real division then it will be a source of weakness, treachery, misfortune and disorder. The vitality of the movement in one form may rouse the other, and on the political side we may get a little more definition in policy shown. I perceive that Social Credit ideas are gradually permeating the more intellectual (or intelligent is perhaps a better word), side of the movement, and thought is concentrating on the Banking system and its relation to unemployment and modern industrial life. Oswald Mosley has been lecturing at the Summer School I see, and expressing ideas and views that readers of the "New Age" have been familiar with these three or four years. Brailsford has been what seems to me to be preparing the ground for a serious discussion of the credit subject for a long time....

The Brailsford "Sprad" mentions is H.N. Brailsford, a distinguished socialist figure of that time. It was he who later contacted "Sprad" to assist a Doctor Marian

Philips set up an exhibition in Westminster's Central Hall to aid the miners' families during the 1926 General Strike which will be referred to in subsequent correspondence. An extraordinary thing happened to me perhaps some 30 years later, when, as a single out-of-work actor, my time in London in the hot summer evenings were very often spent promenading at the Albert Hall Proms. On one occasion I discovered myself being drawn to a woman some considerable years older than myself of tantalising allure. It transpired she was the widow of H.N. Brailsford.

... If you have time I know you will give me some little account of the impressions you get from the Congress and the persons you meet. You dispose of Clynes son rather sharply. I have no doubt you are right. The vitality, the energy (which in a person is Will) of old Clynes was no doubt stimulated very much by the conditions from which he rose to prominence as a labour Leader. Formulating his own opinions they have an intensity that cannot be so great in his son who has been brought up in the atmosphere of Socialistic idealism and who will therefore by reaction be likely to doubt its beliefs to some extent, and look with older more speculative eyes on the people who make it up – as a youngster does – criticizing and valuing those whom he has moved among, comparing their professions of faith with their achievement. He suffers too from the fame of his father – which, giving him prestige in one way, takes something from all he may be capable of in another....

In this particular letter, there follows mention of his mother's (and her bird) return from Dovercourt. Also further reference to Berry's friend Jackson, and the Scroll....

If there was anything in my "Scroll" worthy of your attention, then my reply this time to his 45 pages has three times its merit. I have again kept the draft and I hope if I send you Jackson's painstaking and thorough effort to analyse the Scroll, and my reply to his analysis, you will be able to find time to give it your careful attention, and follow the line of thought whereby I draw what seemed to Jackson, (and possibly you) a medley of ideas into a whole; and answer some questions he imagined unanswerable; reconcile some points he considered irreconcilable....

... I am not surprised to hear that Scarborough has most of the objectionable features of over-popular seaside resorts and regret the smell of fish but I feel sure it must have a picturesqueness Blackpool lacks; have points of historic and antiquarian interest; and a few miles out some charming coast scenery – I have seen some of it painted. Is not Robin Hood's Bay nearby – a spot much favoured by artists?...

13 Sept 1925

My dear Jim

I expect you are just home from the Congress at Scarborough and a most interesting affair it must have been – with several points of excitement.

The vitality of the movement, the hopes and fears that it raises among its friends and enemies, and those with the welfare of the world at heart, or with an intelligent interest in their times, has been apparent in the tone of the newspaper reports – such as I've chanced to see. It is now a power that is very gravely attended to by all.

I am sure you will have learned much and found food for thought in what you have seen and heard. I wish I had an opportunity of discussing it all with you: it would be most entertaining and no doubt instructive.

However you will no doubt give me some brief report: – your own personal impressions of things and people is what I should like, and I shall look forward to something of the sort.

Yesterday I was best man at my niece's wedding! Her fiancé (now her husband) who is a simple fellow, asked me to undertake the duties and although I have refused many friends and even escaped attending their weddings I could not refuse this chap who was so humble about it, nor fail in any way to oblige and please so good a girl as my niece. I felt rather nervous about taking so important a part in the ceremony even though it was with such simple folk and among relatives. Ceremonies want to be done properly or not at all and I usually feel I don't know enough to do 'em properly and that in the main they are unnecessary and for many folk meaningless. However I found out what all the duties were (from a friend who has officiated in this capacity several times) and I conducted the matter efficiently ("though I says it as shouldn't"). The bridesmaids being nieces also, the kissing of them presented no embarrassment. I got the bridegroom to the church in good time and as he forgot his gloves I lent him one of mine (brought especially for the occasion) to carry, and to the unobservant average eye we both passed as equipped in this detail. I took him to his appointed place of waiting in the front, and I greeted friends and guests as they arrived and showed them to their pews, separating the sheep from the goats (nothing shall make me disclose which are which) his relatives on the right, hers on the left. A good crowd attended. It was at the parish church Woodford and the vicar performed the ceremony.

The bridesmaids arrived and waited in the porch for the bride and her father (Leonard A. Rix – you know the rascal) and as soon as she appeared and they commenced their progress down the aisle, I led the victim to the altar steps where the clergyman awaited us. Of course her dad had got her on the wrong arm and glaring at me he said "You're on the wrong side!" I moved with my victim to the other, although pretty certain we were right. The ancient pew opener then hobbled forward and said in a piping voice "Bridegroom's on the wrong side", so we changed back again. That was the only mishap. At the psychological moment I gave the ring for the bridegroom to put on the book and everything went smoothly. My man said "I will" distinctly and the bride said it very faintly, but plucked up in repeating her duties and promises after the vicar. We went to the vestry and her father and I signed the register as witnesses. I then marshalled those in the vestry into proper order and we "processed" down the aisle to the porch where a crowd of friends and neighbours were waiting to do their darnedest with confetti, old boots etc. Bride and bridegroom first of course, then your humble with the principal bridesmaids on each arm, then a young man named George engaged to another niece with the other two bridesmaids, one of which was his fiancé (a bit of practice for him I thought) then my sister and her husband. The other relatives were in the porch. The car took first bride and bridegroom of course, their bridesmaids and George and a litter of nieces, then grandma (my mother in all her glory) and bride's and bridegroom's mother and father and a small nephew. Then the rest of the relatives except one or two of the bridegroom's male relatives who had gone to get a drink!

My sister had prepared a wonderful wedding breakfast at their house (although her husband is out of work as usual – even dodged a good job the bridegroom found for him just before the wedding!) and the tables were laid out very effectively indeed. The work and anxiety that must have gone into it! It was a triumph. The wedding cake my sister made and her husband iced. It would have graced any confectioner's window. It was a two tier affair. I must get them to send you a piece. Twenty six sat down to the breakfast. By an ingenious arrangement of tables we got 'em all in. The Bride's father toasted the Bride and Bridegroom (he left him out till I reminded him in an undertone) in a few ill-chosen words but well enough in intention, (and in ginger-wine – there being no intoxicants allowed). I returned thanks on behalf of the Bride and Bridegroom who were too blushing and hot to say anything themselves, and added the toast of "The Bride's mother". It being ginger-wine no one else seemed to think it worthwhile to carry on the toasting, so the bridegroom's parents and grandma (my mother) who ought to have had a compliment or two, went unpraised. This did not affect their or anyone's appetite so far as I could see. I put in most of the time waiting and serving as did the bride's father and afterwards in washing up. My God it was a never-ending job. Tea soon followed at which there were 30. We packed them in somehow. The tables were again well stocked and the bride's father and I served the cups of tea from the passage where we had the urns. This effectively prevented the possibility of any more speeches from us. The Bride and Bridegroom did not go till rather late and went straight to their little home at Edmonton. Sustained by ginger-wine and cakes the company kept up conversation, and the children games, till about 10.30 p.m.

Of course as best man I dropped in for lots of little expenses and all the tipping.

I provided smokes for everyone, also the bridegroom's buttonhole. Anyway every-thing went off alright and the general report of the guests and all who saw it is that it was a very pretty affair and satisfactory in every way. A few tears were shed by the bride, the bride's mother, grandma, and the bridegroom's mother. There was a lot of kissing and squeezing and "God bless yous" when they went away.

Bride wore white and a wreath of orange blossom and had a bouquet of white chrysanthemums and carnations. Bridesmaids wore mauve and hats, had bouquets of white and brown chrysanthemums. No children were sick, and despite the num-ber of relations called together no quarrels took place and no unfeeling sarcasms were exchanged.

They (the happy pair) had a large number of presents. Mostly useful and not very expensive things. Many people who knew my niece at the shop where she served sent her little things: one lady who had gone away for a holiday took the trouble to buy and pack a present and send it from Torquay.

But what a game it is!

> Is this not a descriptive gem of a Londoner's working-class family wedding? The reader may think "Sprad" in this letter to Jim Berry is betraying sensitive family confidentialities; hardly so, to one he considered his closest friend. Not filled with the character and haste of his own marriage only a few years later, but hardly similar and so typical of family traditions surrounding his own life at that time.

21st Oct 1925

My dear Jim

Thanks for your letter of Sunday's date. I am sorry to hear of your cold – I'm much the same with a cough into the bargain. However an old student has written to me from New Zealand and sent me six handkerchiefs of ample size and fine quality, worked with my initials, so that I shall not be like the "vulgar boy at Margate" and have "no pocket handkerchief to blow my little nose"....

... Thanks for your sympathy in regard to the troubles my mother occasions. I don't think that her sanity can be seriously questioned – all forms of violent tem-per and passion have something of the nature of madness in them – She is like a naughty child that will scream, kick, and even hurt itself in the street or anywhere in an effort to get its own way and conquer by a display of violent feeling. I have long since reported matters to a local doctor who attends her when she is really ill and can be persuaded to have him – which is very seldom. He examined her very carefully (without her knowing that he was called in for anything but a slight gastric trouble that made her feel queer) and said that she was in wonderful condition for an old lady of 78, her heart sound, her system working well, her constitution splendid and her mentality acute. No one he said could question her sanity. As to her outbursts they were temperamental and resulted from her passionate nature, her determined will and certainty of her own rightness – she had used this means of getting her own way from childhood with success and her power had grown with the use. She had flung aside all control of temper so often that she could not control it or prevent it rising to feverish heights on the slightest provocation etc etc. He was very sorry for me. She could not just be put in a home unless she was willing to go, or became incapable. No home would keep her long without excessively high fees and few would undertake it then. However I asked him to keep and remember the statement I had made in the form of a letter to him, so that if under agitation she occasions any accident happened to her, my position and efforts on her behalf would be clear – for it would be quite possible for a situation to arise in which I might appear almost a criminal on mere circumstantial evidence. Various friends have discussed the difficulty of my situation but short of leaving her again, and leaving her to become ill as she would very soon from lack of attention, and then to be taken to the infirmary there seems no action possible to bear until I break down from the strain of looking after her, and continuing work somehow as well. It would break her heart to be forced in that way – she would not give way until nearly dead – and I could not bring myself to leave her so helpless – for I admire the power of her spirit even though I suffer from it – I realise she believes herself to be right in her motives and determined to stick at nothing to assert this rightness. She is not open to reason unfortunately....

... Since we do not know the future there's room to hope, and the achievement of the past in the face of similar difficulties is not unsatisfactory. I have rendered some service by my work, stuck to principles many consider it impossible to hold and act upon – 'tis a battle with Fate or Circumstances in which death is the only excuse for an honourable man giving way. It is a rest one can always take for oneself when energy is gone indeed.

Now let me turn to this matter of the Communists....

All along in quoting from these amazingly intimate and revealing letters to a loyal friend, I have to balance my own loyalty to a man who was also my father. In revealing the true man it is a path, right or wrong, which I have chosen to follow.

It is also not my intention to document Spradbery's life too much with his views on communism, socialism, pacifism or world affairs which he defended with a conviction that never wavered. However innocent, or brilliant his intellect was, he possessed a remarkable foresight and premonition of the future. His meeting with such a young fellow as James Berry on the barren wastes of the Somme in the concluding days of that final terrible offensive was, it seems, meant to be.

"Sprad" continues in the same letter with comment on his art classes and there is a mention of the remarkable Arthur le Mare....

… I must end – Mr Le Mare has just called to ask me to draw up some account of the proposed course for the Settlement Art Class. They hope to get a Government Grant in connection with it this year. The classes are crowded out – can't get the people in – the local big-wigs (like Canon Lampton) are sending their daughters and folk from as faraway as Highgate are attending. The headmistress of the local High School for Girls has been to see the class and everyone seems quite excited by it. I am told the matter of a local art school is slightly agitating the minds of the local Education Committee; that they came down to the settlement to see the Hall and find out if it was suitable to house an art centre under their control, but that it was so much more adapted to their requirements for Day Continuation Classes that they have decided to use it for that. However the end I set out to accomplish seems a little nearer. It was to demonstrate the need and use of some Art Centre in the town – I began to think that there was so very small a demand that it was hardly worth the effort – we are so near London that the larger and better equipped Art Schools can be attended by most serious students. Anyway I felt that there ought to be somewhere locally where a little interest in the elements of self-expression in form and colour could be acquired by anyone interested, and so I've "kept the flag flying". Of course the Settlement folk are very proud about it....

The installation of Spradbery's art classes, latterly transferred to the Friends Meeting House in Greenleaf Road E17 (popularly known as "The Settlement") under the wardenship of Arthur le Mare was one of a number of public-spirited enterprises that incessantly played very much of a social and cultural role in Spradbery's life. Just another activity that opened up vistas of friendships and feelings of fellowship among men as in the idealistic concepts of William Morris himself.

Spradbery, it must be imagined at this time, was the foremost figure behind establishing a gathering and focus of artists in that part of London and its outlying areas which became embodied in the establishment of the Essex Art Club, where not only a great swathe of fine young artists emerged and made themselves known, but notable Academicians and artists recognised nationally became contributing members. "Sprad's" thoughts even then must have focused on a local museum and centre honouring such a national and local figure as Morris himself.

A definition of the spirit of Friendship – potential political power – tips on public speaking and a first sighting of my own mother!

19th Feb 1926

My dear Jim

… It is good, strong chum, to watch you grow, fulfilling what I have felt to be your possible part, to see your inevitable rise, and new manifestations of the power and ability in you. It has been said "character is destiny". By a consciousness of your character I have been sure from the early days of our friendship that you were destined for a great part, working for the welfare of your fellows: that what you did would be just, healthy, good, sane, thorough, touched by a noble disinterestedness – whatever sphere of action you were in. To feel that you were and are my friend, that a close sympathy is between us makes me rejoice with pride and share in all your achievements, your satisfactions, your hopes.

One can feel a unit with all men in some degree, a relation to all living creatures. The marvel of living experience is in this oneness of a living spirit so divided into creatures that act and react on each other – so that one may cry "Hail brother – creature of one substance, part of one Whole – Hail shadow form, other-self" in combat or more marvellous agreement. But in friendship, this division yet oneness – how can one describe its joys and pathos, its wonder! There is the feeling of something so beautiful, so near, so akin – strength and support is in it. It is a vision seen in a glass darkly, where men may see themselves face to face – yet breathe courage and hope to each other.…

More wishful or imaginary thoughts within the same letter:

… By the way of course I am beginning to look forward to the happy days when affairs of State will bring you often to London, and when I shall expect to have tea on the terrace with the Rt. Hon. James Berry and his admirers just as often as can be arranged.… After all Jim I see no reason why our days of adventure are over – all those lamentations you raised some time ago about youth and enthusiasm being past! When you are in the Labour cabinet you are pretty sure to go gadding about between sessions like Thomas, Macdonald and even Kirkwood. I might accompany you when you do South Africa – unless you go on a special mission to Italy, which perhaps will be still better – oh I see some very good times ahead yet. Trade Union Conferences at Scarborough won't be in it with International Congresses by the Italian Lakes.…

Still the same letter – hints on speech-making:

… Your remarks on the effect on an average audience of the emotional orator as compared with the reasoning, thought-demanding speaker, express what is generally very well-known and worked upon widely by the wily. Nevertheless there is justice in this superior appeal of emotion for emotion is more fundamental than reason and nearer the set of motive and will. One error in a chain of reasoned thought may lead us God knows where but emotion is intuitive in its relation to the future and related to the past by instinct. The aim of reason is not really known till the end of the chain of logic is reached, but emotion starts from the vision of the end desired and reflects it as a light in all its manifestations.

Emotion, as desire, evolved reason to justify and direct to the ends visualized. Emotion is impatient for action and is the prime urge to it: reason is concerned with means, foresight by deduction and at a point becomes abstract and detached, disclosing the magic and mysteries of its own and in numbers as in mathematics. They are correctives to each other, react on each other and at a point become mysteriously fused as in Christian ethics.

We show reason for our actions in order to be understood by others. Reason is a mechanism of thought. Emotion has directional force: reason is the light by the way…. Conscious emotionalism becomes a falsification of the feelings almost inevitably – the speaker becomes an actor – and when his audience glimpses this his power is considerably lessened if not gone….

> On the subject of speaking there were at least two further pages, "Sprad" goes on to refer to the work of Frank Brangwyn and his own panel-posters for London's General Bus Routes. More home trouble with his mother – and then a mention of my own mother which must have been at least three years before he ever realised he was going to fall in love with her, marry her and conceive me!

…Yesterday I had a hell of a day. She raved ("Sprad's mother) every time she saw me and I had to take all my meals upstairs as she would not have me in the same room with her. However in the evening I went out to a wonderful concert. Rutland Boughton, the famous modern composer conducted a concert of his own music at the Conway Hall, High St. Walthamstow – A friend of mine (Squire – I don't know if you met him) and I got good seats for 6p each. It was up to Queen's Hall standard. The audience was most enthusiastic. Boughton thanked us and said it was one of the best audiences he had ever had. He said our applause had been generous but varied in quality and style – and said he "You were always right" this caused much amusement. The soloist was a Miss Dorothy d'Orsay – she was great. Boughton's stuff is frightfully difficult to sing – no lilting air following an accompaniment, but weird and yet delightful stuff – calling for a great variety of expression. He played her accompaniments himself – he was an artist from top to toe – entered into it – to see him conduct the choir who sang choruses was to see his whole nervous self being abandoned to the music. Well, he said of Miss d'Orsay, who I believe is local talent – that he was astounded and delighted – "She will go far" he said – "Before long her name will be famous on all the concert platforms of Europe". This was not said as an empty high-flown compliment. She was undoubtedly fine – possibly a rather wild prophecy for all that. She seemed overwhelmed by it.…

The General Strike – 1926

The year 1926 must have been a watershed year in "Sprad's" whole life and existence. This is evident from his sympathies and concerns for the working classes from whence he sprang. I can imagine his unrest and desire to involve himself in helping the plight of the miners' families in the industrial unrest and general strike which took hold of the country at that time.

Everything also begins to tie in with his motives to make contact with the eminent artist of the day, Frank Brangwyn, and his thoughts for establishing Walthamstow's supreme monument to the memory of its greatest son, William Morris, a man whose legacy to Britain was to have as much cultural impact on the country as that of Stratford-upon-Avon's William Shakespeare. The fact is that more homes around Britain and for that matter around the world will almost certainly possess more artistic evidence of William Morris than of William Shakespeare! Regrettably it seems never fully realised or appreciated by the local governing bodies within Morris's home-ground boroughs of Walthamstow and what is today the borough of Waltham Forest.

25th May 1926

My dear Jim

… A large amount of time has been spent in getting and reading the Strike news – certainly during the "nine days" one felt feverishly anxious to watch the progress of events so far as one could gather what was happening from the typewritten new-sheets, "British Worker", "Times", "British Gazette" and wireless reports.

What an astounding demonstration of solidarity, goodwill and good sense on the part of the mass of workers. My opinion is that in due course it will bear fruit not altogether bitter: that its ultimate results will prove more successful than many who took part in it realise, and I rather fancy that the "Calling off" was a very sound diplomatic action despite the criticism it has aroused in some sections – which is very natural from the miners anyway. It is quite certain that although the solidarity of the strikers would have been preserved much longer than Government action, "volunteer" action and the rapidly growing distress of a section of the community would have led to breakouts of violence – moreover it was highly probable that the government would have arrested the responsible leaders just when their control of the situation was most necessary and that although there were others to carry on, organization would have broken down and the Trades Union movement been imperiled if not broken....

> Spradbery's observations and explanations go on and on, extraordinary stuff from someone so seemingly far from the seat of power and from such an innocent reclusive background!

... Those railway companies and employers who on the ground of "breach of contract" were hoping to cut wages and "punish" workers found themselves sharply pulled up. Baldwin's pronouncements against victimisation were very statesman-like on this – considering his party and convictions I think he has come out of the conflict very well, so far, but his difficulties are not solved; he has avoided chaos for a time, but the problem of the living wage under modern industrial and financial conditions still confronts him and it is doubtful whether he has the vision or power to adjust matters. The Will of the people as a whole is right and I trust their faith supports their will – if so the way out will be found and fairer conditions for miners and all workers will result.

In some ways it is a great pity that a general election cannot be brought about now – it would probably put the Labour Party in power – but whether they could meet the difficulties of the situation either seems to me a little doubtful. They would at least have authority to Nationalise the mines, if not transport and other big industries, and with such capable men as Wheatley in their cabinet perhaps the root of particularly modern troubles would be touched....

... During the Strike I was much moved to express the ideas that form the basis of the new economics and sent so far as to prepare a paper that I might read at any meeting where a chance to express them appeared – but I have not yet tested my nerve as a public speaker and I did not find an opportunity or make one. However I tried to make a summary of some of the vital points – the seeds of the idea as it were, and determined to throw them where by the remotest of chances they might germinate perhaps – where at least they ought to be considered and cannot too often be repeated. So I wrote to Mr Baldwin and to Mr Ramsay Macdonald thus: (possibly it went straight from the hands of some minor secretary into the waste paper basket – but no matter – I have wasted more time than that given to this matter on subjects of less importance). What I wrote was complete on a page and read as follows:

"A Message of Goodwill"

Sir,

The Real Wealth and Credit of a Nation rests in its power to produce, distribute and exchange goods and services as when and where desired.

The Strike is a demonstration in demand of a Living Income for miners and all workers. It is a sound economic demand uttered with no uncertain voice. Granted it would involve an increasing issue of purchasing power based on the Real Credit of the nation which Real Credit would rapidly increase through the efforts of trade to meet the resulting effective demand.

America has learnt the first syllable of a new word spoken in modern economic chaos, and by high wages and increased consumer-credit facilities has given form to and established a period of prosperity among her people.

An age of prosperity and plenty awaits the utilisation of the Real Credit of the nation to supply fully (as it could) all the needs of those who produce it by their labour and cooperation, supplemented by the forces and energy harnessed by science and creative thought.

The problem of modern times is not to produce, but to make an effective demand to meet production and call forth potential production.

Economic power dominates political power. A wise government would use the economic power of organised labour against the economic force of cosmopolitan finance, and on its own real Social Credit establish a Commonwealth of happily employed people.

Consider these "New Economics" as a solution of the present crisis, I beg you. Goodwill and faith be with you. If you have not examined the Douglas and kindred proposals see:

"The Community's Credit" by C. Marshall Hattersley
"Social Credit" by G.H. Douglas
"Real Wealth and Financial Poverty" by Capt W. Adams
"Cartesian Economics" by Prof F. Soddy
"The Flaw in the Price System" by P. W. Martin
"Credit Power and Democracy" by C.H. Douglas
"The Solution of Unemployment" by W.H. Wakinshaw

These may be had from the Credit Reform Library,
70 High Holborn

Yours faithfully

Nothing happened and I was not arrested under the Emergency Power Act – nor did I get even a formal reply or acknowledgement. No matter. It was no more futile than saying that the Government couldn't manage a whelk stall which is a "gem" that Ramsay uttered which seems to me a remark unworthy of the dignity of his position and the good sense of the whole movement – more in character of a demagogue than a statesman – playing below the intellectual level of the modern gallery....

Extraordinary stuff to discover in later life from the hands of a father whose political activities one had naively considered to be marches, demonstrations and protest meetings! Surely here, naivety or not, are words of wisdom to grace any minister's portfolio. Yet again in the same letter we come across more personal matters referring to another of his greatest pals and comrades, talking of a place he would never have dreamt his own son was destined to travel to in 1982 – preceding the Falklands War by a matter of weeks!...

… Mac is talking of trying his fortune in Buenos Aires – possibly going there with a Capt. Someone or other – a recent acquaintance. He hasn't even got his fare at present, and the Capt. who has a second class passage and £100 on arrival, says if he can't raise it he'll change his second class for two steerage passages. He thinks Mac might do well as a portrait painter out there – it is the Paris of South America. Personally I don't think there's much in it but trouble…. It will be another loss to me – his company and talk at intervals is a relief to me from that of the dull, limited folk one ordinarily moves amongst. However I think we have known each other too long to lose sight of each other altogether and I shall do my part to keep in touch with him….

Back on with the General strike….

5th July 1926

My dear Jim

… I've "just struck oil" – or hope so anyway – motor oil – "Shell". There is some talk of the "Shell" people getting me to do a series of posters of the English villages – "See the charms of England in Shell" sort of thing … cash has not been too plentiful. Finding myself unable to subscribe anything very substantial to the miners' fund and feeling it was too urgent a matter to wait until money owing me for work executed came to hand, I offered Brailsford of the "New Leader" my big Academy picture of St. Paul's to auction or sell privately for the fund. I told him that I thought a number of artists of repute would gladly contribute work for this purpose, and some verification of this has come from John Nash who has offered four wood-cut prints. He (Brailsford) has handed both my picture and the woodcuts over to Dr Marian Phillips who has organized a sort of auction department at 11 Tufton Street and we shall see what comes of it…. The much abused Mr Cook seems to me to stand out as a wonderful leader – a man of wit, intelligence and determination. The miners are lucky to have such a man to conduct their affairs and the whole Trades Union movement is indebted to his spirit for rallying it at a dangerous moment. A less uncompromising leader would have been tricked by the diplomacy of certain astute members of the Government, but his unflinching, fearless attitude has proved a touchstone to disclose the true nature of those he has dealt with or opposed.... Chesterton, a non socialist, in his weekly publication has been a wholehearted and brilliant supporter of the Unions with all the wit and logic that is at his command. Lloyd George's speeches have had more point and fire in them than Ramsay Mac's. and represent the bulk of Liberal feeling....

... Now I must tell you the news about Mac. In my last letter I told you he was thinking about packing up for Buenos Aires. Well that's off, for on the eve of departure a better chance came his way and a wealthy man, an acquaintance of the Captain with whom he's going with, said that if Mac could be a success in Buenos Aires he saw no reason why, given a chance, he should not be one here, and offered forthwith to back him to the extent of £200. He arranged to hire an excellent studio (in which Mac is now situated complete with telephone – KEN 8125 – No 8 Bolton Studios, Radcliffe Road, South Kensington) – equipped him with canvasses and brushes and is bringing wealthy clubmen to have their portraits painted. From these, and folks who will be brought to see the work, commissions are hoped for and expected and big figures will be charged for such portraits.

The man financing is to go 50/50 with Mac on the proceeds of the venture. Mac declares "this is the chance of his lifetime." I have seen him once in his new quarters and I believe he is very busily at work. Next week I shall see him again as he wants me to help him to arrange an effective show in his studio – to which Mr Erskine (ie. his backer) or the Right Hon. something – or other Erskine (he is the son of Lady Erskine) will bring the nobs of society, to see, and become victims....

> Haydn Mackey's friendship and activities especially throughout "Sprad's" pre-marriage and bachelor years were continuously referred to in his correspondence to Jim Berry. They must have been very much three comrades together on the Somme in the war's last days. Mackey was always the bohemian one and outwardly demonstrative in character. There must have developed a closer affinity with James Berry as a consequence of their political and social sympathies. But Mackey nevertheless was someone "Sprad" felt a binding loyalty towards, an allegiance of artistic principle and belief in each others' efforts that was again as remarkable as "Sprad's" newer found friendship with James Berry itself.
>
> Letters at this time pick upon on a new phenomenon known as "Social Credit", a subject constantly emerging in their frequent correspondence. With the endless failing repercussions of the capitalist system in the world today, one wonders what "Social Credit" was all about and where it might have led to?

5th July continued

... Discussion of "Social Credit" goes on in extending circles and I see that Australia has many centres where public consideration is given to it. Theatres being filled to hear lectures on it....

12th July 1926

My dear Jim

You will be very delighted to know that I have had a very satisfactory reply and offer of work for sale and use in connection with the Fund for the relief of miners' wives and children from Brangwyn, and yesterday I had a short chat on the phone with him from Mr Brailsford's office.

I got his address (Brangwyn's) from Spare (the artist, Austin Osman Spare) and wrote my appeal, and yesterday morning I had a letter from Brangwyn saying he was ill and could not undertake to do anything especially for the cause at the moment but enclosing a reproduction of a lithograph which he felt might meet the needs and express the appeal for the miners' wives and children although it had been done for the widows and orphans of the French Army....

... I met Mac's patron or backer, or whatever he calls himself – exploiter perhaps – he is a very nice fellow, fully aware of the prestige "family" gives and told me he was in the direct descent from the Earls of Marr (Scottish) and showed me a book full of portraits of his ancestors in the Garfax Galleries – most of them painted by Raeburn. He told some racy stories.... He has made himself very nice to me and I've been conscious of him trying to sum me up – looking at me on the quiet – trying to get my real opinion on points. He's equally under my survey as it were – for I'm hopeful of what he may do for Mac but at the same time watching the game. If Mac quarrelled with him (as he's likely to do as not) he might put Mac into a very awkward position. Undoubtedly he's a benefactor at the moment to Mac and deserves consideration and gratitude. Also he's a capable man who knows what he's about and that he's trying an interesting but not necessarily successful experiment. Both have tempers I can see – and a liking for whisky – and there will be many dangerous points in the development of their plans....

... I see that rotten hole Blackpool has, through its Corporation, refused to have collections made for the miners by means of a flag-day. "Gadfly" in the "Herald" tells them off as they deserve and his recommendation to folk to bar the place I sincerely hope will be acted upon – it has no beauty and is built by the hucksters to make profit out of the brief holidays of workers who would find simpler and more beautiful pleasures and true refreshment elsewhere.

I am not surprised at their council's action – their architecture and idea of entertainment (the Tower and the Gt Wheel) shows how they lack taste and proper feeling. No doubt by tomorrow there'll be all explanations and apology and injured innocence....

> "Sprad's" whole demeanour and outlook is such as to touch all life's vast spectrum of heartstrings, emotions and tastes from the simplest of souls to the noblest. His intellect, his depth of principle and honesty never falters, yet wit and compassion have and were always with him.

… Spare has again appeared in the Press as a genius in a tenement – Artist, author, editor and wireless expert and inventor – who exhibited at the R.A. and wrote a Bible at 15 years. (Daily Sketch 11th of July). When I got Brangwyn's address from him he was almost destitute. I bought a wonderful drawing from him for a guinea (which was all I could afford) – He is all they say of him and more than they know or really appreciate.

All his household equipment was a plank bed with some scanty and dirty bedding and a single cup without a handle. He had just received a County Court notice for his rent from the L.C.C. nevertheless he is one of the most remarkable men alive – of such influence and full of strange knowledge – both his writings and drawings will be valued more highly than they now are I think in times to come. His history will seem as unbelievable as his achievements.…

> As a child at our home, "The Wilderness", I remember the name of Austin Osman Spare very well. An extraordinary portrait of his hung in the studio until the end of my father's life. As with so much of his artistic heirlooms from friends and fellow artists, things at "The Wilderness" in his latter years when staying on alone, deteriorated and were irreparably damaged by dampness. I latterly discovered Spare was at one time a close student friend of Sylvia Pankhurst at the Royal College of Art – and both were expelled together over some misdemeanour or other. He also served in the R.A.M.C. in the 1914-18 War, his work is also to be discovered, certainly in the archives of the Wellcome Institute and probably the Imperial War Museum. I always understood him to be known as an "artist of the occult".

15th July 1926

My dear Jim

Have had an exciting day today rowing with people in the Labour movement, who have no idea to use a good thing when they get it given them. The greatest living artist in Europe (or maybe the world) gives them an etching bearing dramatically on the subject they are out to help – the miners – and it remains in their hands before a word appears anywhere about it. Then in "The Herald" we get this – today – that his name is put at the end of a lot of artists who although known, are as fleas beside him, and his name is misspelt, his Christian name unceremoniously clipt to F. and his designation R.A. left out altogether. As his name is as familiar in the Art World as Bernard Shaw's or H.G. Well's in the literary and as much a "household word" – not to mention his world-wide reputation – this is appallingly careless to say the least of it. It is quite as ridiculous as if they had said they had an autographed book by H.G. Wells. It infuriates me. I grabbed up all those notes you read on

Brangwyn, and a number of cuttings about him where he is described as beyond comparison with modern artists and like a giant from the Renaissance and dashed off up to "The Herald's" offices and asked to see the news editor. I saw him at once and let him have it (with proper restraint however and allowances for their having been given the copy to print in the form it appeared). He became quite interested I think and saw what a chance had been missed, and took down notes in short-hand at a terrific rate. I said that had he (Brangwyn) done it for some purpose in which business men were interested headlines would have appeared about it in all the press, that it would have been advertised and exploited in every way and probably a big sum realised for it, crowds induced to go to see it, and artists tumbling over each other to have a work in the same show. I said "As it was useful to you in the Social world for the Prince of Wales to give his ten pounds, and in the religious-thinking world for the Archbishop of Canterbury to say some not intolerant words about the Strike, so to the intelligentsia and the art-loving world this was an event and a gesture worth proper announcement. I pointed out that more than any other living artist Brangwyn had portrayed in his work the pathos and drama of the poor and the humblest workers and showed (to those with sense to see it) that their vitality and energy built and maintained civilisations.

I left him the catalogue of the exhibition Ramsay Macdonald opened (in which English and foreign homage to his genius is paid) and buzzed off round to 11 Tufton Street the headquarter of the Women's committee. There I saw Mrs Morel and other good ladies who did the usual gush around me about my "lovely work" and "the splendid way" I had got other artists also to contribute drawings and so on. I then raised the matter with them – they were awfully sorry and realised, they said, as soon as they saw it in the paper that something had gone wrong. I was told to see Dr Marion Phillip who probably was responsible. I saw her – she is a hefty woman – and undoubtedly working steadily and merrily on – she said she had merely sent in the previous day's notice and written F. Brangwyn on the side to be added. She of course has so much to attend to that no one could grumble at her – and I don't fancy she knows much or anything about Art. However I hope tomorrow's "Herald" will have an article on Brangwyn to put things right and give the whole exhibition a boost....

...There are worse troubles and more foolishness to be encountered all over the place no doubt. Had a fairly long chat with Brailsford today – told him a lot about Spare – got him interested I think – and gave him an invite to go and see Mac's show at his studio. He says he will, Mac will do him good – give him "Douglas" hot and strong I expect.

Cheerio

Your affectionate friend

Walt

17th July 1926

Dear Jim

…You will note today's "Herald" has two notes on Brangwyn's work – I expect if it be much noticed the remark "It has been said that he has put down the mighty from their seats and exalted them of low degree on many magnificent canvasses etc" will excite the enquiry "Who said it?" – answer – "Old Walt". That was going the whole hog – for he hath put down the mighty from their seat and hath exalted them of low degree" is from the Magnificat and refers to God really!

> "Sprad's excessive and zealous correspondence surrounding his concern for the country's General Strike and at the same time his anguish and desperation over the lack of awareness and respect of the standing and genius of such an artist figure as Frank Brangwyn within circles he might have expected more recognition from at that particular period of time may appear infinitesimal and of little consequence, even more so within the context of the massive backdrop of the 1926 General Strike. Also the extracts of his letter of the 23rd July, describing the simple difficulties in actually setting up the exhibition in Westminster's Central Hall is at the same time amusing and baffling when one considers "Sprad's" previous experience in that whole field of exhibiting in rooms and spaces which must have encompassed his life at that time.

23rd July 1926

My dear Jim

You would like to know the news of the last few days and I wish I could tell you all about it in person – I could tell you much more – writing takes a long time. I am afraid too it will seem very like what Cook said of Fyfe's book – "How Bill Adams won the Battle of Waterloo" – sort of account.

Well, I think I told you Mrs Morel asked me to go to supper at 11 Tufton Street on the Monday evening before the show at the Central Hall. I went and after supper was requested to go over to the hall to superintend the hanging of the work sent in. When I got there I found an amazing quantity of pictures, etchings, prints and drawings had been sent in – a collection better than any West End Society could have got together – but as a lot of the work was unpriced and no one knew what the relative value of things were there was a lot of confusion. How the work was to be put up on stone walls with no picture rail was another question. There were lots of willing persons to help and there were lots willing to talk and advise in an exasperatingly futile way, and for an hour or so I could hardly induce people not to keep on looking over the piles of stuff. Just when I was feeling that it was hopeless I found a whole pile of folding 6ft tables and with these we fixed up screens all round the walls; on the wooden surface of these we could pin prints and hang work. I then, having had a word or two with Mrs Morel about the need if the show was to be up, took charge like a "dictator" and got folks separating work into groups – black and white – etchings – framed work and so on and picking out a group of nicely mounted prints of Roy Rothensteins, portrait sketches of Labour leaders, I showed 'em how to arrange them on a brown paper background on the table-screens. It was then discovered that there were no pins, cord, nails or brown paper! Shops were closed as it was now about 8.30 or 9 p.m. However people were sent scouting out and a supply (rather limited) was got from somewhere. A futile youth kept drifting round with works and was very nice in his ideas of how things should go but not an atom of real help at that time (he got better later) and Dr Marion Phillips arrived and I told her that we'd enough stuff for two such halls. She told me that as she wanted to show an imitation coal mine too, she'd just made arrange-ments to take the large concert hall also – and that we might hang big work in there. That was good news indeed. By this time I had found one or two capable ladies who progressed with the hanging and arranging very well indeed and I felt very grateful to them – Also a school teacher of a practical turn who helped to fix drawings up and pack stuff behind the tables so that they did not damage the wall they were leaning against. At 10.15 we had to knock off as the place closes then, but things were beginning to fall into position.

I promised to come up the next morning at 11 a.m. – couldn't get there before because of mother and things at home – and left instructions for "carrying on" pending my arrival. When I got there things were very much as I'd left them except that a lot more stuff had come in. Still the supply of cord was missing!...

... At about 2 pm most were up but still a dozen or two things had to be placed and a lady who I did not know brought me her son, a nice fellow, and said I was to make him useful, so I got him on the job – showed him where the remaining pic-tures were to go and how to attach them. I found out after that the gracious lady was Lady Slesser. She struck me as a capable sensible sort. The son had a bit of a struggle with the job but didn't do so badly. Meanwhile some work space in the first room was found when a screen was moved and some clothes pegs, and this was arranged with some more prints, the last nails being driven in when the public began to come in. During the whole of my "hanging" activities every few minutes ladies were rushing up with prints and things and saying "Oh Mr Spradbery how much do you think this ought to be – what shall we ask!" and so on....

... An apparently wealthy lady connected with the movement, Mrs Bonhote, wants me to go motor rides in her car to see some effects of landscape by motor lamps at night! Her chauffeur would be there. Mrs Morel insists in keeping in touch with me, Mrs Shuffrey – art pottery people in Chelsea – will have me visit them some time – oh and lots more. "What we should have done without you I can't think!" has been said by nearly every lady responsible – and it's a scream how many they are and how they feel towards each other. Dr Marion Phillips strikes me as the most capable (except perhaps Lady Slesser whose style I like better), Dr Phillips is cynical but merry, modern in tastes and looks almost like a fat jewess. She insists that when she goes (as I advised) to see the Editor of the "Studio" I must go with her! There never were such times Jim!...

> The pages roll on detailing many of the sales of the pictures and taking the exhibition to Liverpool and Welwyn Garden City where the Edwards, another of "Sprad's" most valued set of friends (perhaps emerging from his R.A.M.C. days) lived. The sums of money talked about are ridiculously low compared with the astronomical sums detailed in today's art galleries and sales. There's a Bill Adams, a bus man, whom he describes as a "real good fellow and a character."
>
> Spradbery's letters to Jim Berry continue unabated leading out of the twenties into his momentous years of the thirties where his personal life so dramatically changed. However despite the revelations of marriage and finding the idyllic "Wilderness" with my mother, his beloved Dorothy, he still contended with his own mother's surviving years, who throughout the twenties managed to relentlessly usurp his own career and whatever social life there was for him. It is only through this hugely intimate and revelationary mass of correspondence remarkably coming into my own hands at such a late stage in my own life that I was ever aware of the terrible problems his mother (my grandmother) constantly imposed upon him throughout those post-First World War years, which I feel duty bound to reveal to readers in the cause of this account of his life, half a century on – ignoring on the other hand Spradbery's own loyalty and great love for her in revealing these early dilemmas in his home life.
>
> In the ensuing months and subsequent years hundreds of written pages of communicating thoughts passed between these friends – comrades. Miraculously I have some of these communications which have helped me to compile some sort of record and history of "Sprad's" life. Here are a couple of extracts again reluctantly reporting on his mother's extraordinary irrational and disappointing behaviour towards him at this particular time. These brief extracts are taken from numerous letters seemingly dealing with the prolonged developments from the initial Westminster Central Hall exhibitions for the miners' funds and subsequent dealings with the Ladies Committee led by Dr Marion Phillips and Mrs Morel; also various political debates and his own current political ideas, plus his concern for Mac's continuing involvement with the shady Capt Erskine and his setting up of Mac's Chelsea studio.

27 Sept 1926

My dear Jim

Under separate cover I am sending some things to amuse Norman (Jim's young son) as a little birthday present for him. In the book there are a large number of amusing ideas that perhaps he will cut out and make up – enough to fill in a good many winter evenings.

You'll have to show him how to set about the jobs – or perhaps his teacher will let him do some in class – they are the sort of things that some schools use to entertain the youngsters. The nail-and-hammer bricks will no doubt also keep him busy (and you!) banging away for hours.

I cannot tell you how unhappy things are at home – only those who have lived along with a tyrannous old lady can guess what the life is – how wretched, miserable, comfortless – my sister who was here a day or so ago had enough of it in a few hours – and she didn't get the concentrated ill-feeling I get poured on me. Poor mother is so helpless at times, so violent at others, so incessantly nagging – I don't know what to do to please her, make her happy and as to get on with work – peace and opportunity to concentrate are almost impossible things to find.…

31 March 1927

My dear Jim

… My poor mother seems to get more and more irritable and depressed – I know not how to please her – nor does anyone else – and my life becomes a burden and spirits fail.… If one received kindness or appreciation or a spirit of helpfulness was noticeable it would be a reward and one could continue with spirit, but there is nothing but complaints, and outbursts of violent temper in which the wildest charges are made, the most false construction put on acts that are of goodwill and intention. My mother's digestion seems to have got rapidly worse and this no doubt makes her so touchy and unreasonable and gloomy – but you can have no conception of the hell life can be made – and how hopeless the future can seem, how impossible to go on it feels.…

Chapter 4

Family Ties

Placing "Sprad's" life in some chronological order, perspective and sequence of events does not give the full picture, or significance to all the aspects of life that filled his time and drove him onwards. It is the revelation of the emergence of "Sprad's" remarkable letters to Jim Berry that colours and brings these occasions, circumstances and backgrounds to light. Spradbery was nothing more than an everyday human being from the poorest London working classes. Although not an undistinguished figure in his well-worn tweed suits, he was a man of quiet demeanour; his personality was compounded by an honesty and integrity which never left or deserted him. This was what was evident to sympathetic friends and colleagues who moved around him at the time. To me his son, in later life, reflecting on his days as I experienced them – and what has been revealed from his own writings, it appears (looking back to those precious years, before the menace of World War Two and immediate subsequent years) that he led an exceptional life, besides proving a man of exceptional concept and values. . . .

His elder sister, Flo, who ran off from the family home to marry at an early age, as most of her other siblings did, "Sprad" loved dearly; and his brother Charlie he had tremendous respect and admiration for; however his other brother, Joe, he seemingly felt distrustful of and lost patience with. These are siblings referred to in his childhood years as was another sister, Elle, who ran away from home and led some existence as a chorus girl or perhaps more likely a woman of leisure, it seems never to be heard of again.

One can easily imagine the torment and oppressive moods of his mother to have affected "Sprad's" whole being at that period of time. To suffer such outbreaks of irrationality and vitriolic behaviour from a mother whom deep down he loved, on top of the general depressing state of life outside their little abode in 36 Turner Road must have filled him with utter despair. Confiding these feelings, and the hopelessness confronting him to James Berry was something he would not have anticipated finding its way into the hands of his own son, three quarters of a century later. A son prepared to break with a rule of family loyalty to illustrate just what "Sprad's" life was up against at that crucial time in his life. Even so, his love and devotion for and towards his mother never faltered, and was always there for her. His misgivings, his sense of family betrayal must have haunted his mind like no other emotions at that time.

When he wrote those words of anguish to his soul-mate – two hundred miles away in the heart of Yorkshire – Spradbery was thirty-eight years old, a man beginning to think of solace and other sweeter things in life. One can only surmise that his devotion to protecting his mother over so many vital years of his life must have impaired much of his material progress in the world itself. His other siblings had flown the nest at their earliest opportunities! Even so, in his local environ-ment, community and surroundings, his influence could not have gone unnoticed and unrecognized. His poster designs were attracting attention with a steady flow of commissions working under the most abject conditions of a small confined house in the backstreets of such a working class borough as Walthamstow E.17 with a mother persistently demanding attention and help. His teaching prowess and reputation within the borough was reaching the ears of the local educational authorities and drawing a vast number of aspiring young artists and students into his fold; he surely was an influential force in leading and gathering together local artists who established themselves as the Essex Art Club with such early friends and colleagues as Fred Parsons, an artist buddy referred to as Higgins, Harold Parker, a Noel Hills and others from further afield. At the same time his intellectual and political involvement and awareness was always thumping away within him; social justice, moral issues and other conscious duties were part of his character and always at the forefront of his life-long held attitudes.

Haydn Mackey

Looking back from afar to the immediate months and years after the Great Miners' Strike and the aftermath of its possible effect on "Sprad's" outlook and prospects ahead of him: his problems with a mother constantly tormenting him and driving him into depths of despair, friendships must have appeared his last salvation! Never in "Sprad's" mind was there a stronger bonding than with James Berry, although situated and living in Yorkshire and very much tied to a closely closeted marriage with his betrothed Edith and a young son Norman. I can only surmise through the tone and nature of his constant flow of correspondence to his friend in Yorkshire, that the future at that time held few briefs other than his posters under the benevolent hand of Frank Pick and whatever destiny lay ahead with fellow artists and students closer to his roots in Walthamstow. Haydn Mackey was one of these....

6th July 1927

... Today I saw Mac again. I met him by arrangement at a little exhibition of an artist's work, a mutual friend, David Baxter. With Mac there was a very nice young

Haydn Mackey

lady, who turned out to be the same one to whom he had given a lesson – painted a pot as a demonstration, you may remember seeing it in his studio and his remarking on it. He was in high good humour, and the lady was most agreeably interested in all he said. He chided me and I was able to retaliate suitably and we were all laughing, joking, discussing things and quite at home with one another. We went back to Mac's studio; the lady put on the kettle to make tea and I went out and bought provisions. We had a jolly feed – another of Mac's quaint literary friends dropped in – (just a little in the way but we put up with him) – and we talked of books and ideas music and poetry – all like a song until it was 8.30 and time for me to go home.

Mac put on the gramophone and even broke into a little dance in tune to a ragtime air. "Eurythmics" said the lady. "More like Rheumatics" said Mac. So you see he's not so gloomy as he has been. What is it that the song in the Beggar's Opera says… "When the heart of a man is all filled with care" about the troubles all vanishing "when a woman appears"? Well Mac felt easy, and the lady was most friendly and a pleasant discreet young person. She presided at the tea quite nicely and took an excellent part in the conversation and seemed to know a good deal about many of Mac's Chelsea friends. We became on merry terms at once and were able to combine little efforts to banter Mac. She told me that she could never imagine me bored or boring; and she knew a certain amount of my work and was surprised to hear that I ever felt uncertain about it – it looked to her so bold and deliberate she said. I gave her some hints for her own development in water colour painting. I hope she is likely to become a more or less permanent interest in Mac's. life – (perhaps this is hurrying things a bit) – anyway I feel such a thing would be very good for him….

… Oh by the way… I've not given you a very good description of the girl at Mac's studio. Well, she was young, about 23 or 24 I should think perhaps less, perhaps more. She has her hair done in plaits over her ears – dark I think – fair complexion – a quiet intelligent face, with the suspicion of a smile and a merry twinkle playing about it from time to time. Height about 5ft 8in or a shade higher than Mac which is a pity. She wore a loose frock, tight enough to disclose her movement. It was of gay flowered pattern. She had very fair legs as far as I could see – I mean to say – Oh Jim! She did not move as easily from the hips and beautifully as Mary did – (Schwab's wife you know) – a slight wobble, a little self-conscious from the back view. My God! These lads! How they do notice! Whatever will Edith say if she's looking over your shoulder! She smoked a few cigarettes.

> Good night my dear lad – and to Edith.
> I expect the boy's abed long ago. Keep well and happy,
> Your affectionate friend,
>
> Walt.

In selecting extracts and quoting from correspondence written so long ago, I cannot help but detect both a certain apprehension and benevolence towards such an early colleague as Haydn Mackey. Mackey was a pal and colleague from his earliest days, as already mentioned, whom he had possibly grown away from in spirit and in terms of morality, yet he was someone whose skill as an artist he respected with the highest esteem and still possessed a close and touching loyalty towards.

Mackey and Harold Parker, the designer of the wren on Britain's new farthing coin, were "Sprad's" earliest friends and artist colleagues of perhaps even more outstanding talents than himself. Spradbery in his lifetime attracted other younger artists to his fold of friends, but those three must have shown themselves as a unique trio of artist figures from such a confined and working class area of local urban life.

Later correspondence after what had seemed Mac's promising future in the new studio in Kensington came to an end, and with him facing charges for unpaid telephone bills:

25th July 1927

… I called on Mac again a few days ago, at his old address, 108 Drayton Gardens S.W. He has given up the studio, since retaining it increased his obligations with every passing day.…When he was moving out from the studio an official from the Telephone Dept accompanied by a seedy looking individual, interrupted proceedings by their appearance and explained that as Mac owed £4 odd for the use of phone they were there to claim it. Mac said "Well I deposited £5 when the thing was fixed: you better take it out of that and I shall be glad of the change."The official explained that he had no information on that point and asked if there was not something that he could conveniently take to recover the debt. "What about this fine picture in this handsome frame here?" he asked "Couldn't I get sufficient for a thing like that to meet the matter?" "You might get half-a-crown at the pawnshop on the frame" said Mac "but if you sell the picture you'll be able to do a thing I've not succeeded in doing for years." "Well then that easel is surely a valuable bit of furniture" said the Official. "It is," said Mac "but as it happens to be one of the tools of my trade I don't think you can touch it." "Well what's to be done" said the amiable official. "My intention" said Mac "is to remove my goods to 108 Drayton Gardens where you will be likely to find me at almost any time for some months at least, so I suggest you enquire what's become of my five pounds". "That seems the only course" said the official "although our friend here (the seedy man) will be somewhat disappointed as he get's 3/6 per day for taking possession." So away went the amiable official and Mac has heard no more. However that's not all his troubles by a long way. It appears that some weeks ago (before your visit I fancy) – yes – because I remember he said it was the 13th) he came out of a public house in the evening, with his brother, and continued an argument, begun inside, on the pavement. This not only attracted passers-by but the police, who advised him to move along; but Mac was inclined to banter the police and argue with them too. His brother on the other hand was rather nervous about the way things seemed to be going and suddenly seizing him by the arm to pull him away, jerked him so unexpectedly that he lost his balance, and tripping over his brother, they both fell into the gutter. The policemen then ran old Mac in, as "Drunk and Disorderly".

Mac, on arrival at the station, was quite furious and, almost incoherently excited, demanded medical examination by his own doctor. However at first only the Police Doctor was allowed and he put Mac through the tests, which he came through alright. But in the course of his talk with the doctor he was (without using any language that could be called "bad") pretty abusive of the police, referring to them as "ignorant louts" which the Doctor said is very intemperate language and I'm afraid I must say you are not sober." So, still demanding to see his own Doctor, Mac was put into a cell. "Stone Walls do not a prison make nor iron bars a cage" said Mac. "No need to quote Shakespeare" said the constable. "It isn't Shakespeare it's Lovelace" said Mac triumphantly.

About a couple of hours later Mac's own doctor arrived (ie a friend of Mac's who happened to be a Doctor) accompanied by another medical man with whom he had been playing billiards at the time he was called. They re-examined Mac and declared that he certainly was not drunk. Then Mac was let out on bail to appear at Westminster Court on the following Monday I think it was. When Mac appeared with all the medical evidence in his favour, he thought all would go well and the case be dismissed, but excited by the account the policemen gave, he incorporated into his own statements so many violent statements, that they were regarded as counter-charges against the police and the magistrate adjourned the case for the police to prepare their defence. This put the wind up Mac for he was not in the position to employ a solicitor himself and he decided when the case reopened to plead "Guilty" and take whatever was imposed. However when the case opened and he did this, up jumped a solicitor on behalf of the police and said that his clients would expect heavy costs, as they had been put to a lot of trouble and expense, and proceeded to rattle out a list of items that rapidly mounted up to "about a hundred pounds I should think" said Mac. The Magistrate, after jotting down some of the items and surveying them critically said "I can't allow all that and fined him 7/6 and 4 guineas costs.

"Always plead "guilty" whatever you're accused of by the police – if ever you are accused Sprad" said Mac "even if it's rape or murder!"

Well, when I called on Mac and heard all this and found that if he did not pay up by the end of the month, to prison he'd have to go. Of course I was a bit worried and enquired what prospect of raising the cash he had. So far as I could make out there were only vague hopes – fortunately I'd not squared up all my little debts and had some of the poster cash still in hand, so after half a day's deliberation I sent enough to pay the fine and costs telling him that if he was able later to raise it elsewhere he could return it, or part.... Fortunately since then I've sold two watercolours for seven guineas, so I'm not "broke" myself. I have sent off five works for Mrs Ratcliffe (of Ripon) to see – framed up they look a good set – I hope she'll buy the most expensive – and sell the rest to her friends for me.

An Essay on Friendship

25th July 1927

letter continues

… Perhaps what one's spirit cries out for from the deeps of the subconscious mind, is the comprehensive and comprehending love of God – an unsatisfied hunger that sends us from experience to experience, so that all friendship and all love, in varying degrees of perfection is a symbol of this deep longing – and so in moods of introspection we abase ourselves and idolise those we love. We yearn for that which is outside ourself to respond and recognise the inner being as its own. We crave reassurances to justify our existence. The recognition of brotherhood, that is the marvellous experience of affection – it can be extended to all living creatures in degree – as St. Francis knew, calling all living things "Brother", communing with the birds and even elemental phenomena.

But only man can love and understand man completely. According to the New Testament even God found it necessary to become a man and to suffer all things with him, so that understanding man he might forgive him, despite "all the sin wherewith the face of man is blackened" – and it is a sublime idea. Omnipotence must experience the limitations of the body to understand the pains, distresses and joys, of its wrestling and strivings in a world of consciousness.

It seems probable to me that even woman, the complement of man, cannot wholly understand man as a man may, although the love between the two sexes is physically creative and impelled and directed to that end, so that they complete each other. There are things no man could make his wife quite understand, that to his friend would be clearly intelligible. The restlessness of the soul of man is very often a distress to his wife, lover, mother. When in his madness he goes out searching into realms of danger – seeking what? – Knowledge; adventure; new experience; the answer to the riddles of life … into the realm of creative ideas, the realm of spiritual creation, (or maybe the wild pathless wastes of unexplored country) then he is in a world she cannot follow – nor does he particularly want her to. She awaits his return in anguish, intuitively feeling the risks he runs, the terror and uncertainties he moves among, She learns to know man as a father and a son – in all his physical weaknesses, his vanity, his need of comfort, support and rest; She can even go so far as to admire uphold and wonder at his heroism and achievement and forgive his failures. She is the breast to which the exhausted must return – the home of "the sailor home from the sea, the hunter home from the kill".

But the true companion and inspiration of man in the realms of thought, imagination and speculative and adventurous action is man. And the love of man for man is a marvellous thing, more rarely fully valued, more strange and terrible than his love of woman, plumbing to the depths and scaling the heights of feeling, self-sacrifice and even folly. To read of the great friendships makes one tremble before a phenomena that overleaps anything else nature can show in her constant combination of the heroics, the tragic and the comic.

The woman who endeavours and succeeds in separating effectively a man (son lover or husband) from his friends and companions lessens his ability, cripples his spirit, dries up his aspirations, accomplishes his degeneration and downfall. A wise woman knows her value to a man – she holds him with a cord nature fashioned – his friendships with his own kind cannot lessen her hold really – and if she curbs any dread or fear of his fellowmen's influence, her generosity and trust is rewarded by the health of his spirit, his unquenched fire, his continued achievement. She has the sure knowledge and satisfaction that she links him with past and future making the chain of life and human development possible; satisfying and comforting, and renewing him in a new generation that may rectify his failures, build upon his successes – great joy is ahead. Friendship has no such plainly real rewards; it gives one no such solid pledges of its actuality, one cannot be measurably certain what it has begotten or will beget. Yet it sustains and interprets life, encourages the spirit, diverts and gladdens it; in the conflict and intermingling of ideas it creates new thought and gives vision, and it is the basis of the relations of mutual toleration and helpfulness whereby communities come together and are made possible. It is a communion as mystic as any, lifting those who participate to heights of self-realisation and mutual understanding, colouring life: its fertility is of the spirit and cannot be measured because unmeasurable.…

A New Brave Friend and more of Mac

Quoted in this letter amounting to 21 hand-written pages and written in the early hours of the morning of the 14th September, 1927, is a sad, but an inspiring and most moving tale of a fleeting friendship that "Sprad" has felt impelled to inform Jim Berry about in almost every moving detail. It has a ring of true Dickensian pathos – and is perhaps a tale of the resources with which the human spirit is capable of overcoming and achieving.

… Besides the visit of the Bull family I've had another visitor, extremely interesting to me and whose story I must recount to you. I wish I could do it in the simple straight-forward way it was told to me; in the phrases of an uneducated fellow, but of a man of spirit, and that I could give you the convincing tones of his voice, make you see the kind depth of his eye and its occasional sparkle – But first – I must tell you who he is and generally what he looks like; also how I met him.

Well, when I got my cash from the Ely poster, I splashed out on a new suit, and when I called at the tailors to be fitted, his principal work-man came out and asked me if I'd tell him about some colours he'd bought – tell him if he's been charged correctly for them by the man who got them for him. He had a very small tube of Cobalt Yellow and was astounded to find it was priced at 1/6. I assured him that was the price of the colour, which was one of the expensive ones and not at all necessary for use generally. I asked him a question or two about his painting, which disclosed it was a recently acquired hobby and consisted mainly of copying colour prints. He said "I wish I could see a real artist paint; I reckon I'd soon pick up something" "Well" said I "if you think I'm near enough to being a real artist perhaps you'd like to come round some evening and look over some of my works and maybe I could give you a hint or two."

I said this because the poor fellow is a dreadful cripple and I was touched by his simplicity and knew that he could not have a great many friends. A week ago today he came, and full of gratitude he was long before he'd received any help, he was burning with thanks it seemed.

I must tell you that he has one leg amputated at the knee, and that the other is so weak and bent that it is always in irons; that long walking on crutches has pulled his shoulders up to his ears; that his movement is most painful to watch: Between those hunched-up shoulders peers a brown monkey-like face, with dark intelligent eyes and black hair above it. A grotesque figure less than a man in body but, as you shall hear, very fully and finely one in spirit – In fact in appearance he reminded me of a nightmare dream I think I once told you of – of a manikin, distorted and on crutches actively pursuing a course along a luridly lit way. Well I regaled him with two glasses of ale and turned out my work which he admired and commented on with a ready understanding and about which he asked questions very much to the point.

I asked him how he came to take up a brush and that set him on telling me his life history – no doubt the ale loosened his tongue – I got it in patches in response to questions put during the evening but I will give it to you arranged in a better or at least a more consecutive sequence. I asked how he became a cripple. He said that his mother was left when he was a baby with nine children to provide for, so she went out charring to do it, and left him, a little toddler, with his elder sister. He was a spirited little boy, and his sister was fond of reading, so while she was engrossed in a book one morning, he ran out into the snow with nothing on, just as he had scrambled from the bed. The result was a severe chill, which ended in rickets and was followed by diphtheria, and then it was found as he got better that he'd lost the use of lower limbs – and a sort of partial paralysis – and it was even necessary to remove one leg at the knee.

As this maimed little fellow grew up he felt he must earn something to bring to the family store – he was far from allowing himself to become a burden. So at ten he was out with a box and brushes cleaning boots and getting pennies or sixpences according to the wealth or generosity of his clients. One old boy always gave him sixpence and spoke cheerily to him. "What are you going to do when you're a man" he asked – "you don't want to clean boots all your life do you? Would you not like to learn a trade at which you could earn more money such as say a tailor my lad?" "I'd like to be a sailor" said the little cripple in all innocence. Several times the old boy questioned him, my acquaintance told me, and as the idea got into the child's mind he thought about it especially after an occasion when the old boy gave him half a sovereign. At the time the lad thought it was given in mistake and said "Hi gov'nor this aint a tanner it's half a quid" "I know" said the old gent "get yourself a pair of trousers, its very evident you want 'em." Well, after this when he again asked the boy if he would care to be a tailor, he said "Yes if he (the gent) thought he could." The gentleman then took him to his own home and sent his housekeeper ("a sort of nurse" said my acquaintance) out for an outfit for him, and then arranged for him to go to an Industrial School, paying £25 for an apprenticeship to the tailoring for him. At the end of his time he went to a job, got for him by the school, on the Cornish Coast.

"I had some real good times there" said he, "I like the sea, and you know, I can swim better than I can walk." "Swim! Said I, "Swim! How the devil can you swim." "Oh yes I can swim better'n I can walk," he reiterated – and proceeded to tell me how he learnt. "I've been lucky in meeting kind people" he said, "Folks are often very considerate to me. And I met some nice young men down there and so I said to one of 'em that went about with me sometimes, "Dick I want to learn to swim!" He laughed and said he'd take me with him next time he went in the river. And he did. He took me out in a boat and some distance from the river bank moored it, undressed himself and swam to the shore and left me in the boat. "If you're going to swim" he says, "you better get in" and laughs, thinking I'd funk it. But I got out of my clothes and slid over the side. In a jiff he reached me and helped me somehow to the bank. I was excited – "Before I got to you" says my pal Dick, "you swam a few strokes by yourself somehow!" "Did I?" Says I, and I really believed him and was so full of it that in the evening I went again to the river by myself and did succeed in making a little headway near the bank. And next morning I went again, at last I was able to swim in the sea right round the pier. I think it was sheer will – for my pal said that he only told me I was swimming when he hooked me out just to give me confidence and please me – which it did." "But" said I with a glance at the leg irons and some hesitation, "can you move your feet at all" – "Oh yes a little and I can move the stump a little helpfully too" he said – "I swim this way" (illustrating the stroke) "and I can row too. Why I was nearly drowned more'n once. Several of us were in a boat with a chap named Bill Bailey, and it was the time they used to sing 'Bill Bailey won't you please come home', and this bloke had a separation from his wife, and I kept teasing him by singing the song until he clouted me one, and as my stump side was to the outside of the boat I lost my balance and fell into the water. It was a flat bottomed boat and I came up underneath it and although I could feel my hand round the side of it I could not get myself from under it. When I came up fortunately the chaps in it spotted my hand and dragged me in."

A little later he came to London to Snaith's the tailor in Wood Street (Walthamstow) where he's worked for 21 years, and lived with the family. He met a girl who became friendly, and at last she became engaged to him. "She was a lovely girl", he said "not like the modern sort; she knew when I wanted a rest when we were walking, in fact she understood me perfectly. I made her no end of clothes" he said "kept on cutting out costumes for her. When she lost her job I was able to pay for her keep and I'd got enough things together for a little home: paid for furniture and all that. We were going to get married quite soon (this was in 1917 he said) and she said before she married she'd like to go to see her mother and home at Southampton. So I cut her out another costume and we'd practically got a fine trousseau as they call it together and I paid her fare gave her £5 to spend and saw her off. It was a month or two before she came back and when she did I noticed something different in her manner. "I couldn't make out what it was," said he "so at last I tackled her with it, and she burst into tears and presently told me that while at Southampton she met a sailor, that they'd become friendly, intimate, and that in fact he'd put her in the way of having a baby." "Oh I was overcome" he said "I didn't know what to do or to say and she was so kind and so lovely." "Well I says" he continued "we'd better part, we can't go on, or be friendly like even now it seems to me. You better go home again to your people and try to get the sailorman to marry you properly." And he said he'd paid her fare home again, gave her some money to tide her over difficulties and even saw her off again. "But when I came back" he said "I felt it worse and worse; I felt mad, dreadful and I drank and kept on drinking."

"Old Snaith," he said to me "You better pull yourself together man or you'll be no use to me" and I didn't care. It was in a pub that a young sailor on leave got talking to me and asked if my disablement was due to the war and I told him no and something about my affairs. He asked me to go home and have some supper with his people, and I did and they were very kind to me. The old lady got round me at once, and soon I went there every week-end and they made me stay, they got me to start saving again, and I can tell you I've got a few quid by me now; and the old boy he paints quite a lot, and it was he who set me on it. Ever since on all holidays I goes to see them. They'd never take a penny from me but I get me own back on 'em. I cut out their clothes and make 'em up for 'em and when I have a good week on the horses, (I always have a bit on the horses) I take the old lady and daughters chocolates and a week or so ago when I'd a big haul I took 'em a wireless set, and me and the son we got a pole and we had it up before the evening was gone and were listening in. I've helped 'em put up a summerhouse 10ft long. I made a section on the ground and showed 'em how to fit it together, and I've been up a ladder on my stumps and sat on the roof fixing the corrugated iron." "You're marvellous!" I said quite sincerely and with conviction. "What became of that wonderful woman, your mother, do you know?" "Oh yes, she's still alive, 81 or 82; she's got most of my furniture in a room – she has one room; I allow her 10/- a week she gets the old age pension of 10/- and that's quite enough for her simple wants."

"Do you ever see anything of any of your brothers or sisters?" I said. "Oh yes sometimes some of 'em, but as I tell you old Snaith he keeps on telling me the Board of Trade have put the price per hour for tailoring down – from 1/9 to 1/7 then 1/5 and now he threatens 1/3 so I can't stand it. When my brother came last time to see me I said look 'ere Jack I've 'elped pay for three confinements and I can't help anymore – not on 1/3 an hour."

He also told me that he had heard of the girl. Her brother used to borrow from him, and he had the nerve to appear a few months back. He told him he could do nothing more for him – but asked after the girl's welfare. Her brother said she had married the sailor. "If that sailor were to die, you know, I'd take her back now" he said "She's not like the girls today, and I'm not one of them that can laugh and talk and drink with any woman. I'm a funny sort" said he. He's thinking of coming to my Settlement Class to learn painting. If you could see him poor fellow! – but what a spirit!

He said "Oh I say, you have been so kind to me" (I did give him a fish-and-chip supper at home with me, that's all, and listened to his most entertaining talk). "What am I to do to repay you – You will come and have a drink up the road with me one day won't you! And I tell you what, if I may, I'll come round one day with my needle and thread and do a little repairing for you. You know trousers can often be put into shape when they're a bit worn & save you a new pair."

He said "I often enjoy myself very much although folk mightn't think it. I go to Southend by charabanc with a pal or two, and they're very considerate; and I have the shilling all-day tickets on the trams sometimes and have a look round."

What an example! I went to bed that night and marvelled and felt how splendid the spirit of man is that can endure so much, face life maimed but smiling and with hope in the heart. I asked what became of his early benefactor, and he said that when he went to Cornwall he sometimes wrote to him but not often, and when he returned to London he went to his offices, and was told the old boy had died nine months earlier.

My clock says nearly 2 am (but is probably wrong as one hand slips) but in any case I better go to bed.

> Contrasting with his moving account of the cripple's life where typically his name is never revealed, there is in the same letter a report of a visit to an early Henry Wood Promenade concert at the Queen's Hall with his most treasured friends, apart from Jim Berry himself – the endless recipient at this time of Spradbery's written words. Quite on a different note: Haydn Mackey was at that time suffering the perennial troubles of failing to sell his paintings and constant struggle with making a living from their life's chosen vocation.

… Higgins took Harold, Mac and I to the Queens Hall for one of the Proms on Friday last.

Mac arrived late and with a breath that would have revived a fainting man, so strong did it smell of whiskey. Also he had sneaked the hat of the host's wife he had been visiting and he arrived wearing a lady's velvet tamashanter.

He was very lively at first and kept time vigorously with hand and head to the Beethoven Overture that was being performed by the orchestra when he came in. But in a moment he noticed that the B.B.C. who now run the Proms, had reduced the number of Sir Henry Wood's Orchestra and became very excited and indignant about it. He kept making comments, which in the atmosphere of silent worship that pervades the progress of items in a Queens Hall concert, were the cause of angry glances from young highbrows and old ladies. He enumerated several of the musicians who were missing. "Only four cellos" he said "Good god! 15 where there need to be 40 violins – They'll never do the Wagner item – it's nothing but a bloody restaurant orchestra now – enough to break poor old Wood's heart." However he exaggerated. During the Pastoral Symphony he nodded and fell asleep for a moment or two, and when he awoke amid the burst of applause that followed its conclusion he declared the audience were wrong to applaud then as there were two more movements to the Symphony that we'd not yet heard. He was disposed to argue about it, till he found everyone got up to go out for a drink as it was the interval, then he came and had a Worthington and seemed soberer after it.

After the concert we had some supper together and he told us that a dealer had offered him £30 and a proportion of the price he finally made on the work, to paint a "Boucher" for him to sell to an American millionaire. He said the dealer had sold a work painted in Chelsea as a genuine "Reynolds" for £9,000 and that a whole "pedigree" was found for it, that it was discussed and reproduced in the papers. "Now Sprad", he said knowing my desperate straits, "What do you advise" – "As a clean-living young Englishman, who sings in his bath – and all that, what do you advise? What would you do in my circumstances?"

"I couldn't do it at all, so should escape the dilemma, if there is one" I said. "Oh no dodging it" said Mac. "Remember how hard-up I am!" "Well", said I, "personally I should turn it down, but if you feel that is too rigid a morality, I suggest you compromise so far as to tell the dealer you can paint a picture in the Boucher manner, but that if he thinks of disposing of it as a genuine work that the responsibility must be entirely his, and you will not share in the deception or profit. Point out you can paint or design any number of Boucher-like subjects to decorate the millionaire's home, if the millionaire wants it and is satisfied with that – but don't be a party to the deception. In fact my sincere advice is, and the more I think of it, the more certain I am, don't do it at all."

"It may be true that quite a number of works in big collections and private possession are faked old masters. It may be true that people who buy pictures just in order to show their wealth and ability to afford old masters deserve to be "had", but dealers should not be encouraged in this. It destroys the chance of a genuine market for the best modern work and the dealer who says he can only sell old masters and not new stuff should be tackled on his pride, skill, knowledge and vanity if his honesty is non-existent, and the matter put to him that if he can persuade people to buy beautiful things he ought to be able to sell good modern stuff – that if he's a skilled salesman, its up to him to create the market".

Something to that effect is what I said – how it was received finally I don't know. Harold said nothing and Higgins seemed to think Mac was justified in taking on the job. I said to him later as we were walking along. "Do you agree that the dealer is a rascal to sell works as genuine old masters" and he said "Yes". But Mac is so hard-pressed. "Well" said I "The dealer might have been when he started the practice: Mac starting later is no better – I think that he might find any job rather than slide into these which seem so much against the honour – I don't want to sound sanctimonious and I know many capable artists have done these things in a merry, bohemian, careless sort of way – but where is all this leading – will Mac's. bright

SOUTHEND
ON SEA

LONDON'S NEAREST SEASIDE RESORT
BRACING AIR
BRIGHT AND VARIED AMUSEMENTS

CHEAP RETURN TICKETS
ISSUED FROM THIS STATION

Did "Sprad" really try to suggest a cheap return ticket to Southend
was anything like travelling to the French Riviera?

ability survive it – if not – well, any honest line will be better than painting at all. He has already painted pictures for an amateur to sign and exhibit as his own work. – We shan't know who paints or writes anything if this goes on, and put trust or powers of judgement into the hands of folk who we believe have done work that in reality they are incapable of.

At supper of course Mac chivvied me and was a long time before he seemed even to realise that I was against it. I had to repeat several times that if he asked what I should do myself, I should, I felt sure, refuse it. I said "You know me, don't you think so." Then he turned on my poster work. "And this is the man who's going to make a poster of Southend look like the Riviera! He said "there's morality for you!" "Any poster of Southend will have my own name on it and people who think I have misled them, if any do, can upbraid me" I said. "Moreover I claim it will be like Southend, although some very favourable aspect is chosen, and as Southend is the sunniest resort on the East Coast according to statistics I shall be justified in making it look as gaily sunny as I can." But of course Mac received it all with jeers. "If you make every thing a moral question what a time you must have balancing fine points on every little matter" he said "Not at all" said I, "It is usually simple to act in a direct straight-forward way – simpler than to be deceitful – but it may be just as difficult to produce reasons and argument to justify justice, as injustice – and with a skilled debate the issue may long remain in doubt.

I said "With a dealer like this, in any case I should think it unlikely that you'll get the share of profit he promises" "Oh yes", said Mac very simply "He's quite honest." Which made me exclaim and Harold laugh. "Oh I mean, he'll stick by those who undertake things for him" said Mac.

I don't know what Mac will do. I can't think that's the only opening. I said what about the book and what about Jim's suggestion of painting horses.

"Oh. I'm going to get out of it all into the country and do that, when I've got something to do it with" he said. In that inconclusive way we left it, for Higgins and I had to run for our train.

… Cheerio. All good wishes as ever. Keep me informed of news. I wondered if Jackson would drop me a card and look me up when he was in London before embarking on his ship.

Remember me to Edith and Norman – your mother and other friends.

Your affectionate friend

Walt

1st Feb 1928

…The Saturday previous (21st) I met Mac and Higgins in town and took them to see "The Way of the World" at Wyndhams Theatre; after viewing the Winter exhibition of Old Masters and recently dead R.A.s at the Academy. At the theatre another adventure befell us, which will interest you. We had hardly got in and sat down to look at our programmes when Mac discovered that the musical director was Jacques Sennoi, who was associated with him in the very early days when they both were about 17 or 18 years. In those days Mac painted the scenery and acted "responsible" with a "stock-crowd" of players, and Sennoi conducted the orchestra, composed certain musical numbers and played an instrument or two himself to help the effect. At that time they toured Wales and encountered the Ewan Roberts Revival there. They found things therefore rather dull if not worse, hostile to them. In any case they only got 23/– a week each and shared rooms to save expenses. It was at this time that Mac, who had entered a chapel to see what was going on, was publicly prayed for and the congregation sang "Fling out the life line, Someone is sinking". Jacque Sennoi gave a birthday party in their one room, and invited the whole stock company and another travelling company that had just arrived in the town, to the celebration. They were crowded on to the staircase and stairs, but were merry, full, and uproarious. The village turned out to watch with mixed horror and amusement, the "goings on" of these "sons of the devil". I regret to say that they left in debt and that they offered the piano (that they had on the hire system) as payment for their arrears to their landlady, who was (for the time being and until she found out I suppose) very well satisfied.

Jacques Sennoi is now musical director for 3 theatres, and employs deputies to conduct at those he is unable to be at personally. He came round to see us when Mac sent him his card. We missed seeing a lot of the play – and Edith Evans who is a fine actress – but Mac was determined to introduce me, and let me hear their reminiscences.

Sennoi has, now, a fine Jacobean House, he tells us, near Pulborough, on a hill mid the Sussex Downs. He has built a road to it and planted 1000 fruit trees; has two cars, one a Mercedes, and generally seems very prosperous. He offered us sketching holidays at his home in the summer.…

… Mac told us some extraordinary tale of an alleged "haunted" studio and of the people who have been driven out of it. He had arranged to spend a night in it with some friends and investigate the phenomena. I rather wondered if it was not a stunt being played on him by some of his Chelsea, irresponsible, pals, and that, having made him drunk whether they mightn't play some nerve-racking trick on him. You know he's genuinely superstitious.…

16th Sept 1928

…Well I don't know why all these details of the domestic upheaval have run off my pen. I have much more interesting matters to tell you about the fortnight preceding this, when, while my mother was at Edmonton, I went and spent 12 days with Mac at the cottage belonging to Jacques Sennoi and his wife, at Pulborough, Sussex.

Sussex is a most glorious county judging by what I saw of it then and from what I remember of other bits I've seen – like Rye and Winchelsea.

This cottage, called Batts, stands on a hilltop and has a fine garden in front stretching down the hill and joining meadows that also belong to it. It has a fine old boxhedge in front of it and a vine growing over it. At the back is a newly planted orchard.…

… Sennoi and his wife can only stay there on Sunday nights. They come from their town flat on Sunday mornings (being called at 6 – by telephone to do so) and motor down, arriving about midday. At 3 o'clock Mondays they have to return, as Mr Sennoi's work in connection with the orchestras of London theatres necessitates his being on the spot – in particular every evening. They are a very interesting, amusing and charming couple. She is a Christian Scientist – but this does not prevent her having a sense of humour and indeed the whole group of us laughed almost incessantly the whole time we were together.…

… As the cottage would otherwise be unoccupied they were glad when Mac accepted an offer they made to house him there; and so, with the material to finish his book, there he is. They intend to build a studio for him over the garage, and the foundation for this is already laid. They seem inclined to want to adopt me too, or anyway made me spend a large part of my time there: their invitation is extended to any time and if I go at a week-end includes the motor trip down.

There is a boy whom Sennoi employs who comes up every day to attend to the kitchen garden and cut hay, make up paths, fetch errands, and do any little things that want doing to keep the place alright. He is a nice intelligent fellow – a simple good natured country lad. He said to Mrs Sennoi some little while ago. "Mr Fielder has some goats for sale: don't you think if you bought a goat it could be company for Mr Mackey." This raised much laughter at the time, but the more amusing part was that the boy was right, for the goat took a great fancy to Mac and he has quite a weakness for the goat. When it is let loose it follows him about just as Mary's little lamb did follow her, and if he calls out from the cottage window, day or night, "Giddy Giddy" (which is the goat's name), it answers with the funny whinnying sound goats make. If it sees him or hears his footfalls it does the same, and when on my arrival, evenings with me instead of taking the goat for a walk, Giddy protested violently by whinnying loudly, imperatively and repeatedly. On another occasion when the goat was loose and Mac was talking to me quietly, the goat thinking herself neglected plucked at the back of his trousers by way of calling attention to herself. It was a funny sight to see Mac (who as you know is no lithesome creature and who has a rather solemn round face, in repose) skipping over the trenches dug for the new studio and dodging behind some outhouses for the express purpose of amusing the goat who fairly danced after him; skipping on her hind legs and curving her neck very prettily to one side. She sprang into a wheelbarrow and climbed a pile of bricks and performed a number of antics in excess of glee at being played with....

... Of course every evening we visited the local pub. Where we met several amusing characters – in particular an old retired Sgt. Major who told us stories that thoroughly delighted us and caused us to chuckle and laugh all the way home across the fields. I must tell you about him and some of his stories another time – or when we meet – and of the amusing situation that occurred when a young chauffeur came into the pub, and blurted out that he was at one time a Sgt. Major in the Army in India – which was precisely the thing the old boy had been – and the two looked with unutterable contempt at each other.

But the most astounding adventure was in connection with an old artist, a recluse of eighty, who has lived alone for 50 years in a village nearby. Exactly how the Sennois got to know him I don't know, but they introduced Mac to him and under the genial influence of Mac and myself the old boy expanded and told us secrets he had long treasured and showed us certain of his valuable possessions. It is a long story and almost deserves a letter to itself, but I'm tempted, having started on this account of my holiday with Mac to give it all.

Well, Mrs Sennoi said to Mac... "Don't forget to take "Sprad" to see old Potter, while he's with you. Now mind you don't. The old dear would be so pleased".

"He's such a quaint little man" she said to me "like a gnome almost – a real pet." Well (once more) we went to see him, walking a mile and a half, over the hillside to his village.

Going through the village I noticed that several comparatively new cottages and houses had quaint carvings of goat-heads, satyrs and such-like grotesques over the doors and on beam-ends, and Mac told me that these were houses that old Potter had built and that he did a lot of carving and incorporated it into these cottages that he set up for sale or to let; also Mac pointed out a fine fairly big house only partly built but garnished in the same way with fantastic carving, and this he said a house Potter had abandoned building because the local people he employed took advantage of him during an illness when he was away for a time in Brighton, and paid out wages week by week to the builders, who did nothing – thinking possibly he was about to die. During the same illness some distant only living relatives of the old boy entered his house and took away his collection of valuable china and a lot of his clothing. He told us that the big house was on the site of an old one that he let to a German before the War and which the German left in 1914, firing it, when he did so.

Now it would need a Balzac or Hugo to describe the old boy and his house and studio properly and indeed the whole story is so romantic and incredible that I expect you will think, as I go on, that I am embellishing it if not making it up. But it's all quite true.

We came to a tall grey-looking house — almost dusty-looking on the outside — and with a great blank windowless wall turned towards us, and a doorway that was grimy and looked little-opened: and we knocked. The old boy heard us and shuffled to the door, and I got the first look at his bent wizened figure, and his shrunken little face with its sudden smile and the little bright eyes that peered up so challengingly and merrily at you. He wore some old check trousers, a loose shirt and tie, and his belt seemed to almost cut him in two. Mr Mackey introduced me; and the old fellow expressed much pleasure and excitement at our visit and ushered us into his studio. It was a large room well lit on the north side, and stacked about with pictures and sketches: others were on easels: and there were chairs of various heavy designs carved by the old boy (but as yet lacking upholstery) side-boards and mirror-frames all quaintly and yet boldly carved. There were some in the Renaissance manner, others rather like Scandinavian ornament, but all had weird creatures interwoven into them....

...We were soon launched into an art talk: and the old boy was telling me in a round about way how he came to retire from the world and live 50 years in this village, painting pictures that he never showed — filling houses with them in fact.

In his young days he exhibited much, and was a fixture in the art world of Leighton and Whistler, an exhibitor at the Grosvenor Galleries and at the Academy. He painted a big picture — "Young men always paint big — too big" he said — that was hung in the line at the Grosvenor but moved up on Varnishing day to make way for a distinguished artist's work, who had complained to the Committee that he was badly hung. But after having had his work hung several times at the Academy and feeling that he was even in the running for an Associateship, he suddenly found all his work "chucked." Dreadful disappointment. In those days they were very serious about it. He fell in a fit. When he recovered he decided to retire from the art world where he was convinced he was the victim of jealousy; and he moved to this village in Sussex and lived his solitary life there. Today it sounds almost funny. No one takes the Academy very seriously. It's a toss up! However that is the dear old boy's story. He told it very indirectly in snaps: mixed up with talk on work shown us and so on....

The scope and depth of Walter Spradbery's life was very simple, but breathtakingly brilliant and spirited. Within these very pages is the evidence of prolific writing, but he was also a prolific reader. In his letters over the years to Jim Berry he is often recommending books to obtain, or what to pursue in the great vocation of reading.

Reading was a massive pre-occupation of his. Few artists were better read – perhaps few other men! I am at a point, as coincidence has it, in quoting passages of correspondence from an earlier era of national depression at a time now of great economic crisis, eighty years onwards where the sudden realisation of it has hit the conscience and minds of all with the collapse of one of Britain's greatest high street shopping institutions – Woolworths!

How remarkable, as this news is reported to us in the year 2008, that I am reading and quoting this letter dated 18th November 1928 commenting on a book purchased in Woolworths some time before 1928!

18th Nov 1928

My Dear Jim

… I am sending you this little book to amuse your leisure hour – if you get any. Bearing in mind your admonishment that it was quite unnecessary for me to mark your birthday by a present and that you did not wish me to spend my money (so hard to come by) on such things, I have selected the book from my shelves. When new it only cost me sixpence at Woolworths! Could one make a more humble offering!

However these things do not prevent it being a very fine modern novel – also a very popular one. Perhaps you have already read it. Anyway it is a well told story of some very Bohemian people – musicians for the most part – and the most conventional folk they fell among. The numerous characters are drawn with penetrating observation and retain their qualities and individualities throughout the work. It has fine humour and pathos and is a very remarkable work, quite astounding when one knows that it is a first novel by a girl.

Indeed it is an accomplished work of a mature mind – plentifully stored with observation and experience one feels, that certainly does not exhaust itself despite the wealth it pours out. How came a girl to know so much, to be able to balance characters so admirably!

Having read a second book by the same author I can say that she certainly did not exhaust herself on the first, it is equally entertaining to my mind: just as original, just as powerful – Margaret Kennedy is a wise and brilliant woman.

Of course you know that apart from the book being a "best seller" and running into countless editions; staged as a play it has been as popular and played to packed houses ever since it was put on….

Reading this brief letter of my father to James Berry written on 18th November 1928, I was reminded of Margaret Kennedy's play, "The Constant Nymph" which I encountered as a student myself at RADA some 22 years later. RADA was

London's Royal Academy of Dramatic Art where I was hopefully about to redeem myself in the eyes of my parents as one to emerge as a fully-fledged actor!

Lewis Dodd, the leading role of "The Constant Nymph", was at one time played in the West End by Noel Coward and subsequently by John Gielgud and in the film by Charles Boyer. In our student production at RADA I shared the role of Lewis Dodd with fellow students, Ian Holm and a dear friend of mine, a Peter Dixon. In those student days it was common practice to share roles. Ian Holm went on to some serious success in the cinema and theatre, while Peter, who remained a friend of mine all his life went on to become a popular vocalist in London's nightclub scene of the fifties and sixties.

Strange that such a letter should revive my memory of a student production now over 50 years ago. RADA of course for my father and mother was seemingly the salvation for me after some years of concern and worry over what course my life was going to take.

So typical of all "Sprad's" constant writing, his letters are so diverse and full of contrasting matter and ideas. This particular letter was one of "Sprad's" shorter ones, but it still managed to describe a recent visit with the letter's recipient (with some remarkable perception) to the House of Commons:

… I trust you found all well on your return and that Edith and Norman enjoyed the chocolates – or did that smart young lady who left her lover on the station (just when we decided they were off for their honeymoon) sneak them from you. I'm sure you must have felt you'd like to comfort her – but not with Edith's chocolates I hope…. I was very interested in our visit to the House of Commons – It intensified my feeling of what a pathetic forlorn little creature man is, striving to deal with forces and complicated interactions he does not understand. These mighty politicians look very like Canute bidding the waves to go back, before the problems they professed to deal with.

That is the singular and brave thing – that a man should go on and do his little bit to establish order and justice as he sees it, in the face of forces he can so little control – in such a brief span as life allows. But I must not wax philosophical … but get this posted or I shall be belated with my greeting. I hope (since this year is almost done) that early in next I shall have a chance to come up and see you all and that you will come tramping with me over your Yorkshire Moors – that we shall have more time to talk together too.

Cheerio. Your affectionate friend

Walt

In this particular seemingly simple everyday letter to James Berry, "Sprad" once more typically conveys his philosophical approach to life and the great value he places on friendship.

As already intimated and quoted in "Sprad's" own confidential words to James Berry, words that he never dreamed some three quarters of a century later might find themselves being exposed to print, Emily Spradbery demanded an unnatural possessive hold over her son, Walter's, life. Even before Joseph Spradbery's tragic death in a London fog, she wanted her Walter solely to herself, and she was generally scornful of friends of his; she would it seemed set out to humiliate him in front of them if he should ever consider entertaining them within the confines of their humblest of homes in Turner Road, E.17.

A Death in the Family

The following extracts of letters to Jim, excluding his overwhelming problems with his mother, relate to his brother Joe's unreliability, a young nephew's tragic death and the discovery of a young niece's hidden musical talents, all family items he communicated to pal Jim within a matter of months and days, not long before his life, unexpectedly, changed for ever with his renewed acquaintanceship with my own mother....

The following letter to Jim Berry is dated 12th January 1929:

My dear Jim,

I ought to have written to you before to thank you for the cigarettes! They were very good in flavour and my brother and I soon disposed of them. I regret to say my mother did not accept the chocolates, being determined to regard you as an enemy. She flung the box into my studio, and I picked them up and put them aside with the intention of either persuading her in a better mood to take them, or pass them on to my sister with a word of explanation. However they disappeared from the place in which I put them so I suppose mother has handed them on to someone....

... But my mother has not been the only trouble lately. Did I tell you how dreadfully ill my sister's boy, a stout lad of eighteen, had been looking, and how I'd had a little talk with him, thinking perhaps that his pallor was due to some of the troubles that affect adolescents, and that a little brotherly (or unclish) advice might be helpful! Anyway I did so attempt, but he did not seem inclined, I thought, to give me his confidence; and professed himself well informed on sex subjects and not desiring to read any books about it.

He looked so bad, so troubled, as if some dreadful secret was oppressing him —

so I did not pursue the matter but merely said, that I hoped if he was in any distress, mental or physical he would regard me as a reliable pal willing to help in any way I could and let me see if what might be worrying him was not some simple matter that could be cleared. A few days after this talk I saw him again and his pallor was absolutely alarming and he confessed that he was unable to run or ride a bike because his heart was so bad and his breathing short. His parents and everyone noted his condition and he was at last persuaded to go to a doctor. It is remarkable that at this time he still was very industrious and made a fine gramophone cabinet and polished it except the lid, and fixed it all up so that it gave splendid results.

The doctor treated him for anaemia and gave him liver oil. He also took a blood test. The result was that he at once advised the lad to go to the London Hospital. Here it was immediately recognised that he was very ill indeed with a rare complaint – incurable – a germ that destroys the blood, being in the system. He was put to bed and subjected to X ray treatment but he steadily got worse. On Boxing Day his sister was married and he very much wished to come home but was persuaded not to. I went up to see him every Sunday, as he constantly expressed the wish to see me, and I hoped the doctor's forebodings were wrong and that he would beat the disease. I don't think he realised he was dying or likely to die soon. Whether or not, he was extraordinarily patient and seemed only anxious to avoid worrying his parents.

A few days after Xmas the sister of his ward sent word that they must give up hope and that if they (his parents) would go up to see him daily it would comfort him as he seemed to fret for them.

His father then decided to have him home and the doctor lent his car to bring him. I went over to Woodford and found him fixed up in the front room, very comfortably, with his father and mother as devoted nurses. He was better for the move, and taking food well. He was sitting up and talking and joking, but he was very white, with a pinched look at the nose, and his eyes looked dark and unnaturally large, and his hands (which had been hard-working and much begrimed hands a few weeks back) were like pale wavering flowers – with a dreadful sort of beauty.

I sat in the room with him alone, having supper: and I was much overcome by the shock of finding him there, I had felt that while in hospital he had stood a chance: all the resources of science were available, and I felt that the sentiment of his folks was taking away the last chance. I sat with my back to the light, and so he could not see the tears which ran down my cheeks.

The next day I took over the gramophone and records which Higgins had loaned me (while away on his holidays in the midlands) and the boy was delighted with the first-class music. He asked me to put the records on the cabinet gramophone he had made, and although I felt fearful of doing so as the things were not my own and I felt should only be used as Higgins intended, yet I did. He was tremendously pleased with the result – much greater volume of sound – and we had to go through the whole programme again.

He asked me to bring them over again on the Tuesday evening, which I did, but I found he was fast failing. His breathing was noisy and his sight uncertain. He asked his father to come to bed with him and put an arm around him. He was still anxious that no one should worry – and patient and uncomplaining.

Wednesday I was unable to get over: Thursday I helped my brother (from Hong Kong) move his things to new rooms at Woodford, and then went on to my sister's place.

The lad had died at 6.20 that morning.

It is all astounding and terrible – but my sister and brother-in-law are bearing up remarkably well – he is their only boy. He was a well-built fellow and somewhat stolid. How he came by the disease is a mystery. It is called Acute Myclobastic Lenerennia (I copied off his chart, but can get no information about it). Being a germ in the blood all the organs were affected in turn – and I understand the spleen is the centre of the trouble. He had bleeding from the nose and one eye was blood-shot and I am told that a valve of the heart leaked.

I cannot help feeling still that some shock or overpowering worry beset him – that he was keeping some unhappy secret. It is regrettable that he left his employment as a cabinet-maker to join his father in the decorating and painting. They've had some filthy jobs to do and the boy had done the brunt of the work.

> "Sprad's" letter goes on to debate the problems that may have afflicted the young lad's mind and emotional state at the time. Also a couple of incidents, one a charming girl he was infatuated with, and another regarding a contretemps with a taxi driver which might have preyed on his mind. Also in "Sprad's" same letter there is yet another mention of his brother, Joe:

Another surprising thing and something of an anxiety is that my brother has persuaded the doctor to say he is unsuited to foreign service and so lost his job in Hong Kong and is remaining over here.

Apart from the trouble we are likely to have with the poor lout over here, consternation will be created in his family in Hong Kong. His wife has a business over there – a Soda Water Factory. He is annoyed because he is allowed no control or interest in it. His son has just married as I've told you – his cousin – who went out in Sept – and done the thing in extravagant style. His daughter is engaged to a young fellow out there, and his youngest boy, who was to have been put to school in England he sent there in Sept too.

He has no idea what he's going to do. He has just moved to new lodgings. I had to help him pack – and all the rubbish he has gathered – books innumerable on all sorts of subjects – all unread. Clothing in about five boxes and portmanteaus. Patent foods and medicines – filled a big motor so that there was hardly room for us.

He gave me a letter asking me to find him a job of some sort – And having eased himself of the responsibility of looking for one, I suppose he will go on getting up at 1 pm daily until he's hungry and penniless!

I've told him to join the Commissionaires: that he'd look alright outside a posh cinema with a uniform and rows of buttons and nothing to think about in particular – except opening doors of motors and taking tips – and that as the cinemas don't open until the afternoon he might be up in time for duty.

He has an Army pension of 2/6 a day – that's a trifle. I hope his wife does not come over and shoot him – she has some temper....

> This is an extract from a letter dated 3rd May 1929. "Sprad" mentions an Old Comrades' Dinner and includes news of local students of his, and an appeal to the Artists' Benevolent Institution to help with costs towards his artist friend, Austin Osman Spare's show at a London gallery. They gave a grant of £25 towards the cost of framing his pictures.

3rd May 1929

My dear Jim

Thanks very much for your letter of the 25th inst.

I was sorry you could not come to the Old Comrades' Dinner, but I did not expect you would be able to come all the way from the north for it. Mac was also unable to attend.

I gave your message and Mac's, and several wished to be remembered. In particular Hedges, who was with us you may remember on the stunt that got some of us decorations. He is a gardener at Redhill, and preserves much of the countryman's ways and appearance. He was genuinely glad to see me for "You are the only one I know intimate-like" he said. "Quarter Bell" took the chair and was the life of the proceedings. He insisted on my sitting beside him and as there were few others that I knew well I was pleased to do so. Sgt North was found in great distress and brought along to the dinner. Despite his hard-up condition he looked one of the brightest of the party. He has a kind, merry eye and a good honest look – perhaps that accounts for his misfortunes. The Benevolent Fund will provide him with a little cash to carry on with, and perhaps among the members someone will be able to find him a job.... I made my toast to absent friends....

...You will be pleased to hear I have a picture on the line at the Royal Academy again this year; and two of my students from Walthamstow Settlement are also exhibitors here this year. It has caused a little excitement. John Higgins also shows, and although I cannot claim (as in the case of Miss Baylis and Miss Harris) to be entirely responsible for his training, I have had a good deal to do with his encouragement and development. His work is to my mind the best of my friends' work showing there. Walthamstow has done pretty well. The Essex Grosvenor Art Club – the exhibition organizing and secretarial work – has eight of its members in – including those already mentioned. Tom Kennedy, Mary Burgess, Margaret Flanders and Miss Delafield are the others; another old-time student of mine is showing – Gladys Bennett.

You have probably seen the notices in the Herald about Spare's show at the Le Terve Galleries. I was able to write a letter to the Artists' Benevolent Institution, which gave him a grant of £25 which partly paid for framing of work for the show....

His exhibition was really a wonderful display of the most subtle draughtsmanship. But most of the critics "jibbed" at his mystical ideas. The first purchase was by Hannan Swaffer the famous dramatic critic. It is not often that a critic backs up his appreciation by a practical act of this kind....

... The director of the Tate Gallery – Aitken, came down to the show and has asked for three works to be submitted to the Committee for purchase for the national collection of British Art there. But in all Spare has only sold £160 worth and will get in cash probably a little less than £100. Of course indirectly he may get a great deal more in the course of time. But it is a small reward for a year of such an extraordinary fine standard.

Tell you more about it all when I see you. Also about my brother, Joe (from Hong Kong), who is taking over a small shop – "Tobacco and sweets" for which my mother and I will advance the cash.

Owing to his unreliable nature I fear we shall lose – but hope not. Anyway he seems unlikely to find employment and the shop is "going cheap" and seems a possibility, and to have captured his fancy for the time being.

A thing more likely to have satisfactory results that I have succeeded in finding the cash to do (and I hope keep up) is to start my young niece Iris at the Metropolitan Academy of Music. She has made a lot of progress in the first few lessons and her teachers are enthusiastic.

Her playing delights me when I have a chance to hear it. Some time ago I took her to Frank Griggs who is a first-class pianist, and he kindly heard what she could do. With me, he was struck by her quick reading and taste for good stuff. He said she had, too, "a perfect ear" and a hand naturally adapted to the piano. "There is the making of a musician in her" he said and recommended the training she is now having....

It is impractical for me to quote the full range of Spradbery's abundance of letters to Jim Berry at this particular time. The contents overwhelmingly dealt with his trials and tribulations with his mother, caring for her as well as avoiding her hysterical behaviour towards him. At this time he slept at 36 Turner Road, overseeing her needs and cooking breakfast for her. She was now in her 81st year! It seems "Sprad" had acquired a studio close by, somewhere else to work. The rest of the family were reluctant to take on any responsibility towards their increasingly irrational matriarchal figure of a mother.

Brother Joe

Walter's brother, Joe, was yet another concern! This is an extract from a letter to Jim Berry dated on the 12th May 1929:

…When last I wrote I told you, I think, that I am putting up £25 towards buying a shop – or rather the business of a little shop – for my brother, and that mother was giving him £20. Well, on the very day that I wrote to you and when everything was arranged, he disappeared. He went on a bicycle that he'd bought for 15s and left his lodgings at Woodford just in the state of untidiness that it was in when he got up at noon. The shop is at Leyton and he had already engaged rooms nearby to which he would have moved that day.

I received that night a letter that reads thus – "Dear Walter, Will you please forgive the trouble I am giving you, but I feel I cannot go on or I shall go off; so I am taking to the road in the hope that I may be better. Could you please look after my kit for me if you could stow it away somewhere it would be doing me a great favour for I cannot go on like I am any longer. Your affectionate Brother, Joe. P.S. I know I am a lot of trouble to you; but I really don't know what else to do, but I hope to be alright and will write again soon. I have paid my rent to 4th May inclusive" (his letter is dated 3rd). "I feel this is the only thing to do as my nerves have been so bad. Yours, Joe. Don't worry about me I shall be alright now but not before."

That extraordinary "epistle" came at 9.30 after I'd done a good day's work completing arrangements for the Essex Grosvenor Art Show. I went off to my brother's (Charlie) at Woodford and called at his lodgings on the way. They had nothing to tell me except that he had taken no clothing but what he stood up in, and had given no warning of his intentions.

I suggested to my brother, Charlie, that Joe's mental condition was perhaps unsound enough to call in the police to trace him – for I may say he'd taken mother's money with him and I was anxious to get in touch before he spent it recklessly or was robbed of it. My brother Charlie was of the opinion that we were well rid of him and said that he had no doubt that when the cash was exhausted he would return. We decided to await the promised letter.…

This extract from another remarkable 11 page letter to James Berry at the height of his electioneering campaign for his local candidates must have been a curious if not unwanted distraction! The outcome of "Sprad's" domestic troubles with his brother was that Joe did eventually emerge from his temporary spell of despair and disillusionment after travelling to as far afield as Eastbourne and was persuaded to pick up the reins of his new business venture in Leyton! It seems he had travelled on his newly acquired bicycle all over London, landing on various friends' doorsteps and begging or pleading for a night's rest and then merrily going on his way to catch up with someone called Mabel near Eastbourne, slowly dissipating what money he had on the way. He at one point knocked on Haydn Mackey's door. Mackey it seems, had no idea who he was. Eventually the promised letter did arrive. Included is a further extract from this same letter to this long enduring best pal in the North!

… On the 7th I received another letter "Registered" as it contained the key of his old lodgings. It read: "Dear Walter – As you will see (it was on an Arum Hotel paper), "I found shelter on Saturday night and have been treated very decently (total cost 10/-). I left London Bridge about 5 pm and arrived at Streatham at Rose's sister about 6.30 and was invited to stay the night. I left again about 10.30 am and arrived at Mackey's about 8.30 after a struggle with wind and rain necessitating a good deal of walking in the wet but otherwise none the worse for it. I am now going on to Eastbourne via Lewes, but cannot say when I shall arrive. I have chosen Eastbourne as it is near Mabel and I shall try to settle there. I expect I have been and am a trouble and worry to you and mother but I hope you will forgive me. I felt I could not remain another day at Woodford my nerves being very bad so this was the only thing to do. I am sending the key if you would be so kind as to deliver it for me. For the rest I must continue on and hope for the best. Your affectionate brother Joe. Love to mother." Well I rather congratulated myself that he had not got my money too; so under the influence of Mr Parker, who often changes my cheques for me, I opened an account with it at the Midland Bank….

… On Thursday I had a busy day … and arrived home too tired, almost, to get my supper ready. However I set to work and fried an egg and made a pot of tea. It was then about 11.30 pm and just as I sat down to feed there was a knock at the door and there stood my brother Joe with his bicycle loaded with things he had acquired on his travels. He was tired too – having come up all the way from Brighton that day – so I made some more tea and cooked another egg and listened to the sketchy account he gave of his tour. I did not indulge in any of the sarcasm I might have done: he looked to me a bit chastened….

… He (Joe) spent a restless night on the sofa in our kitchen – kept me awake by making tea at 3 am and bumping about for various purposes, and got me in a nervy state myself. I felt as if I'd got a lunatic in the house – to add to the night's horror, a picture fell in my mother's room and disturbed her and me – and I was glad to see daylight.

However in the morning he had a little interview with mother … she convinced of his ill-health and weak-mindedness, was quite kind to him – and he set off to carry out my suggestions. He is now established in Leyton and on Monday I hope the final arrangements as to the shop will be made. Then perhaps I can leave him to struggle along for a week. God help him!

I may say that we had an interview at the shop on Saturday night and after it was over he wheeled away someone else's bike instead of his own which was standing outside. It turned out to be that belonging to the shop-keeper. He stopped us when we'd got about 200 yards away.

Now of course I've got to withdraw from my "account" most that I put in.…

> Within a busy period of time for James Berry fighting a political election in the north of England, "Sprad" bombarded him with a succession of letters, and a further mention of his brother, Joe, is revealed. I quote here some less critical words of his brother from a letter written to Jim Berry dated between 27th and 28th May 1929. A letter incidentally which referred in the main to "Sprad's" own train journey home from visiting Jim in Yorkshire, and news of visits to other friends (the Schwabs), prospects of candidates in his own elections; also his admiration of Jim's own electoral work in the north.

… This evening I have been over to see how my brother's getting on. He was still there and the business seems to progress although the turnover is not nearly enough yet to be satisfactory. He has had someone buying the business off him for £70 – so if he sold he'd probably make more than he will do by continuing for some while. However I am glad to say he is not giving up so easily as all that, and has not closed with the offer – he is going to experiment a little longer anyway.…

… I had supper with him in his rooms at Leyton and saw his landlady for the first time. She is an amusing character – Very fat and with golden hair. She was at one time a dresser at a theatre. She smokes a pipe on the quiet – and demonstrated to me that although she was so very stout she was not inactive, by touching her toes and doing a few other physical exercises. She said "You see until a few years ago I was a teacher of swimming."

The home is very clean and my brother is being well looked after in a quiet way I think – but the world is full of astoundingly funny people – one is always coming across some new specimen of humanity – Just as when one feels that one is pretty familiar with all the common flowers one finds two or three delightful kinds that one has never seen before in some out-of-the-way field or hedgerow.…

Amongst a multitude of correspondence to Jim Berry at this particular period of time, I have highlighted personal family matters which he would never have dreamed of imparting to anyone else. That I am quoting these confidences now is to draw a picture of the domestic background "Sprad" was almost encased in. It is also a time when he was approaching his fortieth year and perhaps he was beginning to have some romantic notions. However there were other letters still flowing betwixt him and Berry before these momentous occurrences in his life became apparent.

36 Turner Road, E.17
12th June 1929

My dear Jim

Although it is again turned midnight I must take a few minutes to write to you.

I trust you are feeling very happy about the Election Results – It seems to me that Labour is in a very good position – a majority big enough to carry through a lot of good work but not big enough to tackle anything rashly nor so big as to allow splits in their own ranks.

I am sorry your candidate did not get in, but he improved the position in the Skipton Division and no doubt, ere long it will put in a Labour representative – perhaps, who knows, it may be James Berry J.P. who eventually carries it! Or Sir James perhaps!

You will have noticed that both our men got in. And I'm glad Dr Marion Phillips pulled it off against the odds.

I stayed up with the crowd on Thursday night and till 2.00 am on Friday morning seeing the results flashed on the screen. It was exciting and cockney humour was at its highest – rattles, trumpets, bugles etc were used to emphasize the opinions that the results called forth. I thought of you, but I expect you were in bed sleeping long before I was.

Mother is still away at Woodford so I'm getting on with work and have found an opportunity or two to visit quite a number of friends. I told you that I visited Alfred Schwab and his wife, and the Parkers, I think. I have also been for a weekend to Welwyn Garden City to see Edwards. Had a very pleasant time and received a fine rucksack as a present – which was just what I wanted. Come in handy if we do some tramping later!

On the Monday I came up to town with Edwards and as we were coming out of Kings Cross Station someone came up to him and said "I suppose you don't know anyone who could design me a good cover to my paper "The Land Worker" do you? "Well yes" said Ed. "The fellow on your other hand is just the man for you – Let me introduce you to Mr Walter Spradbery."

Walter Spradbery design for cover of "The Land Worker"
magazine in 1929

So I went straight to the office with Mr H.B. Pointing, the Editor of the "Land Worker", which is the official organ of the National Union of Agricultural Workers, and have since then designed them a striking cover which pleases them very much and which they say will be the first thing of any artistic quality to appear in Trade Union journalism....

... I took my niece and nephew to the Natural History Museum on Friday. I had to go there to make some more studies of insects for my floral panel designs for the "General" (bus company), and as they (the nephew and niece) were at home from school, thought it a good opportunity. They enjoyed it immensely. It was undoubtedly an education to them and opened their eyes to some of the marvels of nature and the antiquity of life in its many strange forms. We took Edwards to lunch with us. The rascal returned thanks by buying me a copy of the cheap edition of G.B.

125

Shaw's "Intelligent Woman's Guide to Socialism and Capitalism" – which I had happened to say I should like to see.

It is a wonderful work. He has never done anything more thoroughly conscientious: and the concentration, information and wisdom he has just put into it is remarkable. It will be not only an education to many women but to men too....

> Yet again there is another letter, posted to his aspiring political friend and confidante, Jim Berry – just weeks or days before what must have been the one and only great romantic partnership of his life, that of the singer and musician, Dorothy d'Orsay, my mother! This particular correspondence dated 1st July 1929 has no reference to my mother at all, yet it must be only weeks away from his life-changing event.
>
> It is yet another example of "Sprad's" characteristic whimsical nature, revealing once again his exceptional warmth and admiration for James Berry, and hidden within this extraordinary mass of hand-written correspondence, a rare glimpse into Spradbery's own feelings surrounding his award for bravery in France, and perhaps his truest reaction to receiving it and of his thoughts in later years.

36 Turner Road, E.17
1st July 1929

My dear Jim

Thanks for your jolly letter. It is beautifully characteristic of you. What a dear honest lad you are! I chortled over it – and wished to goodness you were sitting in an armchair opposite me so that I could pick up your arguments and discuss things fully, with humour and banter and all the ragging you deserve. Dear old Jim explaining his natural modesty – that is as clear and as transparent as the day you went speech making and I came back to London – (by the way, my dear lad, your description coincides exactly with my visualization of what was happening and what I felt you must be seeing, feeling and doing – for, as I sped through the country in the train the beauty of the day was absolutely poignant, and I thought Jim with his sense of the beautiful will be enjoying all this, motoring through the Yorkshire Dales; and heightened by the excitement of his purpose and prospects of speaking it will be an absolute inspiration to him....

... One day the reputation you are unconsciously making in various parts of your county will flow together and you will be surprised at the estimation in which you are held and the enthusiasm with which you will be received. Which brings me back to the point under discussion –Your modesty. I quite realise your feelings and your expression of them coincides with what I know of you. I can imagine you blushing a little and feeling self-conscious when you went by the placards with "Earby Hero Rewarded" on them. It is a very proper sensitiveness and belongs to the same fine nature that would do the deed meriting the recognition itself although you'd hate a song to be made about it….

… Of course my attitude to decorations and honours is just the same as ever it was – as I said or rather quoted – "the rank is but the guinea's stamp, it's the man's the gold" – but when the stamp is put on the genuine metal one cannot help feeling a little satisfaction. It is hateful to seek cheap and tawdry honours and hateful to see those who pursue every opportunity to get the marks and awards without troubling particularly about the merits or the services they should render when they acquire the honour. But one is grateful to one's fellow men when they applaud one or put some trust into one's hand or show one honour.

I understand your anxiety not only to remain unpretentious but to avoid in every way appearing so. Although I banter you I agree with you and applaud you. Nevertheless my dear boy you will find someone who will accuse you of office-seeking and excess of pride of place some day – there are always mean spirits who make unwarranted accusations and the best men do not escape them. The more important your posts become and the more you make your integrity felt, the more you will be likely to find jealous and unjust folks to misrepresent you. As for all your palaver about my D.C.M. why you make me out to be as modest as yourself!

Certainly I never expected such a fine medal for so simple and natural an action with my best friends at my side. Indeed I was surprised at the general appreciation of our little exploit. We were often in as great a danger I think. I know that more than once I have been in positions where death seemed as imminent, and after all nowhere on the western front was very safe – to any thoughtful person calculating the chances there, the position was not inconsiderably worse.

Of course everyone was pleased when I got an award because everyone wanted the unit to have as many medals as possible – besides Capt. Hall was not a popular fellow and another D.C.M. to tone him down was rather favoured and "Sprad" was not a bad one to wear it for that end.

For my part I was surprised but genuinely pleased to have it – the only bitterness in it being that you who were with me did not get the recognition you equally deserved. I was pleased to have it for a real number of reasons and I still am glad I've got it – and only a few days ago showed it to my nephew who had rather taken my breath away by saying – "were you in the War, uncle – not in the place where they were fighting were you?"…

… When I was sketching for the Imperial War Museum at Oxford an old Professor came and looked at my picture and said to his colleagues "there is not only a very able painter but a brave man. I see he is wearing the ribbon for distinguished conduct in the field" – and I thought he was a dear old fellow and glad he recognised the ribbon, and glad I had it – although I blushed and upbraided myself for feeling pleased and busied myself in my work with even more determination.

When Col. Silver, the H.D.M.S., came up to tell me that it had been awarded me – at Virny – (a place I remember more keenly and vividly because it seems to me that there amid the most desolate country, with mine shafts in ruins and the ground torn to shapelessness by shell holes a sort of lost world all round us, our intimate friendship flourished; and to have so good a friend, so rare a thing as friendship, seemed indeed a gift from the Gods bestowed amid man's desolation – for that Virny is most dear) – I greeted his announcement (Col. Silver's) with some remark expressing my surprise that such a highly valued award should be made for easily performed actions – meaning that in civil life one may be called to endure more – suffer indefinitely and yet no medal nor applause, perhaps only finally be worn out and stigmatized as a failure. (In fact – for my own part if the actions at Mametz deserved a medal – I think I've then deserved rows of medals for tackling difficulties in the case of humanity on the home front). However Silver misunderstood me and no doubt thought I was affecting modesty that was not proper to the occasion – for he said "If you do not think you have earned the award which has been made to you, your only course is to do some deeds in the days ahead that may justify it so that you can wear it without humiliation."

I was a bit flabbergasted – but I felt it was a proper rebuke for my sententiousness.

I still have letters come addressed D.C.M. from folks who have looked me up in "Who's Who in Art" where it is recorded on information supplied by me. Nevertheless I know it is a vanity – a bit of metal to trick a fool into thinking he's some fellow – and I don't for a moment imagine that it is a record that I am any better than another – I accept it and value it because it means that someone at some time thought I behaved myself creditably. When I am abused by those who should know me well and whom I've tried to please or serve, and am weighed down by the sense of my inadequate qualities, I gain a certain amount of help from this and the other evidences I have of the approval of my fellow men and my friends....

And later in this same 12 page letter "Sprad" turns to the inevitable question of women!

… Another backhander is all that paragraph about not expecting perfection in the women I might contemplate proposing to because I am not exactly perfect myself.

My dear fellow – I admit that in excited moments I might feel a fairly presentable attractive fellow but at others I am very far from having any illusions. Any woman I ventured to propose to would think I was trying to put her off I expect for I'm sure I should feel bound to tell her the awful risks of unhappiness she would run into marrying such a one as I. I should tell her I loved her – God help her!

I should not like perfection – a long way below perfection. There are folks one feels a natural delight in – who are in time with me as it were – and folks who leave one cold or repelled. I don't imagine that to find an affinity would be to find perfection – I imagine it might be to find someone who could without causing great pain or troubles correct some of my weaknesses and lead me to fulfil some of the promise that I felt within me in days gone by and that is not quite dead yet….

Chapter 5

Life with Dorothy

Extraordinary Admissions and Confessions

36 Turner Road E17
24th July 1929

My dear Jim

I am most sorry to hear of your illness and am anxious about you. I am very sorry you have been disappointed of your holiday, and Edith of her rest, and to hear of all the pain you have had to endure. I do hope you get free of this nasty thing soon and have no reoccurrence. I hate to think of any flaw in your splendid physique, and if you suffer in this way again I hope you will get special advice. Nowadays inoculations are performed from a culture taken from the patients' own blood, in cases of persisting bad boils and carbuncles, and with permanent success I fancy.

I wrote you a brief note to Birmingham. No doubt your brother will readdress it to you. As you are unwell you will no doubt be glad to be amused by some account of my philandering and I will give details of what led me to make the cryptic closing remark of that note to Birmingham, that you "must wish me joy – in case I didn't get it".

Well, my dear old lad, I do wish you were here to advise me. I might be able to wring some expression of opinion from you then, or judge from your visage something of what you thought anyway. But I doubt if you'll advise me at all as it is. You may write an amusing word of comment, but I doubt if you'll be really helpful. Of course to be that you ought to see the lady in the case – or the ladies perhaps I ought to say.

The swift results from my slightest moves when I show any interest in girls or womenfolk convince me that I have only escaped a life of continuous and complicated love affairs by my determined attitude of never entertaining thoughts of any particular one for any length of time and never getting within arms length – as Jackson put it – never showing preferences or allowing myself to be too deeply sympathized with. By contenting myself with the most detached friendships except with any men friends, and indulging my subtle and powerful sensuality by my own imaginings only – to the injury of no one but myself I hope.

I can see that fastidiousness as to personal association and a romantic mind have kept me from "fun with the lasses" in my youth, and from a wild career of mixed pleasure and misery. And I could always think of something better than actual conditions seemed to offer. Once I had got familiar with the other sex God knows where I'd have ended.

I hope you are not allowing Edith to read these confessions as I propose to make them pretty full and there may be one or two Rabelaisian touches – although so far as that goes there are no "consummations" to report – only a little nearer approach to the fire – Picnics seem particularly unsafe for me. My susceptibilities seem a little less guarded at these free and easy gatherings in the intoxicating air and summer sun. And other people's! You know the awful time I gave myself for falling in love with Mary Bonner – and a matter I had to keep almost entirely locked up in my own breast except as so far as confession to you was made. Mary showed a feeling for me that will forever be sweet in my memory. I think – just on that one brief afternoon – an idyll – "I did but see her passing by".

I now have to deal with a much more determined lady I think – distinctly more sophisticated, more clever, more vigorous – and I have already been hurried through a variety of violent feelings; and temptations to take risks are increased by my realisation that life is passing, by a certain regret for my unselfishness before – and because one can never tell – the proof of the pudding is in the eating – and friendship and love in the wear of life.

You have heard me speak more than once of an excellent singer named Dorothy d'Orsay – (not to be confused with an Australian singer comedienne and dancer of that name who is trading a little on the high artistic reputation of the D.D. I am speaking of … who took part in the "Immortal Hour", and was a principal in "Cosi Fan Tutti" and is well known in oratorios, operas and character songs with Frederick Woodhouse). Her great artistic skill and enterprise in organizing a series of first class concerts in Walthamstow a few years ago, prompted me, as an expression of appreciation to send her a set of colour prints. They were handed to her by a facetious Chairman – and coming from an "Unknown Admirer" and she publicly thanked the "Unknown Admirer" for them from the stage.

When she examined them of course she found out who they were from, as I had not omitted a note of appreciation of her art. From that day she tried to get to know me; and I met her once for a few minutes when we had an animated conversation – while I excused myself from accepting an invitation to join a party she was making for a theatre. I tried to hint what was the truth, that my admiration was purely for her art – nothing personal. But invitations to one thing and another kept coming. I sent her invites for local picture shows and she notified me of her successes and engagements. A party of my own friends went to see "Cosi Fan Tutti" and everyone agreed as to my estimate of her art – the party included Mac, Higgins, and Harold Parker. We congratulated her on the whole thing. More recently she sent round to me by hand of her brother, two tickets for a recital of old English songs (sung in costume) that she gave at the Aeolian Hall, I asked Higgins to accompany me to the performance which he readily agreed to and did. And I could not let her gift of two 7/6's go unacknowledged so I sent up a box of Fuller chocolates in the interval with a card saying it came with compliments of Higgins and I. I dragged him in for safety. We both thought she gave an amazingly good show – and she received the most enthusiastic applause. However the pianist and a classic dancer who shared the programme evidently had more wealthy friends present and they got three or four bouquets each to her one – from her family I think.

This annoyed both myself and Higgins who declared he should have got one tied up with blue ribbon and sent it up when she sang the well-known old fashioned song – "Oh Dear What can the Matter be".

So after the show, when I got home I penned one of my enthusiastic criticisms of the whole show and sent out and posted it so that she should get it first thing in the morning – a 7 am collection from the Postman's Office being especially to enable local letters to go out on the first delivery at 8 am.

This overwhelmed her I fear. Higgins and I were promptly invited to a picnic with a party she was organizing. I was asked to choose the route the party should take – 14th July – the date. Well, Higgins excused himself with many humorous excuses – in fact he was just then consulting a doctor about pain he was in, and before a week had gone by – was in the Walthamstow Hospital being operated on for hernia. I hesitated about the matter so long that it was with a day or so off the 14th before I wrote accepting and saying Epping Forest was near and cheaply available and giving a variety of routes for the party. I thought I may as well see this lady without her make-up and after all no doubt she only wants to be just friendly in a kindly condescending sort of way. I excused Higgins on the ground that he was in Hospital.

I got a quick reply expressing great pleasure and asking if I would take her to see Higgins in hospital some time – as she wanted to thank him for his share of the chocolates. I was to meet the party at her house at 12 noon.

At noon I was there and introduced to the family – father, mother, and a bevy of sisters and two brothers. All received me with familiar homeliness – eyed me a lot and were very merry. I took a big rucksack for provision – carrying – some fruit and another box of chocolates which I also blamed on to Higgins – saying he'd sent it as he couldn't come and relating the blue ribbon idea he had expressed. The rest of the party soon arrived – in all about 20 – all simple merry folk – and Miss d'Orsay consulted me again about the best route – said everyone was truly very poor so that I must make it cheap as to journeying and where we could get cups of tea to have with the provisions carried. Well I'm at ease in most company that is not snobbish and in three minutes I found I was practically in charge of the whole affair, explaining the items of interest on the way – exchanging ideas with everyone and although giving D.D. a lot of observation on the quiet and backing up her efforts to entertain and organize the affair – not singling her out for attention oh no! We fed twice, covered 6 or 8 miles and played games with a bat and ball – smoked and talked – I took in a lot about D.D. – I may say she has a fine firm figure, shapely legs (as modern skirts allow us to note with ease) auburn hair, an intelligent face, an animated manner – crossed now and then with a certain tiredness – and is practical and downright. She is well read and has some artistic taste as is shown by the delightful fancy costumes she has designed herself and her mother has made – and of course in the realm of music her taste is unquestionable. In fact as I go over her points I must concede that she is in every way an attractive and charming person and a distinguished personality. Her dependence on me and her frank friendliness made me feel delightfully flattered and glad I'd come – with just a little tinge of uneasiness as to whether I was not encouraging "the lady's" tendency towards I fancied affection. However, Damn it all I thought – I've been on brotherly terms with dozens of girls and let'em get no further. But I wondered whether I was feeling as brotherly as usual – the note of points on the figure and so on made me suspicious of myself.…

… I was asked home to supper with the family – and made much of. The old boy is a butcher. It is an appalling home artistically I may say – but they were all a jolly homely lot. I was treated like one of the family almost – or likely to be perhaps!

After supper of course we went up into the drawing room and D.D. was asked to sing. She asked me if I liked Brahms and when I said "Yes" she sang a song in German about a girl telling a fellow who will have nothing to do with love, how important it all is. She sang another – also a love song, and then Schumann or Schubert's – "I will not chide" which we all applauded and she then declared we knew nothing about it for she'd sung it badly; and she then burlesqued a passage in a very excited way and said "Oh I can't sing – I'm too too tired". I felt she was almost a little hysterical and so said I could well understand her being fagged out after our day's outing and that we had been unthoughtful in asking her to sing – that I would go at once for they must all be in need of a rest – in fact I'd absolutely played the brothers out – they looked exhausted.

She gave me a book she wanted me to read and it was agreed I should call for her to take her to see Higgins next day. I did. She took him a bunch of roses and poured out tea for us both – he had a private ward. He was by then well on the road to recovery and in fine humour. His face shone with pleasure at her visit. He asked after my mother and a certain amount was let out about her temperament, age, and my numerous daily duties. D.D. said couldn't she come and see her and perhaps take her out – and might she come and see my work. She told us a lot about her work for the B.B.C. and some trouble she'd had with them. She proved very practical and sensible in all she said about it. I managed to leave the matter of when she should come and see my mother open – I felt I was getting into dangerous waters and that her personal charm was beginning to work on me too much. However a note came within a day or so. "Dear W.E.S. When can I come?" – and would I go to another picnic with the same party at Northolt then next Sunday – and let her know soon and don't put the matter off – and "yours Dorothy".

Well I was afraid mother would be rude to her and the situation was becoming so exciting – However I thought (for thinking of a person away from them is most dangerous) she must come but she must be warned and I'll try to make her realise my situation, how poor I am, and generally cool her ardour a bit. But I was secretly rather elated by her keenness.

I got a letter back by the next post "My dear W.E.S." this time and full of praise for my character, and regret for my misfortunes – "I don't think, my dear, I shall ever bemoan my personal lot any more." And would I let her help me to look after "mother and the house" – especially as she was quite free for two months and could give a lot of time. She could come on Monday, "wear long sleeves" and I must do my best to make mother like and trust her.

My God! That almost turned my head – quite probably – with the heat too. She occupied my thoughts continually all day long and the greater part of the night – I imagined her beside me – I will spare you all my long continued imaginings. I began to feel positively ill with my own sudden passion. I had an idealized visionary idea of her always before me. I saw that I must smarten myself up; how I had slacked and fallen away because uncared for, and I felt full of song, although also with a certain physical pain I became dreadful. Had an awful idea I might be struck impotent – Felt that I was being carried away too quickly – That, like the selected bee of the queenbee, I should be carried to bliss and death at the same time if I was not careful.

God these vigorous wenches how damned urgent they seem. What could she expect – God bless my soul, a well known concert singer coming to do household duties for me, and nursing my mother! Quite impossible of course unless she married me and then mother! What the devil would she say to it all!

The girl must have lost her head! Her letter said that as I wasn't going to Northolt she didn't think she would (but she did) and was signed "Yours always Dorothy." I was tremendously touched too – but had sufficient sense left to know that she must not be allowed to be so precipitate – that she must know more of me and my affairs. I wrote a long letter saying "how profoundly I was affected at her kindness and her desire to rescue me" I even called her by way of start "My dear fair rescuer" and joked at the idea a little, but I told her a lot more about home affairs and ended by saying, I was Peer Gynt, and that the Button Moulder would have me. "A poor fool my dear who you must not worry your head about any more". I pointed out that her career and a happy life was what she must look to – which would hardly be helped by aiding me. That I could carry on in spite of difficulties.

I am afraid I was a bit pathetic and I know I was in a terrible state. However she would come, and I said I'd call for her.

I broke the news to mother that I'd asked a lady to tea, and she took it well, and was even interested, smartened herself up, and we prepared the tea in good time. Mother was curious. I felt it was all very fateful. I felt ill almost. I even went to the extent of looking for omens and signs. I opened my bible at random to see if the verse I should read would have any bearing on events. It did, nearly knocked me out – appalling. It was Psalm LXXIV 10. "All the horns of the wicked also will I cut off: but the horns of the righteous shall be exalted" my God – hardly decent – I hoped I was not wicked – I felt I had some ground for thinking I might be right-eous. However feeling that this was a bit too violent. I tried again determining to see what a whole page had to give me. Psalms CIII and CIV – lovely things full of comfort and beauty for me.

I felt I must pull my socks up and go and meet my beloved. I went. I waited in the parlour till she came down. She came in and when I looked at her, I felt as if my illu-sions melted. My face must have fallen – My desire was not only dead but in flight. I am sure she saw something. She went out to get her hat. I carried on a flat conver-sation with her father. I determined to pull myself together.

This must be a reaction. "40 if she's a day" said my instinct. We set off. I knew she was as bright and clever as before. Her figure was as good, she seemed as animated. But something repelled me – cried out against her. We got home and had tea. She was delightful to mother. I watched her closely – her style her animation. Why did I not feel drawn? I still admired and liked her – but the idea I'd been entertaining of asking her to be my own had fled shrieking. Mother liked her it was easy to see – she talked wonderfully – was the charming old lady full of reminiscences. After tea I showed her my pictures, my poster, my war sketches, your photo and your boys and she was interested in it all – but conscious of my nervous coldness I'm sure – and she came and sat near me. She went into the parlour and sang the only songs we had that were worth considering "Summer Time on Bredon" and then "Coming thro' the Rye" I turned over. She swayed about a little. I felt she hoped, almost expected, I would kiss her while she sang "need a body tell" I felt I couldn't. "Too old at 40" or what is it I thought. I was courtesy itself, and felt full of unhappy sym-pathy and we talked long and I told her a lot about my brother and my family gen-erally. Then she began to urge me to allow her to help me. She said it made her feel she must weep when she thought how my time and ability was wasted. She was very serious trying very hard to persuade me. I could not say definitely why it was impos. I said "you may take mother out sometimes, if you will, and if she will let you. It will save me a lot of time and be a most useful kind thing". But household matters are too complicated – beside I could not bear that so fair a lady should do these tedious things at the peril of gossip and reputation – (I did not say so directly of course) the only way would be to have a natural right – which I did not feel I could offer her. We fairly wrestled in argument. Then we went into the kitchen where mother sat and she asked her if she might take her out....

... And then there is another young lady who is extremely charming – whom I've not seen for a couple of years until Sunday, but who had remained in my memory by reason of her attractions and familiarity towards me. She is a second cousin of mine ... I've known her from a baby but seldom seen her. I told you a lot about her once. A very witty vivacious girl who said she wanted to cultivate personality and be "Vivid" and who said her favourite author was Anatole France. Well I've always felt it would be almost kidnapping to think of her! She can't be much more than 20. Unexpectedly she came to see us again on Sunday, and we were as merry as ever. Her conversation sparkled. She is a lovely girl. The conversation was distinctly flirtatious. I couldn't help it – she led it so. When I happened to say I was 40 she refused to believe it. "You don't look it anyway" she said. "You know you ought to be married – you must consider the surplus females" she said – and after a pause "I'm a surplus female you know". Then when she was helping me with the washing up she said – "Oh I feel so foolishly young now – it is a shame."

I teased her about a soldier cousin who I rather thought was paying her attention – she denied it. I felt she was a delectable bit of goods and much more manageable than D.D. However I had not received my shock then, and felt I was unsettling myself rather badly.

She told me that she often wanted to write to me about various subjects and ideas in books that interested her but that she was afraid to take up my time. We discussed a number of things she'd read – quite lightly. She had gained a prize in some London Readers' Union for an essay on Hamlet and wanted to write plays. I had no hesitation in kissing her when she left – claiming a cousin's – if only a second cousin's privilege. I did not kiss her when she came in – I was thinking a bit sentimentally of D.D. and so hesitated. I explained the hesitation to her later, on the ground that she'd grown and I thought she might not like the familiarity. She said she noticed my hesitation and regretted it. "Kissing is good for the heart; you ought to put in a little practice"....

Marriage

It was at this time of family turmoil, frustration and despair that Walter Spradbery's whole outlook and life took on a momentous change. Happiness and a married future reached out to him like never before. This with the temptation for him to escape from his impoverished and humble surroundings of working-class Walthamstow. Suddenly, miraculously, he found himself coming under the spell of my mother, undoubtedly driving him into a new magical world of make-believe and happiness beyond his wildest dreams. Even so, his eighty year old mother's care and well-being was not far from his thoughts and responsibilities....

This union of such spirited souls, both past the bloom of actual youth, yet embroiled and embraced in their lives with the hope and optimism of the whole philosophy of creativity, a voyage, inviting undreamed-of happiness together; perhaps as much a revelation to themselves as to their friends around them. Their coming together in the whole field of art was such – opening up new dimensions, acquainting each other with their own professional lives, linking the visual, musical and aural aspects of their art like never before. Above all else it must have been the eternal spring and font of what is called love....

Once again through his most intimate correspondence with his pal, Jim Berry, the original doubts of a partnership with a womanly creature emerge, this prior to his joyous union with my mother, a union and ever-growing life together which despite my mother's sudden death in 1952, seemingly only faded some 18 years later in "Sprad's" memory in his own very last moments of life itself.

"Sprad" was perhaps never a man of this world. If ever there was another soul awaiting Walter in another world, it must have been Dorothy's in that moment of Walter Spradbery's own death on the 31st December 1969.

Though never having blazed such a trail in history, fiction or fantasy as Romeo and Juliet, Troilus and Cressida or Abelard and Heloise; it is perhaps no coincidence that Dorothy d'Orsay's finest and most dramatic role was in Purcell's superlative romantic and musical masterpiece "Dido and Aeneas". That Walter and Dorothy's passion and love held sway in the most privileged of life's circumstances with the discovery almost simultaneously of their idyllic home, "The Wilderness", hidden away from the rest of humanity, in the very heartland of north east London's great natural preserve, Epping Forest, was just another stroke of incredible fortune! I quote here "Sprad's" very words at the time:

A friend once said "You have invented this (The Wilderness): you dreamed it and it became true", and certainly with love and marriage, life became more real and at the same time more dreamlike, for "we are such stuff as dreams are made on" and ere I fall asleep I must set some part of it down, for the encouragement and joy of dreamers yet remaining or to be....

To Dorothy....

> "And thou singing in the Wilderness
> The Wilderness were paradise enow".

Quoted here are the last two pages of another letter to James Berry, where his heart and passion for my mother was conclusively resolved! Somehow the letter's first ten pages are missing. It's date of writing almost certainly the later days of the summer of 1929....

Yet again it might appear to the loyal family reader that I am unworthily breaking the unwritten code of family loyalty in disclosing such intimate and honoured tales and details of the most explicit relationship between two souls lost in the most entangled emotions of desire, passion and a state of affairs called love. A shameful betrayal. Today, I perceive it differently. Time has elapsed and I look upon the exposure of such written words as providential and as something rather miraculous to be celebrated in the true nature of life!

... I am in an awful state. The thought of Dorothy D. I perceive still affects me in a far more vital way than the little cousin. The only way to escape temptation is to flee from it perhaps – but where, how – it is within myself.

Mother, who is in a bad mood today has just said that she's too ill to go out Thursday and I'm to write and tell "that woman" not to call. And thinking over this and how I could completely warn her off troubling herself with me and my affair, I find myself turned inside out again and burning with desire – I feel, let me confess it – that I should say to her "Damn all this rot about helping in my household duties and giving me time for my work – it's me you want and I want you – Let us leave the troubles, the curses, the duties to take care of themselves as they must and would have to if we died – let us come away now to some country place on a honeymoon – to ease ourselves and try out our love. Then we can return to all we have to do with chastened spirits perhaps and face the problems with less fear and a united confidence. All the world will after – there will be a new orientation. Hope will spring anew. We shall, perhaps have answered the cry of our unborn children that wail in our flesh now and a blessing descend upon us.

'Ere it is too late I will give you what you desire – love – and forgive me – whatever lies ahead.

Well now, if I sat down and wrote that to the lady I believe she'd come almost straight away – but then damn it, when I saw her I should feel the reaction again – that I had made a mistake. It is the abstract idea of woman – an intangible creature of the imagination, ready to take into herself any and all of the charms of persons we may see, that call us and that we love. One should shut one's eyes, love in the

44ª Dover Street, W.   Vaughan & Freeman.

Dorothy d'Orsay

Dorothy d'Orsay in costume portraying some of the repertoire of musical and dramatic roles she undertook in her early performances around the UK. She set many of these engagements up on her own initiative when touring with the great musical comedy star of the twenties, Josie Collins, in the popular musical of the day, "Maid of the Mountains". In the right-hand corner is a particular shot of her and Frederick Woodhouse in one of many musical duets they performed in those early years. A duo, absolutely unique in their time – and unheard of today.

dark, treasure a vision an ideal – the eternal Eve, mate of the eternal Adam – the persons are but the imperfect embodiment of the thing – the passing experiment that goes on down the ages, carrying on, shaping and re-shaping humanity.

W.E.S.

It was after the extraordinary letter to Jim Berry of the 24th July 1929 that "Sprad's" passions and thoughts for my mother changed dramatically like no emotional experience he had ever encountered before. I was to be the blessed offspring of such a partnership not long after the union of two of the purest of souls and spirits ever to discover each other – albeit perhaps beyond the bloom of youth! However, legend, mythology or fantasy will never be able to describe their eternal youth. Living my earliest childhood with my mother and father in the idyllic home of "The Wilderness" – nothing could have better exemplified to a young mind the true nature of the values of the gifts of life itself, even if at the time such thoughts and imaginings were beyond me.

Above all else these two individuals were gifted and dedicated to the purest craft of their contrasting artistic pursuits; one combining the magical elements of the singing voice and the full embracement of the natural heritage of English music, the other – the whole impact of the country's traditional aspect of visual art. A merging of the arts in an ultimate romance and marriage, overwhelming their existence like never before.

As their first offspring under the unique circumstances of my childhood, I was never able to live up to the artistic heritage and background I came into! As a child I was to struggle with the violin and later the oboe. The paintbrush at school gave me some childhood pleasure, and acting and the theatre subsequently took over, but learning lines and a growing sense of stage fright were ever-present.

Ironically, under the encouragement of theatrical legends such as Lindsay Kemp, Maguy Marin and others, my latent talent as a "magician of lights" did emerge! Perhaps an artistic legacy of my parents' genes that did not surface until later years!

However, back in the days when I was just a passionate dream, "Sprad's" letters to Jim Berry in that turbulent time followed fast and furious!

25th July 1929

…Well I am not going to write you a long letter now – things are happening so rapidly, so excitingly that I hardly know where they are leading nor can I believe that they are leading where they seem to be. Anyway wish me joy in case I don't get it – now whatever can that mean!

Patience yet a bit my dear lad – Give the Gods a chance.

27th July 1929

My dear Jim

After writing to you I thought what a brave lass Dorothy was – and that my fear was silly – that her age was much younger than her anxious look expressed to my fevered imagination and I wrote such a letter as I've never written before, on the lines of my post-script only much nicer and having disclosed exactly my financial position my wish for children and a lot of other things, I said that if she was fool enough after that to want to marry me when I asked her well she'd got some pluck! About 14 pages of it! She sent me a note to say she must have the night to think about it, but would I call the next afternoon. Felt father might be there with a chopper! Sent express letter saying a little more – and arrived – and hardly got in when she put her arms round my neck and said "it's all right" – I gulped – kissed her and then we went off for a wonderful ramble in the forest – had our tea out and discussed the whole problem. I swear if you'd seen us with our arms about each other stepping through the leafy lanes you'd have said we were as pretty and merry a lad and lass as you ever saw.

1st Aug 1929

My dear Jim

Am to be married at Registry on 21st Aug at 11am. The wonderful house, perfectly situated almost furnished by the fittings, has appeared. The owner would almost like to give it us only he's gone broke and his solicitors would not let him. He has suggested a line of action which by marvellous luck might bring it within the realm of possibility – but it seems altogether too good. However come what may something must be arranged soon and something affording opportunity – Rooms would be hopeless – Dorothy's practice would wake the neighbours' babies. My word she's great – If I'd designed her myself I could not be better suited – the more we talk and are together the more amazed and happy I am. My health is getting better now. I've had a little sleep. She has conquered all my relatives – the youngsters are disposed to worship her. She had been gay and witty and philosophical and full of cute observation. I have walked her footsore. She survived an attack from mother, and has softened her heart a little. From me she has had to stand a lot of cynicism, a little moody despair, a lot of imaginative nonsense. She has met it all and holds me firmly now. By God it is to be a great adventure. Her family have received me most kindly – they are homely – a big crowd – everyone is surprised incredulous and marvelling at us – we marvel at ourselves but we go on – it is too good – but it must it shall be maintained – I invoke the Gods!…

Dear Jim send me your congratulations – Higgins sends me splendid ones and, all about me, even down to some who are nearly strangers seem most pleased.

We look lovers – we can't help it – Bus men smile at us – severe married women with their husbands look scandalized – folk grow sentimental and thoughtful after we pass – Ha! Ha! Amazing!…

2nd Aug 1929

My dear Jim

Thank you for your kind letter of congratulations which I shall show to my love today. Knowing you want to see her and wanting you to do so myself I begged a photo of her for you and enclose it herewith – it is one of the innumerable ones taken of her – they vary very much as they depict her in various parts and she can do anything from the sublimely tragic to the absurdly comic and from the austerely pure to the fearfully wicked – but this is one that shows her as herself in her serenely serious mood and wearing a simple little hat and so looking altogether as I like her best. Just as she does when she talks with me about life and what we are going to do.

Oh Jim behold my love, is she not fair, is not kindness and determination enshrined in her countenance. May she always look so when she is near me. May I make her heart glad and full of a rejoicing peacefulness.

You will wonder why I could hesitate or feel qualms perhaps – except at my own unworthiness. Well half of 'em were sheer fear of the situation – which after all is fraught with difficulties that I am fast acquiring the spirit to face – in fact I appear a most resolute and foolhardy fellow to all onlookers – it is only in my secret spirit that anxiety rises shrieking every now and then. I am as one born again, for alas my spirit was almost dead, my hope of a reality in life gone – not that this seems quite real but it is a cleaner finer more inspiring, laughing, shouting, triumphant dream – I am resurrected from the dead, my dear strong friend – and I am glad and thankful and I see you are too, with me.

The practical problems remain unsolved although things move. The wonderful house exists as I told you, stands waiting for us on the forest edge – it is called "The Wilderness" and 'twould certainly be "paradise enow" for me, with a glass of wine, a loaf of bread, a book of verse and my love singing by me – as Omar says in immortal verse to me.…

"The Wilderness" Years

…The dear girl went and sold her mink coat for £22 to buy little things for household use. Did you ever hear of anything so overwhelmingly devoted, on such short acquaintance. I feel absolutely humiliated and exalted at the same time. I must meet this generous spirit with all my best.

I hope I am physically up to giving her all the pleasure that is good for her. She is passionate and eager. I feel I must delight her in a hundred ways. My doctor assures me I am alright. I went to see him when I felt so ill and am still under his eye for a week or so.

I wish I could have you here to talk to intimately. I am almost as ignorant as Daphnis in the story of "Daphnis and Chloe" or anyway if not as ignorant (with all literature and text books available) as inexperienced….

(undated)

My dear Jim

Everything went off splendidly on Wednesday although we arrived at the Registrars (by bus) twenty minutes late. A telegram of congratulations from Harold Parker in Rome, was waiting for us there and about 30 more arrived during the excellent meal Mr Horsey provided for our near relatives – some 26 or 28 sat down to it. All was merry and full of song. Dorothy sang and I sang and one or two others. I made two speeches, one in thanks on behalf of the bride and myself for the "health" rendered to us with musical honours and another in proposing the toast of the bride's mother and father.

We have furnished "The Wilderness" and it looks splendid….

… Need I say we are delightfully happy – that we understand each other, delight and amuse each other, love each other profoundly. How can I explain all this. Dorothy is an artist in loving as in everything else. She can be ravishing.

I can now add my commendation of her cooking and qualities as a housewife to the other more rare charms I have outlined. I long for you to meet her, and hope and expect you will like her very much.

I am an amazing lucky fellow. As to the house and garden too that is a delight to us both – we breakfast in our dressing gowns on a balcony overlooking a fine expanse of forest – we have mulberries from our tree at nearly every meal and apples and pears will be laid up for the winter. The place will need a lot of attention before it is in shape; but five of Dorothy's brothers weeded a patch the Sunday before we came in and that shows what can be done.

Visitors in great numbers we shall undoubtedly have. Twelve came to tea on Sunday – seven more on Monday two came today and our list of friends, all determined

Poster design by Walter Spradbery published in 1929

to see us, is enormous. We shall try to survive the expense. It has not cost too much so far....

... I cannot tell you all the adventures that have befallen us – they have all been great fun and you shall hear them as soon as you pay us a visit....

... I bought Dorothy a pedigree Airedale for 25/- ... a fine looking dog ... called "Peter" he is a good house dog and is already very affectionate towards us. He is full of spirits and play – as we are. Dorothy gave me a wrist watch. Those were our mutual wedding gifts. My only real extravagance was in buying her a platinum wedding ring which cost about two and a half times the price of gold....

... I note what you say about the fruit trees. Whether we shall develop this side on any lines except for personal use is doubtful – the idea is that I shall get forward with my work as an artist – not become a market gardener. It seems to me the products of the garden will be a source of relish for our many visitors and save us expense in that way. Anyway the mulberry tree which is loaded with delicious fruit, has done good service this week. We shall make jam too.

The Roses are all coming out again and crowds of Michelmas Daisies – among the weeds and nettles that have sprung up we keep finding fine plants, Hydrangeas, Carnations, Snap dragons, and bushes of Rhododendrons – all sorts of things – if we are lucky we shall "make the Wilderness flourish like the Rose" next year....

... Like a good husband I have chopped a big supply of firewood and quite a small pile of logs for winter use. We shall be able to get some wood from the forest nearby.

We have found Dr Stopes book not without useful advice. We are both nearly as innocent as Daphnis and Chloe ... but make progress. But I must tell you no more....

"The Wilderness"
Buckhurst Hill, Essex
30th Sept 1929

My dear Jim

We have been so overwhelmed with company that it is difficult to find time to write or do my work. Our little home is so attractive that when friends call they tell all their relatives and remote acquaintances and we seem to have a continual procession of callers. Our average to tea on a Sunday is about 15 but has arisen to 20 on a Sunday when we expected no one, and the daily callers have numbered about seven – it's a strain on our resources although very merry. We managed to give 'em all a bite of something and a cup of tea – talk and singing and an exhibition of sketches is the usual procedure. Dorothy looks a bit worn out sometimes. However in spite of this of course we have done some work. One of the callers was the Advert. Manager of the North Eastern Railway, who motored over with his wife. They were delighted with the place (as is everyone) and he was delighted with my work. As a result I have the order for a poster of Flatford Mill, which is Constable's birthplace....

... Harold Parker is home from Rome. We gave a little party here for him on Friday – Higgins, Hills, Miss Burgess and one or two more. Mac. was invited up for the weekend but has not replied so far. Harold stayed the night. He has done some remarkably good work while away....

... The biggest event here was the 21st Birthday of Dorothy's brother when we had a party of 30, with dancing in the studio and on the lawn – which we have had cut, for it was a hay field – and young couples found the hay very nice for flirting in – the younger ones for a hay fight....

... I printed 30 little lino-cuts of the house and gave one to each guest as a souvenir of the event. Herewith is a spare one. The square building in front is the studio, and to the right of it the suggestion of a white figure is the sculptured knight that I told you stands near the gate....

... Dorothy has got a principal part in "The Barber of Seville" to be produced at weekends at various south coast resorts a little later on. She is now practicing – And as soon as I've finished this I'm going to finish my Flatford Mill design – so we're both busy – worked to death in fact. However we are very happy and a source of amusement to all our friends. How we laugh!...

Perhaps I should remind readers that "Sprad" cultivated and gathered a unique collection of other valued friends – apart from James Berry, family man and aspiring labour politician of the north – around him. Quoting from much of "Sprad's" copious correspondence to Jim Berry, I am naturally pinpointing reference to my father's own affairs and goings on, rather than quoting his equal interest and concerns for Jim Berry and his own family who are constantly referred to and inquired after. Amongst "Sprad's" other close crop of friends, closer to his home in Walthamstow and subsequently Buckhurst Hill's "The Wilderness", his letter writing must have been legendary. However I cannot believe his literary accomplishments could ever take on such confidential and intimate tones with anyone else other than Jim Berry!

I find it inconceivable to think that while in the throes of the greatest emotional turmoil, culminating in his happiest days, anything else in his life could have noticeably suffered. His art classes flourished and were as popular as ever, his poster work continued with some acclaim, and stirrings must have been afoot for local recognition from the iconic figure of William Morris and the awareness of the part someone like Frank Brangwyn might play. Spradbery, never a figure of false bravado or to show any signs of bullish patriotic fervour, may very well –

with his life distracted by a love of such poignancy and the thoughts of bringing up a family of his own – have played down in his mind the approaching implications and dangers of a second world war.

26th Aug 1930

My dear Jim

Life is so full nowadays that I find it difficult to write all I would to you and many other folk, but I must add a word or two to my postcard giving you the news of the birth of our son.

Dorothy had a bitter set-back due to an abscess forming in one of her breasts. This necessitated a minor operation and occasioned her great pain, but the operation removed the troubles and she is now home with me (she returned on Saturday afternoon and we hung draperies over the gate and a Welcome Home notice) and is doing very well although it will be necessary for her to take things as quietly as I can induce her to for a week or so.

The babe has been put on "Cow and Gate" food and this seems to suit him very well and he has a great appetite for it. He has gained in weight, turning the scale at eight and a half pounds after his bath yesterday.

The proceedings of his feeding and toilet occupy a lot of time and energy and call us to action at unearthly hours although we strive to be stern disciplinarians. You know I think I told you his name was John – the voice crying in "The Wilderness". I regret to say he has justified the title one or two nights lately – but he's not too bad and his mother thinks him perfectly lovely. She is like a great child herself and works away devotedly at all the little duties she is called upon to perform on his behalf.

He looks very knowing but his main energies are obviously centred on matters of digestion at present. His hair will probably be the colour of his mother's – auburn – and he may be labelled ginger one day (his eye lashes are the same colour). His eyes are blue and look very dark in his fair-skinned face. He has long fingers to his hands which are very nice for so wee an infant. His voice is strong but not so tuneful yet as his mother's.

His is likely to be an expense for some time to come I expect but we hope one day he will be a profit if not a prophet. And he is lucky to get "Cow and Gate" rather than locusts and wild honey. We hope no one will ever demand his head on a charger....

... Last Thursday was the anniversary of our wedding day and I took the opportunity to write a love letter to my wife in the Nursing Home and she wrote me a reply all too flattering in her appreciation of my affection and our life together for the year. I cannot tell you all I told her nor all she wrote to me now, but when I had written my letter (which she declares a masterpiece) and quoted the greatest poets

Walter cutting the lawn.

and the Bible in her praise I felt inspired to write her a poem of my own – and I wrote just as the words came to me, something which I think has the character of poetry – unrhymed verse – free verse as they say, but not quite blank I hope. I will copy these lines for you – here they are.

To My Wife

My love burns within me like a fire,
As affection it warms, and as passion it consumes;
It flames like a sacrifice to the glory of the Immortal God,
Who gave thee to me, and who have accepted it,
In pledge whereof is our dear son born into the world.
Gloria in Excelsis

What honour can Fame bring more than this:
The deserts of Industry and Toil are less;
Be thankful, oh my heart, and humble:
All-Topping Pride cannot encompass such glory,
Kings and Emperors have no loftier crown.
Gloria in Excelsis

Let me delight in your beauty and your countless graces
And tremble with joy and with thanksgiving;
And pray that what has been so bounteously given
Remain with me to the end of time, always
So may our life and love, flower to new splendour in our son.
Gloria in Excelsis

From her husband.

An artist's poetic ode to his beloved is perhaps the most poignant gesture a man can offer a woman. His expectations towards his son at such an early age though would somewhat have daunted the poor lad in the future if he had known anything of it! But then the poem was never revealed to me (his beloved son) until its personal discovery some 75 years later!

"Sprad's" constant flow of correspondence to Jim Berry through the depression years of the thirties, reveals the hardships and struggle such folk endured to keep their lives afloat in the idyllic surroundings of Epping Forest where my mother Dorothy and my father Walter had made their home. In his correspondence "Sprad" repeatedly writes of Dorothy's singing engagements up and down the country and her many broadcasts at the time. There is also reference to his local art classes and poster commissions from Frank Pick's London Transport advertising services. Spradbery had strict moral principles plying his art in advertising; he would never consider accepting a commission if he did not believe in its honesty and worthiness! However money was extremely short and earnings so ridiculously low in comparison with everything today.

His mother, Emily, was very much on his mind and came to live the very last years of her life at "The Wilderness" in accommodation specially set aside for her. The birth of Walter and Dorothy's children added to the burden in terms of work-load and demands placed upon them! In those precious days from their marriage in 1929 to Dorothy's sudden and shocking death in 1952, foremost in "Sprad's" mind from the day they made their home at "The Wilderness, every-thing else in his life must have paled into insignificance. His devotion and happiness to his beloved Dorothy and budding family was paramount. At that period of time he must have made many sacrifices in the wake of his many other responsibilities and activities.

Dorothy herself was a woman of a similar nature and so I suppose for those idyllic years of childhood we enjoyed at "The Wilderness", both my sister Rima (named after a famous child character in W.H. Hudson's Green Mansions) and I must have been given the most privileged of childhood delights. Again in his never-ending letters to James Berry, "Sprad" never failed to pay homage and

Early days at
"The Wilderness"

"The Wilderness" in Winter and in late Autumn or early Spring.

affection to James himself and his family – and furnish them with gifts whenever possible. This, alongside his generosity to many other friends and colleagues, despite a constant lack of funds and cash; it seems both my father and mother also lavished hospitality and hosted many parties on this abundance of friends and relations under the most difficult of circumstances.

While the spring, summer and autumn were months of mostly fine weather and conditions of warmth and some comfort, the winter seasons within the remoteness and the natural wildness of the forest were at times most severe. Log fires could not allay everything.

At that particular time in "Sprad's" life – of love and the births of a son and daughter, the great motivating causes of later years lay hidden, though not far from the surface of his thoughts....

Spradbery's letters during these early years in the thirties, leading up to the Second World War, covered mainly his family life, his mother's last years, his painting, teaching, his poster commissions and concerns for Berry's own family. His correspondence also featured two remarkable occasions that made contrasting deep impressions upon him which are quoted here.

9th Nov 1930

... Dorothy left Euston at 8.30 a.m. on Saturday for Liverpool where she sang in the afternoon – a recital with Frederick Woodhouse – a complete programme. At 11.50 p.m. she set out on an awkward journey to Hawick in Scotland, necessitating a return to Crewe and a wait there, then to Carlisle and another wait, and eventually reaching Hawick at 5 a.m. Sunday – in the evening singing the contralto part in "The Messiah" – leaving by night train for Birmingham, where on the afternoon of Monday she gives another recital with Woodhouse – of old English Songs in costume and involve several changes of dress and make-up. I am glad to say she will have the Tuesday to rest. On Wednesday she comes to your part of the world – to Keighly. She will arrive in the afternoon or evening and give a recital of old English Songs in costume by herself – This she repeats in Wakefield in the evening and there will be little time for her to get from one place to the other. It will be a great strain. She will leave Wakefield for Manchester to give a recital there with Woodhouse I think on Friday. Friday night late she will be back in London....

... I have dug up the big bed of poppies that goes the length of the studio and sown it with Delphinium seeds gathered from our plants last year and surrounded this with lupin seeds.... The show we had this year are mainly from the cuttings I took last autumn from a few big plants in the garden.... The garden is a big problem. There is too much for me to handle – it is a one man, full-time job almost.

However headway has been made and next year ought to show a great improvement on this....

... Looking in on my mother and doing little jobs for her – my real work does not get all the attention it should.

Mother looked remarkably well but is making a lot of trouble by accusing almost everyone who goes to see her (except Dorothy and myself) of stealing things from her – most ridiculous things sometimes. She is indeed a most pathetic figure and I should like to be able to arrange something comfortable for her last days. It is lonely and unsafe for her there by herself. Dorothy with some trepidation even was good enough to ask her if she would, at a push, come to live with us. What is to be done remains a problem....

9th March 1931

... Several things have happened to keep me very busy here. We have decided to have my mother live with us permanently, and Dorothy has given up the music room in order that she may have a downstairs bedroom filled with the most valued of her possessions. The music room is now incorporated with the studio....

14th July 1931

... I have not told you much about how troublesome my poor mother has been, but it would be the repetition of an old story I told so often in the past. Her mind, which for long has been uncertain, is now even more confused and changes from mood to mood but remains mostly despairing and gloomy. She imagines that Dorothy is poisoning her and refuses to eat much but boiled eggs and milk. However she is not quite continuously so bad as this, and we do our best to make her cheery and comfortable. Little John is a great asset in this – but she "wishes she could take him to heaven with her"....

Lunch with Gandhi

Some 15 or so years after serving under the command of Lt Col Josiah Oldfield in the early part of World War One, Private Walter Spradbery was uniquely remembered by his former commanding officer in his initial training days in the R.A.M.C. in the peaceful surroundings of England's Anglian countryside of Peterborough. As it transpired, Mahatma Gandhi, recognised throughout the discerning minds of the world as well as the overwhelming populations of Asia as the greatest and most influential political figure of his day, was the guest of honour at a luncheon presided over by Josiah Oldfield himself at London's Grosvenor House Park Lane Hotel. Spradbery's words to James Berry at that particular period of time are quoted from a constant flow of correspondence. Not only finding himself apparently lunching at such a large gathering in such close proximity to Gandhi, it revealed "Sprad's" extraordinary capacity to be remembered after so great a distance of time by his former commanding officer some 15 years or so later – and present at an occasion honouring someone as internationally illustrious as Gandhi himself.

Quoted here is an extraordinary detailed account from a letter dated 12th November 1931 to James Berry, written in the middle of seemingly domestic chaos at home: "Sprad's" remarkable memory appears to recall all of Gandhi's actual words; also describing the emotions and nuances that accompanied such words must be utterly unique and as revealing of such an illustrious figure as survive anywhere today.

… "The doctor advises sending her to the Infirmary but I don't like to do that (referring to his mother). She would go completely mad – as it is she is in a very decrepit mental state. Anyway a week or so more may give me a chance to see what alternative can be found. It is quite certain that Dorothy's life, the children's and our home must not be sacrificed to her.

"She is so impossible to handle – she means well at times but can be, as I have every reason to know, the very devil. It is most disappointing that the matron of the Nursing Home did not make a greater initial effort to keep her. Had she stayed a day or two the advantages of the place – the care and attention would have been evident to her and she would have been alright. I fear now that even if I could induce her to reconsider the matter the Home would not take her – they see her strength of will and body – it was amazing – we were all exhausted but she seems none the worse – a little more colour, that's all.

While Dorothy was at the Nursing Home where the babe was born I went to lunch with Mahatma Gandhi! – it happened thus. Dr Josiah Oldfield, the Colonel of the 2/3rd E.A. Field Ambulance which I joined in 1914 is President of the

Fruitarian Society. They gave a luncheon to Gandhi at Grosvenor House Park Lane, and invitations were sent out by Dr Oldfield, who remembered me. We had to pay 5/6 for our lunch I may say – however the occasion was worth it – it was a great entertainment and I was very glad to hear the speech that Gandhi made and to see him and his associates at close quarters.

I sat opposite Miss Slade (a matter which has given Dorothy the opportunity for much arch fun) and about three paces from Gandhi and Oldfield, so I had a good opportunity of hearing everything. Next to me an Indian Dr named Shah sat and we had some interesting conversation.

Dr Oldfield who also is a born swanker and an enthusiast and wit, made a speech containing all three. He told us that it was forty years since he had met Gandhi. They were then students sharing rooms. He told us how he (Gandhi) became a lawyer: and how he was thrown off a train in Africa merely because he was a coloured man – and how he could get no redress. He told us that Gandhi served in the field as a stretcher bearer during the war. And went on to say something of his character and powers. He said threats left him unmoved – even death; prison was not unknown to him; bribes did not tempt him; that he had a passion for justice which he pursued with relentless logic. "He has" said Oldfield "only one weakness, it is a woman's vanity in the matter of clothes. He will wear nothing but this beautiful material which you see rises to his neck from his knees and which he calls a loin-cloth". Gandhi laughed. Having built up this picture of a noble character Oldfield then went on to say that a vegetarian diet produced this sort of thing, and spoke of fruitarians being of a higher class – that Fruitarianism was for the higher-classes and that meat should be left for "the lower orders". It was annoying to listen to, and I longed to rise in defence of the noble meat-eaters and the humble folks who hardly got enough of anything. All this said in Park Lane too, with sumptuous surroundings, waiters and braided flunkeys about! However Gandhi did it for me – with more competency, cold logic and beauty than I could have mustered. Flamboyant Oldfield who had stood and gesticulated, was pricked like a bubble, all his weak points were calmly revealed, without apparent malice – only a quiet mind expressing simple truths. Gandhi spoke sitting – spoke slowly and hesitatingly at first, and never quickly but with greater distinctness as he went on and developed his subject.

He said "First I must thank you all for according me this reception and lunch but I shall not call you the Fruitarian Society for a reason I will explain presently". He said that when he first knew Oldfield there was one matter of diet on which they differed. Oldfield would eat eggs, he himself would not, because they contained potential life – or in a great number of instances did. He said I have given great care and thought to diet and tried to find a simple one I could recommend to everyone and one to cause no pain or suffering to dumb creatures: but I have had to include milk in my diet because I find that although I can go without it for a few months, I lose strength and cannot recuperate without it. I hope to find a vegetable substitute one day and appeal to those here – who study diet to inform me of anything they know. I feel that cows conveniently carry milk for their calves but are uncomfortable and inconvenienced by distended udders and the treatment they receive at the hands of dairymen. Moreover the poorer folk of India could not have milk because they could not find or afford the grain to keep cattle. Goat's milk he took because goats had an excess in nature and were relieved by it he was told, but he would rather find a substitute.

Turning again to the matter of eggs he said he saw that practically the whole society ate them, and therefore in respect to Dr Johnson and Webster he thought they ought not to call themselves Fruitarians – nowhere had he found eggs included under a definition of fruit!

He then went on to say that he failed to understand Dr Oldfield's reasoning about nobility of character built on fruit diet. He did not remember having ever suggested such a thing himself or having said anything that could be so represented. He claimed many men of noble character and the highest integrity among his friends who were meat-eaters and he knew of many sorry fellows who were vegetarians. As to classes, he felt it ill-behoved anyone to claim a superior class for himself or his kind: it was impossible to weigh values of natures and services; and who was humblest and who highest was uncertain to a philosophical mind. Certainly in India it was the lowest classes as they were thought, the poorest, who were vegetarians. They could not afford meat. The more wealthy and high-placed ate it.

And so this interesting philosophic discussion on food came to an end and Oldfield hastened his guest of honour away, since there was no replying to what he had said.

I regret to report that Dorothy has been gambling! She has secured for herself and others tickets in the Irish sweepstake and so we shall all scan the results with excitement in a few days time. The race is on her Birthday which she takes to be a happy omen, and her most popular song is called "The Lottery" and concerns a maid who purchased a ticket for a guinea and hopes thereby to win ten thousand pounds – failing which she will fall back on Roger who is courting her and will be lucky if he gets her. She will sing that song on the 28th – the fatal day, at a concert in Ealing and whether with secret jubilation or tearful regret for her lost money remains to be seen….

There is an uncanny similarity in the pattern of Gandhi's mind and thinking that has been so well-documented and Spradbery's own seemingly undocumented existence. War? Was the war Oldfield reveals Gandhi was in as a stretcher-bearer the Boer War in which Spradbery's older brother Charlie served? It could not have been in World War One as according to the World Encyclopedia, Gandhi returned to India in 1914. But then according again to the same Encyclopedia Gandhi was in India in 1930 – leading The Salt March to Dandi and was constantly involved in acts of civil disobedience in India until 1934.

The excitement of dining in the presence of Gandhi for "Sprad" must have been irresistible in the midst of all his own domestic turmoil with his beloved Dorothy having just given birth to a second child and his hysterical mother refusing to be moved into a nursing home.

Similarities in their moral consciousness and passion for justice followed uncanny paths, Gandhi on a world scale – and "Sprad" very much at a grass roots level and unexposed to the world. Through Gandhi's friendship with Josiah Oldfield, it is just possible Gandhi was not unaware of Walter Spradbery's existence, as may be surmised with one other great political figure of the twentieth century, Winston Churchill.

Bankers and Politicians

A particular letter "Sprad" wrote to Jim Berry on the 7th September 1931, referring to the bankers' crisis of that era, coinciding with today's seemingly similar crisis (!), showing the reader nothing has changed; lessons have gone unlearnt, greed, fraudulence, ineptitude and corruption is as prevalent as ever in the world of banking, presenting a state of distrust and despair throughout the world like never before; this brought on inevitably by the invention and introduction of every conceivable device and contraption to allow man every chance of temptation; dishonesty, deception and corruption. Civilised society appears almost certainly on the verge of collapse, the signs and symptoms of which more prevalent than ever in the higher reaches of politics, banking and global big business.

In the course of quoting so enthusiastically from Walter Spradbery's letters to Jim Berry on tales and anecdotes of a perhaps more appealing nature to any reader, my selective quoting from his correspondence has missed out on his early political and economic observations and comments, which may very well be judged naïve of me, however, that will be for readers to decide for themselves!

Reading back through my father's writings, especially to James Berry (one cannot fail to recognise his visionary perception) there also runs a constant reference to the American, C.H. Douglas's, "Social Credit", something in my political knowledge I know little or nothing about. A theory and financial alternative to the western world's capitalistic system to assist and help the working classes. For myself I have to confess a complete lack of understanding of what is projected as the mystifying world of financial dealings, and looked at as beyond the comprehension of we working class mortals. However, Walter Spradbery's words uncannily seem to have some resonance today!

7th Sept 1931

…The furnishing and curtains were taken from a roll of material originally bought to make curtains for the studio – to divide it in the winter, so that the room should not seem so big, and to make it cosier round the fire.

So you see, with the usual round of weeding, lawn mowing, household jobs, poster work, sketching etc. I have been pretty hard at it.

Of course I should like to write you a long letter on the Bankers' Crisis. I heard (Ramsay) Macdonald's speech on the wireless. I am sorry for him. He has done what he believes to be right and inevitable, I suppose, at the cost of his more dearly held principles. And he's wrong and been "had" I believe. It is a crisis that must inevitably recur if the problems are not tackled on different lines to those favoured by bankers. How is it possible that economics such as is advocated on all sides and foreshadowed by rumour can aid a world in which there is a greater surplus of goods (household necessities in particular) than the world has ever known before, and unemployment at home and abroad on a scale ever increasing.

The debts under which the world is supposed to be suffering, and our nation in particular, are created by a money system that is designed to cripple the many and put power in the hands of the few. They can never be paid off since no production of goods will meet the demand for gold, and the whole chaos and confusion of the financial world is due to its unfair and impractical effort to shackle mankind – it cannot even apply its own principles now – the errors are so flauntingly apparent that all sorts of juggling has to be manoeuvred to cover its utter foolishness. Prof F. Soddy has produced another illuminating little book on "Man versus Money" that should be widely read.

Just before the "crisis" the 'Sunday Express' came into my hands with the front page article, headed "Too much of everything" and pointing out that tons of coffee were being burned and almost every household necessity and many luxuries were in excess of demand by an enormous amount.

It was too much for me – the explanations and remedies offered too piffling – I wrote a long letter to Beaverbrook putting the position to him, of the failure of banking to function as a distributive medium and the absurdity of the economy campaigns and outcry against expenditure on public works. He was in Canada his sec. replied. Send the letter on and let him read it with or to Montague Norman who has also gone on holiday there – I said.

But I don't suppose he's seen it or if he has troubled to think about it. Those who are at the top of a rotten system cannot be expected to see how bad it is. However, if I'm to catch the post I must cut this short, or the fruit I am sending at the same time will be rotten too.

> As I remember, Lord Beaverbrook was later the great pal of Churchill and the proprietor of the Express newspapers. He later held a government appointment during the Second World War. I cannot remember who Montague Norman was? Perhaps the Governor of the Bank of England!

A Trial for Murder

> It is I believe well worth quoting Walter Spradbery's words from a letter he wrote to James Berry sometime in the early thirties regarding a murder trial he served on as a juryman in Chelmsford at the Essex Assize Court. I do not have the actual date of the letter or the trial; the letter does not divulge these dates, although "Sprad" pasted newspaper reports of the trial on pages of the letter. The first part of the letter is missing, so I could only pick up the contents of the correspondence from page 13! The final page of the letter was page 30. From reference to the health of myself and my sister, I am able to deduce the year to be around 1932 or 1933. The whole course of the trial with "Sprad" as a serving juryman is very indicative of his humane attitude to both victims of crime and in this instance the perpetrator of the crime. The description of the jury's summing up has echoes of a famous Hollywood film much later – "Twelve Angry Men".

… I should have really liked to write you a full account of the Trial at Chelmsford, but I can't manage that now – time will not allow, and so I am piecing together cuttings from the paper and will add some details myself. The newspaper report does not give you the atmosphere of the whole thing, one or two important points are left out, and as the man was acquitted I suppose the "news" value was less and therefore reported more shortly than it would have been had a different verdict been given.

To give some idea of the judge I put in the cutting below. He impressed me as an agreeable fellow administering laws reasonably and not without mercy. I noted that prisoners pleading guilty and those who gave no trouble got better treatment than those who ventured to struggle in the meshes of the law. Here is an account of the opening of the court and the cases I heard on Friday 3rd Feb. They may, if you care to read them, give you some ideas of the Judge's nature – in particular I was pleased with his brief and humane treatment of the last.

Spradbery here inserted in the letter more than two pages of newspaper coverage of a number of cases that preceded the case "Sprad" was there on jury service for. A variety of cases....

And this is the trial for which I was "Sworn in" as a juryman:

> "At the Essex Assize at Chelmsford on Monday – before Mr Justice Charles – William Robert Stannard Munday, 35, a dealer, was indicted for the murder of Everitt Elliott, at Foxearth, on January 3. – Mr F.W. Gentle prosecuted on behalf of the Crown; and prisoner was defended by Mr John Flowers, K.C., and Mr George Pollock."

F.W. Gentle, the prosecuting counsel, seemed to me very able and presented the case very clearly, carefully and fairly and did not fail to impress on the jury that if they had reasonable doubts the prisoner was entitled to the benefit of them and should in that case be declared not guilty.

John Flower for the defence did not seem to me quite so able nor to put the points in the prisoner's favour with sufficient force, nor to include all he could have done – Pollock said nothing. The Jury were supplied with photographs which showed the interior and exterior of Munday's caravan – a ramshackle shed, and surrounding details connected with the tragedy – also a photo of the dead man, just as he fell, with his head half blown away and in it (the photograph), it was noticeable that he fell with his hand in his trousers pocket. We had a sketch map of the camp and district also.

Here, within this thirty page letter, Spradbery pasted a full reported newspaper account and detail of the court proceedings, the shooting of the victim and the circumstances surrounding the tragedy of the incident neatly and closely informing Jim Berry of the Trial's drama right up until "The jury retired, and after an absence of only twenty minutes which the newspaper column reported, the Foreman ("Sprad") announced that they found the prisoner not guilty, The prisoner was accordingly discharged." "Sprad" then continues....

At mid-day, (1.00 to 2.30) after the evidence had been given but before the counsel's speech and the judge's summing up, the case was adjourned for lunch. We were provided with a good feed and a bottle of beer apiece – I declined the latter, and the meal gave me an opportunity of examining my fellow Jurymen, taking their measure and some idea of their opinions although, very properly, little was said about the Trial then.

I noted one elderly man who had a sense of his responsibility anyway, who was quite agitated by the seriousness of his duty; for the most part they took it all very easily and all ate a good meal – some thinking the beer ration might have been more. Some had suffered badly from being in the box from 10.30 to 1.30 and were in agony to relieve themselves of water. I felt that their examination of and attention to evidence must have been affected by their condition. During the trial a rather loutish sort of chap next to me said, quite early on, "I don't think he stands much chance, do you?" "Yes I do" I said "so far I can see little evidence that is at all damning".

When we retired to consider our verdict, a confused conversation began, everyone looking very nervous naturally, and a rather wordy fellow began to develop the evidence with theories of his own. Moment by moment I could see confusion creeping in so I spoke up somewhat in this manner.

"There are a great number of points of reasonable doubt I think, and we ought to consider these and the conditions of the alarming awakening of Munday (the accused); the lonely situation of the caravan the darkness of the night and several other details – particularly the condition of the gun which we have been told is 60 years old and adapted from pin firing to a modern cartridge by an amateur – we saw it fall open every time it was lifted.

I think we ought to consider this man as if he were our own brother and not get any idea that he is of a particular criminal class – in fact the evidence proves kindly since he gave cigarettes and beer to the folk he met only a little more than a week before the "tragedy".

Various folks approved these sentiments and I again launched out. "Munday, roused by his wife's cries in the middle of the night, heard the threats of the gypsy outside. Any man would be excited and not too clear for a moment or two, of what was happening – even if he said "I'll blow his bloody brains out" that might not mean a serious intention to do more than frighten the gypsy. How many of us have used threats when excited that we did not seriously mean."

A young fellow heartily supported this and said he's often used similar expressions. I pointed out it was quite dark outside the caravan in which Munday stood and in which there was a light that Mrs Munday had lit – a poor light probably, and possibly a mere hurricane lamp, since the child in her evidence said that her father, in springing out of bed, knocked it over, and she picked it up and stood it on the table again.

Outside a man would see in and see if a gun was raised to the shoulder to take aim – it would be hard for the man inside to see to take aim even if the intruder was near the caravan. A man seeing another take aim, would it seems to me, in a moment make an involuntary act to cover or protect himself – he would not let his hand remain in his pocket – as the dead man did.

If the gun fell open, as the prisoner said, he would not see the cartridge in it, even if he was awake enough to think about it, because his back would be to the light – and in pushing up the gun when it fell open, I think such a ramshackle gun might very well go off.

More discussion took place here and a tendency to "manslaughter" was evident in the minds of some. So I proceeded to show that the chances of accidental discharge of gun were clear – that the child and prisoner both indicated the gun as being near the waist, not raised to fire. That the statement made immediately after the tragedy was not a clearly thought out one – agitated and anxious as the prisoner must have been.

I pointed out that the police treated Munday (whom they evidently knew) and acted as though they regarded the affair as an awful accident and not as though Munday was a dangerous criminal – so that putting him in with the railway clerk and allowing him earlier to return alone to his caravan showed this – and was not therefore as curious as the judge seemed to think. We had been told too that when the Essex policeman came Mrs Munday and Mrs Elliot were having some tea together in Munday's caravan and he was seated outside – which indicated that the women were trying to calm each other, and that no real hostility existed.

At this point debate began again, and again began to wander – when a fatherly-looking old chap said – "look here we must have a foreman and get down to some decision" – turning to me he said – "Will you be foreman"? So I said "Yes" immediately as I could see a lead was necessary and would be more difficult to give from any other position.

At once I said "Well can we agree to the most humane verdict. This man does not seem to me to be criminal in intention or nature and even if he were given a manslaughter verdict I can't see that he, his wife, family or the community would be any better for his imprisonment. Are you willing to give him the benefit of the doubt and bring in a verdict of "Not Guilty" – and I went round, pointing my finger to each man in turn – commencing with the nervous kindly man already mentioned and so from those who seemed most intelligent and humane who fortunately were together against the harder nuts and more uncertain fellows, and they agreed one after the another until I got "Oh alright" from a fellow at the back of me and the chap who had sat next me in the box. The moral force gathered as I went round – and so complete agreement was reached in short time.

"Let's have a smoke" someone said and several lit up. "Don't be too long" I said "remember a man whose life has been in jeopardy awaits our verdict" – "and if we're too long the judge may adjourn." That hurried 'em a bit. Three men then told tales of how guns had gone off in their own hands – in one case nearly killing a child and another in the midst of a group of friends.

We went out and I had the satisfaction of announcing the verdict – which I had to repeat and assure the clerk of the Court that we were all in agreement. There was some cheering. The judge just said to the prisoner "You may go."

And running his finger round his muffler, giving his head a violent shake twice, Munday turned and was led out.

I felt that the legal fraternity expected a manslaughter verdict – and a week later I had evidence that this was so. Yet if such a tragedy had occurred with a wealthy, well-established man whose wife had been frightened by a gypsy in a lonely place under circumstances at all similar the matter would never have gone beyond the inquest, when it would have been treated as a terrible accident and possibly some comment on the retribution that had befallen the violent drunken gypsy, with nothing but commiseration and excuses made in regard to the man who fired the gun....

Spradbery as far as I know never served on another jury where any defendant might have been fortunate enough to have had such an understanding and humane juryman on his case. Some years later however, he was called before a judicial court himself, a local rates tribunal to explain his own failure to meet his rates arrears (another touching story, told later, with "Sprad" on that occasion the recipient of a more beneficial outcome).

However my sister did recall an instance of another court appearance many years later. This when a young fellow she knew and felt had unjustifiably been taken into court on some charge she was concerned about. The story was: "Sprad", without a penny in his pocket, almost certainly guided by his white walking stick, trudged many miles in rainswept conditions to the courtroom to plead on the young man's behalf. This same young fellow admitted later to my sister that he wept like a child, seeing and hearing a rainsoaked old man like "Sprad" pleading for mercy for him in such harsh circumstances as a courtroom. This unpremeditated appearance on the young man's behalf, some thirty or so years after his officially summoned appearance as a juryman in a murder trial was something that so moved the heart of this hardened young man, it seemed it possibly lived with him for the rest of his life! No-one had done anything like that for him ever before.

When one looks back half a century later, it is such little unrecorded deeds and actions that stand out and maketh the man. This was a typical instance of "Sprad's" charity, morality and total belief in the spirit of fellowship towards all men. A constant morality and belief that reverberated throughout his life, part of the legacy of "Sprad" that will forever linger on.

"Immortal Hour"

Extract from a letter to Jim Berry: 15th Feb 1932

… Dorothy, as I think I told you she would be, is now singing every evening, and two matinees a week, at the Queens Theatre, in "The Immortal Hour". Rehearsal time, when she had to be away a lot in the daytime was the most difficult for us, and Joe being here was in some ways a help – Although we can ill afford to help him.

I went to the first night of the revival of the opera. I had never seen or heard it before although I knew a good deal of it and was familiar with the Fairy Song, so popular on the concert platform. I believe, by the bye, that the first time I heard it was at a Queens Hall Concert which we attended together. "How beautiful they are, how beautiful…" you may remember or know it.

I enjoyed the performance very much although I had many things to criticize. Gwen Francom Davies is a charming actress but she has no voice – it was painful to listen to her at times. She does need a big or powerful voice, but has a small sweet one suggesting her fey nature – but not only is her voice small but she was positively out of tune again and again. In the first act where Dalna stands a terrible time in a dark wood, singing of himself and his powers (his touch turns men mad or kills them) I felt that for the successful preservation of the atmosphere it should be shorter. It is in this scene that Dorothy's voice rings out pure as a bell, as lovely and as startlingly beautiful. She is a Spirit voice and an oracle voice speaking from the Fountain of Youth. You do not see her, but I was thrilled when I heard the quality of her voice, comparing it with what I had heard till then. In a later scene she plays the part of an old woman but has little singing only a good bit of character acting to do to create the atmosphere of foreboding and the terror of supernatural things. The principal parts are played by Gwen Francom Davies as Etam; by Johnson Douglas (who gives the finest performance of the lot both as singer and actor) as the dream-loving King and victim of Dalna (played by Arthur Cramner); "Midir the Prince of the lordly ones" was played by Bruce Hegg, a young Woodford tenor, recommended by (and engaged on) Dorothy's recommendation. He has some concert reputation but this is his first appearance in Opera and is a great opportunity for him. He has a good voice but everything to learn about acting yet.

Well, you might think my thrill at hearing Dorothy was natural but a prejudiced affair so far as a disinterested judgement was concerned. However I was delighted to find that Alfred Toy who writes musical critiques for the "Morning Post", and on whose word everyone was hanging, expressed in sober language opinions exactly at one with my own.

He said that although Gwen got through her part with skilful acting, her voice would not win her a second or even third prize at a musical academy – he said "a word of congratulation must be given to Dorothy d'Orsay, the tone and quality of whose voice is worth all the cast put together, for her rendering of small parts that fall to her". Rutland Boughton the composer congratulated her on her voice – he said he had never heard it better, and Arthur Fagg, the conductor of the London Choral Society, to whom she had been in connection with a concert production of Berlioz's "Faust", said she was in excellent voice also.

You can guess this all pleased me much, as I have been most anxious that her domestic duties and her experiences as a mother of two children in so short a time should not rob her of her powers or ability. She has had little time for practice, although the most that my help could afford her. She has been anxious too herself, and the authoritative praise has "bucked her up" a good deal. I am sure she ought to do remarkable things and greatly extend her reputation – she has not yet had an opportunity to show the extent of her powers. The best she has had, I think, was in "Cosi Fan Tutti". It will come no doubt. She is in every way a great girl – the merriest pal and loving wife a man could have....

A Steinway Piano

Extract of letter: 20th Dec 1932

... I am not sure whether I told you of our great acquisition in the face of our serious financial position. I mean the Steinway grand piano which Dorothy secured as an astounding bargain. I urged her to get it with the remaining trifle of her legacy, which was fast disappearing for household expenses, so that she should at least have something substantial left and something she longed for. Worth about £250 it was on sale at 45 guineas (as it is hard to find homes for grand pianos that are much too big for ordinary houses) at Murdock's great piano sale, and Dorothy persuaded them to take our own piano (which is one of their own recent makes) in part exchange – so for £20 we got one of the finest instruments made and it is Dorothy's great pride, pleasure and delight. Steinways are considered even better than Bechsteins or Bluthners – and are pianos that stand harder wear. So there in the studio stands this massive piece of furniture, work of art, and source of artistic expression – and it is only because I could not cut the block well enough to please Dorothy that it does not appear on our Xmas card this year....

... My four posters executed two years ago – prints of which you saw when up – were displayed in September and October and I got more letters of congratulations and praise than usual – and I often get a few. When I visited the Underground Offices, Duncan, the Publicity Officer, told me that they had had a large number of favourable comments and that Fred Taylor had rung up especially to tell them how

"The Silent Pool" as I remember was exhibited at an international Industrial Arts Exhibition in either Paris or Milan in December 1932. It was acclaimed an outstanding poster of its day and praised by notable artists, such as Fred Taylor, among others.

167

fine he thought them and to ask for copies. I wrote to Taylor to thank him for his generous and useful tribute, and he replied that my "Silent Pool" poster appealed to him more than anything he had seen for 25 years – that he had secured 3 copies of it, one of which he had sent to Genoa, one to his son, and one to Prof Lloyd James of the B.B.C. This was rather overwhelming praise to receive from an artist who occupies the foremost position in British Poster Art and who had been so conscientious and fine a pioneer in the development of artistic advertising – Especially as in many ways our field of work overlaps....

An Affinity with Death

From "Sprad's" earliest years he had been no stranger to the confrontation of death. His father dying by his side in a London fog. The premonition of death that must have hung over him when witnessing the departure of troops for the Boer War from the Quayside in Yarmouth when a boy. The First World War – his orderly hospital duties towards the dying and the wounded, his own imminent prospect of facing a firing squad for refusal to remove his one symbol of peace, the international sign of the Red Cross and comrades dying around him on the battlefield of the Somme itself. It was significant in later years with the death of a young nephew from some mysterious debilitating illness and later the even younger tragic childhood death of Jim Berry's son, Norman, an innocent life he probably held almost as preciously as those of a father himself; and then his own deep feelings for his mother, despite her hysterical and cruel behaviour towards him for such a long period of his bachelor life.

Did Spradbery have a strange affinity with death that drew him closer to approaching death than others? His old Colonel, Josiah Oldfield in the R.A.M.C. wrote one of his last letters to "Sprad" from the comforts and warmth of the Caribbean Islands shortly before he died, and also Frank Pick, London Transport's doyen figure of the twentieth century wrote one of his last letters to him before his own sudden death in 1941. Some I cannot vouch for, but others it seemed would turn to "Sprad" very much in their closest spiritual needs. Quoted here are excerpts from a letter to James Berry, consoling him with the irreplaceable loss of his son, Norman, and later also his restrained compassionate final thoughts on the eventual passing of his own mother.

The word serenity would not have been misplaced in describing "Sprad" in his natural countenance and many other ways.

19th April 1932

... But you must combat it in yourself and in Edith and turn to what has yet to be accomplished in life – find comfort in what there is to do and what the future holds, and remember Norman as the lad he was, thinking how grieved he would be by any excess of sorrow that distressed you on his account.

I am sure he would wish his own cheerful spirit to come to you to comfort you, and strengthen you at all times – so that in all future efforts, trials, troubles and difficulties he might stand by, a silent, loving watcher, lending the strength by his love and admiration to you.

What has been can never be really lost – it remains like a record, like a cinema picture in store for eternity – such is the whole of history and life for us all – his is an episode of youth, a cheerfulness and beauty that can never be stained or spoiled or go on to any more unhappy ending. Regard it as that. A brief life you engendered, which if it has not gone forward to fulfil the promise you expected, nor undertaken the great work you would wish, has closed before the passions and pains, the sense of great wrongs and the burden of great labours settled upon it, that looked up at the sun, and round at the green earth and saw all the lovely heritage of beauty that is man's, but never had that vision clouded by the toils, doubts and despairs that man is also heir to it seems.

If we would remain as pure and simple as children – as full of trust and faith – as unaffected, frank affectionate without self-consciousness – as eager, fresh, enthusiastic – if we would remain or become as little children – then indeed could we enter upon a heavenly Kingdom on earth....

Contrastingly "Sprad's" brief note to Jim Berry, notifying him of his own mother's death was delivered with a somewhat relieved state of mind touched with some remorse and obviously some early heartfelt memories:

11th Jan 1935

My dear Jim

I am writing to tell you that my mother passed away on the evening of the 9th about 10 o'clock, being unconscious for several hours ... she passed away quietly and now in death looks very peaceful and lovely, despite her 86 years of age....

... I am very glad to have seen her through with patience and I hope every kindness we are capable of, to the very end – I am grateful, very deeply, truly, immeasurably grateful to Dorothy for the wonderful part she has played, and to Mrs Tanner.... I am blessed indeed that the end should have been so peaceful in parting and leave no final memory other than of the parting like a slipping away of a ship from the shore – of the final wave of the hand in farewell that can hardly be seen....

Writing and Delivering Speeches

"Sprad", Spradders", or "Walt" to his great friend in the north, Jim Berry, was acknowledged to write fine speeches, but perhaps did not realise, until his wife brought it home to him, that there was an inadequacy of delivery and presentation in his voicing of them. Dorothy, my mother, the totally professional artiste was suddenly aware of his mumbling and rushed delivery which must have been undermining the whole impact of the vision and intellect of his written words on the pages before him. In a letter to James Berry in March 1933, "Sprad" quoted a speech he had delivered as Guest Speaker at his old school, to the Old Boys' Annual Dinner on 4th February 1933.

As a consequence of my mother rehearsing him and making him aware of his vocal shortcomings, it seemed the speech made something of a stir....

March 1933

... I had received an invitation to be the Guest of Honour at the Annual Dinner of my old school – St Saviour's Walthamstow – and so had to prepare a speech of thanks.... Sat up till 2 a.m. getting it into shape and on Saturday morning made a fair copy of my notes (which I send you herewith) and recited it to Dorothy and my brother Joe. Dorothy said I delivered it abominably – I mumbled and spoke far too quickly and gave no emphasis to any of the admirable points that she felt it contained. She made me rehearse it three or four times, the last time just after tea before I set out for the dinner. By that time I had learnt a lot, and why some of my most effective lectures (so far as matter and expression of ideas is concerned) do not impress students so much as my impromptu easy talks – because I had raced through them in a torrent of words that could hardly be heard, much less grasped.

However I appreciated the criticism I got and acted upon it so that I delivered my speech fairly clearly and it made a great impression if I may judge by the reception it got and the fact that my notes were grabbed from me and only recently returned with type written copy after being sent to several interested people – but not reported as I intended because I was following up, in the local paper at the earliest moment, a letter introducing an element of Douglas's Social Credit and I thought a report of my speech would help. However it did not appear – I think myself typing a copy made it too late for the issue.

Anyway I put in a letter on "Social Credit" the following week, that covered more ground and gave more information than my speech would have done....

... Dorothy was amused at the idea of you thinking that only a fortnight to prepare an address was inadequate – she expects everything to be prepared and done at the shortest notice – gives so little preparation herself to big efforts – trusts to luck and her genius – that she is impatient of long and careful preparation. But a life-time's study is long enough perhaps to speak authoritatively really I suppose – but just wisely and with trepidation.

Anyway here's my effort on Sat 4th Feb....

Dear Mr President and friends,

I thank you very heartily for the very great compliment you pay me in making me your guest of honour this evening, and feel all too unworthy of such distinction.

In a reasonably modest man, high praise given by friends produces a slightly uneasy sensation, and while to be honoured is gratifying, it leads one to re-examine one's record with a critical eye.

Whatever one may have achieved and be proud of in exalted moments, when it is named, seems to shrink in one's own conscience; and before the ideal conception that friends sometimes put forward, the real self stands a little shamefacedly.

And so tonight I hope the record presented to you by Mr Cox, who proposed the toast, has not given me a glamour which I must altogether dispel. In any case I should like to say something to you on an occasion like this, that is sincere, unpretentious and cheering – for these, as we are constantly reminded, are times when we must brace ourselves with ideals and go forward with faith and hope.

For my part, I truly believe that we are living and have lived through wonderful times: times that are no less glorious for being perilous: historic in that they are full of change and trouble, some final pangs of which we have still to endure perhaps. Folks in a happier future may envy us the adventures of our struggles and salute our travail as a prelude to the birth of an age more orderly, reasonable and secure.

Horrible, mad and agonizing as the War was, we that have survived it know that it revealed to us how common are the great qualities of comradeship and heroism in the masses of men: how amazing their endurance for what they believe right: how splendid their almost light-hearted cheerfulness in the face of great dangers and how beautiful the close kinship and sense of equality that can exist in such conditions. Well … rightly inspired, directed to goals less confused and contradictory than those of war these qualities will yet, I believe, establish the ideals that seem to be disappearing in the gloom modern economic conditions have brought about.

The men who endured the war have not yet passed away, and although the youth of today may be impatient and despairing over the conditions they find about them, their true heritage has not been yet clearly revealed to them – and we have yet to claim it for them and they to help get it.

I am not going to allow my expression of thanks to you to develop into a political oration – Far from it "Confound their politics, frustrate their knavish tricks" – but I have this to add, – We have witnessed ourselves, since the days we were at school, the progress of science in the making of labour-saving devices and in increasing production, so that today goods are super-abundant and labour less required than ever. The rapidity of the developments that science has brought about in industry and agriculture has been so fast that Economic Theory and Practice has been unable to keep up with it, and the problem of distributing these gifts of plenty and leisure that science has bestowed on us is the important one of the moment.

Plenty and leisure are the heritage that our forefathers in remote times have, by their accumulated patience, experience and ingenuity, bequeathed to us and the future. Today we are getting some part of the leisure without the plenty in the form of unemployment. But since an artist or a poet is allowed to indulge in vision and prophecy on occasions, I will say that we shall get both properly allied ere long.

Major G.H. Douglas by his theory of Social Credit has shown the way since 1919! The light has spread and his ideas have percolated to all parties. Technocracy in America is another pointer in the same direction. Currency and money as a distributive mechanism will be brought up-to-date at long last, so that consumption may keep pace with production and goods brought to market will find purchasing power there to meet them. The strange hold of debts to a financial monopoly will disappear: the gold standard be remembered as an historic bar to prosperity that the swelling tide of scientifically produced goods swept away.

These are the darkest days, darker perhaps than those of the war, but the dawn is near I believe. It would not be right, and probably prove tedious, to develop or explain the theories touched on, now: you can study them yourselves in the literature they are evoking. I have given you what I believe to be a message of hope and a direction in which to look.

Let me turn to artistic matters that have occupied the larger part of my life's endeavours and for which you commend me.

There in the field of poster work I have tried to play a part in putting decorations upon the hoarding to enrich rather than disfigure the place where they are displayed. I have recognised a duty to the public even greater than the advertiser. I have avoided advertising things which I could not recommend to use myself, and avoided, I believe, exaggerations or untruths in regards to things my work has advertised. This has helped to restrict my work very largely to Railway and Bus Advertising – travel generally. To recommending and portraying the joys of the open-air and countryside.

I count myself as lucky in finding so pleasurable a way of earning a living – precarious though it may be.

The pleasures of contemplation have always been recommended by philosophy; and the problems and difficulties of portrayal and of interpreting what one contemplates also have fascination. To have been born at all, and given the marvellous experience of consciousness – to see and feel some proportion of the wonders and beauty the world holds, is a blessing to excite the deepest religious emotion: to have made the contemplation of these things, their study and portrayal, a principal occupation is to be doubly happy; to have one's efforts appreciated, and to know that they carry some part of the feeling their subject-matter inspired is to be thrice blessed – and your kindness to me here is a seal upon that, and for it again I thank you.

Finally I thank, right heartily, those masters and instructors of my youth – Mr Farmer, Mr Lewis and Mr Cox for all the encouragement and help they gave me in my school days, and for their goodwill and kindness which continues, as you see, to this day.

W.E.S.

It seems to me today an extraordinary and remarkable address from a former pupil, even though an artist of some repute at the time – and from such a background! There seemed at the time from those present that "Sprad's" words made some impact. An irony throughout his life, to me, has been that his presence, views, whole philosophy and idealism didn't reach a wider audience and public generally. Spradbery's whole life was intermixed, obsessed with talks, addresses, debates, lectures and pleas for one thing and another. As my mother, Dorothy, pointed out, he was not the most dynamic and inspirational of speakers in the physical sense nor did he possess the fiery nature of a George Bernard Shaw or a David Lloyd George, but I have no doubt as my memory serves me that he was a man whose personality was charged with passion, an honesty and a humility that in my own eyes raised him apart from other men.

His written words surely impregnated many occasions and events which surrounded and affected his life. By the providence of God or just good fortune I have held on to masses of his papers, of his memorabilia, where in an instance such as this, as I am chronicling the life of a man who was my own flesh and blood, I can quote words he wrote and delivered in an opening address that he made some years later in the presence of the country's Prime Minister at the time, Clement Attlee, at the civic opening of the Borough of Walthamstow's William Morris Gallery; "Sprad" himself gave fifteen years of his life to ensure the museum's existence. I discovered only recently a speech made almost sixty years ago and certainly forgotten today. A speech I quoted to certain prominent figures in a recent campaign to save this same William Morris Gallery from what looked likely to be its shameful closure just over fifty years from that locally historic day!

Spradbery never was in a position to excite great attention nationally, internationally or in any great forum – other than in the most insignificant and smallest of meetings, either locally or some great protest meeting where public opinion and newspaper reportage was so biased and prejudiced as to ignore the most noble and inspiring of efforts.

The following words are quoted from both a handwritten and typed draft discovered most recently amongst papers I have managed to hold on to. It came to light in my own personal efforts to draw attention to the recent campaign to yet again save the William Morris Gallery from closure as recently as 2007/8. An opening address supposedly spoken before Britain's Prime Minister of the day, Clement Attlee, and other local dignitaries at the museum's official opening. The question is: did "Sprad" give the address? Did he actually give this speech on the same platform with the country's prime minister present? It was certainly drafted and prepared. However, amongst all the newspaper cuttings and reports of the day, there is no evidence that the speech was delivered. Of all the mountains of correspondence Spradbery wrote to James Berry and in those later years to Elinor Pugh, there is no mention of it.

Walter Spradbery was a fellow of the humblest stock. However he radiated a charismatic presence that could not have been unnoticed or ignored. If he had delivered his speech (it is not difficult to believe there might have been some dastardly plot afoot to deny him from speaking those words), it would have been one of the proudest and most fulfilling moments in his life. In recent years I did inquire with Waltham Forest's local Guardian newspaper, but heard nothing from them. A paper at the time very observant of municipal affairs and occasions as it still is today.

Whether this intended speech was ever delivered or not, I think it is worth quoting extracts from the one delivered 17 years later for one of Spradbery's most gratifying moments – the long-awaited opening of Walthamstow's William Morris Gallery!

21st Oct 1950

Mr Chairman, Mr Prime Minister, Your Worships, Ladies and Gentlemen:

I need hardly say that this, to me, is a doubly moving occasion, and would be at any time. It seems to me at this precarious moment in the world's history to be particularly charged with significance and emotion: for, in this opening of a memorial to the artist, poet, and socialist William Morris, a brave faith in the creative arts of man is restated; and a project of certain of his artist friends and associates who have laboured themselves with motives as high and generous is coming to fruition. A candle of vision lit here long ago, today shines forth with renewed light. The donors have put into our care a collection of works of art varied and rich, that includes a range of examples of their contemporaries; some part of their own design; and works by their forerunners in both East and West, which they collected for their own joy and study, and now pass on to inspire others.

I am the more moved because I have the privilege and honour, beyond my deserts, of having the confidence, friendship and affection of the late Arthur Mackmurdo and of Katharine Bruce Glasier, whose burning spirits in life, and in memory, have been and are encouragement to high endeavour; and the same regard from that artist of outstanding genius Sir Frank Brangwyn....

> "Sprad" went on to detail much of the gift so uniquely and generously given to the Borough of Walthamstow, its value, its place in cultural importance and its standing in future years. He also thanked the staff of the museum and libraries, the council itself and its officers in undergoing the conversion of the building (once Morris's old home) into the museum it is today. Quoted here is the final part of his speech. His concluding rhetoric in its textual contents is moving, passionate and of an inspired mind. I imagine my mother may very well have given him a guiding hand in delivering it before the British Prime Minister and other dignitaries who were present....

Nothing could crown and dignify the occasion of its opening more properly, nor confer greater distinction, than that the socialist Prime Minister, the Rt Hon Clement Attlee, Member for this Division, should perform this ceremony.

That one who has so nobly borne the burden of the post-war period, who has with such patience and quiet determination led us amid the unsettled and critical conditions that inevitably follow such holocausts of war as we have witnessed and endured – that such a man, bearing such responsibilities, can come amongst us to do this for us is a great joy and honour, and I am sure that to him this is an occasion after his own heart – a constructive effort to support, strengthen and perpetuate the work and spirit of Morris and the artists, humble and great, who understand his purpose and lend their aid to forward it – centred in the town in which Morris was born, a house that knew him well, and a Boro' that bears as its motto his dictum of biblical quality: "Fellowship is Life, and lack of Fellowship is Death".

ART, as Morris has said, is the expression of joy in work, possible to every man: a joy which makes work a service, the shaping and designing of things to a perfection of fitness, worthy to offer one's fellows, and to praise creation.

This then is our happy hour when, as a Trustee, with my fellow Trustees, James Laver, the distinguished Authority and Keeper of the prints and drawings at the Victoria & Albert Museum; William Stewart, the artist friend and neighbour of Sir Frank, and Mr Blakeley, well known to you all in his capacity of Town Clerk, I offer for us all our thanks and appreciation to those who contributed to the establishment of this permanent exhibition – and in particular to the few who opened the way for it by their earlier public-spirited efforts.

Their thoughts, acts and undaunted persistence have brought it into existence, and high among these I place our retired and retiring Boro' Librarian and Hon

Secretary to the trustees, George Roebuck, who took a most vital part. The present Boro' Librarian and Curator, Mr Overall, has taken up the burden of endeavour with the strength and enthusiasm of youth – backed by his assistants Miss Weaver and Miss Halford, who will by the information and help they can give make the Gallery useful to the wide public that will come from near and far to see it.

In all it is a great co-operative effort, a gift of generous goodwill that has met and evoked co-operation and goodwill, and gathered the distinguished company present in person and spirit today, to attend its opening. May its purpose and influence grow with the years to an effectiveness that will not only be a memorial to Morris and his friends, but a force that, by the preservation of such fragments of beauty as escape the assaults of time, brutality, war, ignorance or greed, will sow seeds for the renewal and new harvest of man's efforts to attain truth and beauty, and make it the substance of everyday living – for Art has a language that speaks to all times and civilisations, and a spirit that endures. Endow it with your utmost support.

On behalf of the Trustees, I ask one and all to accept our thanks, and to be assured that we shall continue to serve with such advice as we can give and such influence as we can bring to bear to ensure the achievement of its high purpose.

W.E. Spradbery

Brangwyn and the William Morris Gallery

"Sprad's" letter to Jim Berry dated the 5th May 1935 not only must have had a revealing significance for my father himself at that time, but as it happened, to myself also some 73 years later on a rendezvous in the village of Ditchling with a sterling group of hardy campaigners from the Friends of the William Morris Gallery, on a sunny October afternoon, visiting Sir Frank Brangwyn's old studio and home "The Jointure". I stayed there as a child on one brief memorable summer holiday with my father, mother and sister Rima in Brangwyn's Jointure cottage adjoining his imposing studio. This letter was one of Spradbery's typical 17 page scribbles written in the late hours of two nights. Besides the extracts quoted here, there is particular mention of a surprise visit by London's great entrepreneurial figure of London Transport fame, the doyen, Frank Pick, and his daughter, in their tiny Austin car. Mentioned is Pick's keenness for a picture of "Sprad's" and "Sprad's" insistence he should have the picture as a gift. Spradbery at the time was burdened with unpaid bills and deep debt with an overdraft at his local bank!

5th May 1935

…The thing that I have to decide now is where to start – I will start now, and work backwards towards January when I last wrote, I think.

Well yesterday we finished a big spring cleaning – have had the sitting room papered and the ceiling repainted, the kitchen repainted and the scullery, and got rid of the accumulated dirt that oil lamps and fires have deposited thickly in a little over two years. As it is usual on such occasions we have had a great clear-out of rubbish, and rearranged everything, and now are preening ourselves, and looking about us with renewed satisfaction…. And I have started on the garden again, which has been left since the autumn but is full of flowers and weeds, and which twice in March was invaded by a herd of cows! They walked all over my dug beds, they chewed off the tops of the bulbs that are rising very promisingly, and gathered on the lawn to chew the cud and deposit what they might more conveniently have left on the beds to work in as manure! Twice I rose from my bed, and once in pyjamas, and once after dressing more fully, I chased 'em out, "Bunny" our dog being of the greatest assistance – for he is a very intelligent fellow….

…We have just had the 36th Annual Exhibition of the Essex Art Club – which is as you know run under my Chairmanship of Committee. I think I have told you from time to time of its wavering fortunes but I am glad to say now that it seems re-established with better prospects than ever and a better balance in hand than for many years. This year the Dowager Countess of Warwick did come to declare the exhibition open. I had the pleasure of conducting her round the show. We also had the Mayor of Leyton to give the affair civic importance and he made the most appalling speech – ignorant and rude, and Councillor Heather (of a different party – Labour Mayor) made another almost as bad from the chair which he occupied as one of the Governors of the School in which the show was held. Sir George Clausen R.A. our President was with us too for the first time and gave a good speech, rather long and hesitating in style but very agreeable to listen to after the rubbish the other two had mouthed….

Was this early meeting, with Arthur Heygate Mackmurdo, where the true seeds of the William Morris Gallery sprang from?

… Following the Essex Art Club show Mr Mackmurdo came with his niece to see me again. I had at Christmas told Brangwyn in a letter that Mackmurdo was still alive and on friendly terms with me and this is what Brangwyn had said: "had I listened to his advice in my youth I should have been a better man and a better painter". In his reply, he also asked me to press him to come to see him again.

This Mackmurdo did the day before the E.A.C. show, and he told me that

Brangwyn would like to meet me and that I must go down to see him, as since an operation of about a year ago he could not travel, he had at all times to sit upon an air cushion....

... Recently Mackmurdo said, he (Brangwyn) had given up the big studio he had in Hammersmith which he had not visited for eight years and had the large collection of work housed there brought down and stored in four extra rooms he had built for it on to "The Jointure" at Ditchling. Mackmurdo said to Brangwyn: "How despite your generous gifts of pictures to various galleries and despite the demand of your work will you not place all these before you die and then dealers will not squabble over it, benefit by it and it will be scattered – Could you not give a small collection of work to Essex – and Brangwyn agreed – if Mackmurdo could find proper housing for it.

With this Mackmurdo consulted me and I suggested no better place than Walthamstow by reason of its connection with Morris – and Mackmurdo's and Brangwyn's relation to Morris, and that Roebuck, the very active Librarian and Secretary of the Antiquarian Society would be just the man to seize the opportunity and find ways and means of saving the bequest for Walthamstow and housing it suitably. Mackmurdo asked me to open negotiations and on the 21st of this month I have arranged for him to meet Roebuck, see the Library, the Museum and hear of the various accommodation that could be made available for the collection. After that has been agreed on, I am to go down and see Brangwyn myself.

This is all very exciting and will mean the acquisition by Walthamstow of works valued today at many thousands probably and which later on will appreciate in value in all probability. It will inevitably, I see, (since I know most about the matter now, and from Brangwyn's letters think it likely that he will ask me to act as his agent in the matters relating to this bequest), mean a lot of work and time given without much hope of thanks, appreciation or understanding on the part of most of those in official positions – and the suspicion of the baser minds that I am making something out of it. Or am at least not disinterested except as an art lover and appreciator of their master painter.

Nothing ever happened, by the way, in regard to the William Morris Centenary poster. I did the design, made no charge or fee for it, spent at least a fortnight on the work and got not even a letter of thanks from the Council, much less the public acknowledgement it should have had. In addition someone went round saying "it was a shame, I'd received £50 for the job"....

> Despite the hardships of having very little money, bills piling up, the loss of the last of their parents, the advent of the thirties for both my father and mother was the apotheosis of their lives, and their newly discovered home "The Wilderness" was the apex, the glorious binding homely paradise for the next

twenty-two years of their life together. As their first-born and being steered through those early years of uninhibited childhood at "The Wilderness", I look back on those days as the apotheosis of my own life and everything that was to follow. As a child growing up within a wild forest and the small and personalized world of such gifted and loving parents, a subconscious independent spirit must have lurked within me. My mother was more conscious of this than anyone and felt it more. Only in her last moments, twenty-two years after my birth, when she was struck down by a massive stroke in front of my eyes was I able to throw my arms around her and show her for the first time my depths of feelings for her. Did she realise my desperate love in those last moments? I would never know. What I do know is: she died, leaving my father bereft of his world, his heart and soul. While my mother lived, it seemed as though an ethereal spirit had descended upon them.

Dorothy Horsey, oldest child of a Dorset butcher's large family of eight offspring, came to reside in Walthamstow with her family, possibly sometime in the early twenties. She took the singing name of d'Orsay because at the time there was a popular song entitled "Horsey Keep Your Tail Up". Around the same time in Australia, legend has it, a young Australian Vaudeville star also took up the professional name of d'Orsay. A popular restaurant in Melbourne was named after this Vaudeville lady and called – "The Fabulous d'Orsay"; coincidently in later years I found out that "Bistrot d'Orsay" on Collins Street was managed by another Spradbery, a distant cousin of mine!

As Dorothy d'Orsay's own son, readers may take my undiluted praise for my mother with caution and disbelief; but even if my own talents and ability have never reached any great heights, I speak out in honesty with the voice of someone whose words have been critically respected in a long and not uneventful career in the theatre.

Reflecting back, it is impossible for me to think of any more determined or multifariously talented woman endowed with such vivacity and inspiring qualities. Walter Spradbery with all his own exceptional qualities was the luckiest of men!! Legend had it that my mother's piano teacher relinquished her teaching lessons when my mother was only seven years of age, saying that there was no more she could teach her! Child prodigy or not in her younger years, she was a regular singer, singing lieder on the B.B.C.'s earliest radio programmes, also singing in concert under the baton of Sir Adrian Boult, Sir Thomas Beecham and Rutland Boughton. In her acting, she possessed a striking facility in both dramatic and comic roles. While taking on the arduousness of a supporting role in her earliest days, on an extensive tour of the popular musical "Maid of the Mountains", she relentlessly set up for herself a series of solo musical and dramatic recitals following on from that first excursion of the English provinces.

Her association and friendship with Rutland Boughton has already been touched upon and there was an operatic season sometime in the thirties with Sir Barry Jackson's Birmingham Repertory theatre, at that time the most prestigious provincial theatrical company in Britain.

Sadly there are no proper recordings of her voice in existence today. Whatever recordings did exist, have disappeared.

Her new-found home, "The Wilderness", and marriage to my father changed the whole pattern of her life and career to even more astonishing boundaries and dimensions. "The Wilderness" in the forties during the war years and up until her death in 1952 became the focus-point and attention of her own operatic productions and musical activities, opening up opportunities and scope for both local amateurs and young aspiring professionals alike. Never has any single musician or musical figure produced, conducted and sung such a repertoire of predominantly English opera as she did, in the summer months especially, during those war and post-war years. Ranging from the works of Rutland Boughton, Ethel Smyth, Thomas Arne, Vaughan Williams, Henry Purcell, not forgetting rarely performed operas of Gustav Holst, Bach, Handel, Schubert, Gluck, Humperdinck, John Gay and Martin Shaw, as well as a local composer John Cole Stokes whose opera "St. Joan of Rouen" my mother sang the title role in and produced as well. "Sprad" was forever there painting the sets and making the props, and on one occasion taking on the role of the one-eyed giant, Polyphemus in, if I remember, Handel's "Acis and Galatea". My mother took on the role of St. Joan simply because musically it was a most difficult role for anyone else within her Group to take on, leaving the conducting to John Cole Stokes himself. It was a challenge and effort which exhausted her and she never really recovered from.

Over those extraordinary years, her conducting was a fascinating feature of her whole musical life; no conductor was ever more animated. In performance – if a flautist or horn-player missed or hit a wrong note – Dorothy would mouth the sound or sing it. Many of the instrumental scores she arranged and wrote out herself. Forsaking her singing career, she undertook many operatic productions centred around the summer months in the open-air theatre my father had built and constructed in the upper reaches of the garden. Miraculously the sun always shone on performance days – and it was known as "Dorothy's weather".

Running for many years in parallel with the garden activities were the Wilderness Orchestra and Opera Groups' other local concerts and performances, besides singing tutorials and wide-ranging musical classes at one time at Walthamstow's Friends' Hall. Other independent productions and roles intermingled with operatic events in the grounds of Pollards, the beautiful renaissance garden in Loughton and the garden of the Mathieson family house in neighbouring Woodford, a rich Quaker family who were makers of the famous Clarnico sweets. My mother, looking back, was a woman of indefatigable energy and character. Her following, friends and fellow-enthusiasts locally in the world of opera and music were equally passionate and loyal. She exhausted herself for the cause of bringing rare music to the local area in perhaps a time of great need. As a young boy I certainly never appreciated my mother's remarkable versatile talent and tremendous selfless energy and dedication. Only on reflection now half a century onwards do I look back with wonder. How did I fail to show her the love of a son at least? Never did she stop persevering to find me my own foothold as an artist, if not a musician, then subsequently as an actor.

Some brief extracts from two later letters to Jim Berry dated four years before the Second World War. Mention in one of them of a young German girl, Sigrid, a beautiful young German woman who came to stay with us as a family-help. A young German very much caught up in the hysteria of German youth, running amok with the Nazi peril overtaking the German people at that time. The second letter, quoting an extract surrounding another crisis of that time, the monarchy crisis surrounding King Edward's approaching abdication!

15th Sept 1935

…Your last letter with its account of conditions in the cotton trade was of great interest to the young German girl, Sigrid…. Social Credit is getting some publicity just now owing to the Alberta experiment, but I do not find any very intelligent or intelligible accounts given of it in the press.

As to the international situation, we seem precariously near another European conflagration with a lot of colour feeling burning amid the fires.

Oh for the peace and prosperity that seems so possible, so desirable, so sane, civilized – this wearying bickering, quarrelling lack of generosity and goodwill – lack of co-operation and good sense – it oppresses the spirit! There is no lack of sensible and pleasant things to do – but an uproar of snatch and grab, vulgarity and profanity prevails in the world.

Life is made such a sordid struggle for so many, that even a war seems a glorious release in comparison – it has the glamour of heroism and heroics anyway – and so they slip to the final barbarity of slaughtering each other.

King Edward and Mrs Simpson

7th Dec 1936

… One touch of nature in the form of a modern woman from the New World sets the Old World quivering and the whole world talking. The "bonds of Empire" we are assured are strained unbearably. Garvin more pontifical than ever in "The Observer" (which from being open-minded has become fascist) is lofty, reverential, so near the ridiculous and sublime in a most precarious way, and Bernard Shaw "blows the gaff in the Evening Standard".

Well the outcome is not settled as I write. The King holds the trump cards and we can't foretell how he'll play 'em. But in playing the man he has jangled the whole puppet show – and having showed his humanity on several other occasions, whatever he does he will endear himself to a scandalized nation – all the world loves a lover and those who can't believe in love, love scandal – they will run the gamut of moral indignation, enlarge on social and political indiscretion, fall by easy stages to sentimentalism – and in due course find something else to wax noisy about. I am of the opinion he will be a better man and a better King if he has his way than if he is thwarted or persuaded to "self sacrifice". As to the lady – Dorothy thinks she looks like Sigrid (a German girl who stayed at The Wilderness) – and so do I, This means that Dorothy works her out to be a designing minx who would stop at nothing, and I think she appears intellectual, witty, with grace and charm, and I hold with charity in all judgments.…

An Unwelcome Intrusion

Without confusing readers too much with correspondence not always flowing in chronological order, I must recall a late-night incident which occurred in the darkness and isolation of "The Wilderness", contrasting with the tales and recollections of happier and more joyous times that prevailed for the most part there in the thirties, forties and early fifties, perhaps a kind of "Lewis Carroll" fairyland. The intrusion of the uglier world outside! But then one can believe life at "The Wilderness" despite any material wealth or money was a way of life between the great European Wars that existed widely in the English countryside. This innocent existence, protected by a society with some sort of civilized awareness, if not devised by history or order, developed from a growth of ideas, intellect, a recognition of the choice of good and evil, and not least, some appreciation by discerning minds of the beautiful and finer things.…

Included is an account of a frightening incident one night at "The Wilderness" which I recall from being a young child but have never found any written evidence in my father's correspondence of that time to substantiate. It must have been a Christmas night in the late thirties, when I was old enough to have some realisation of what had taken place.

The night on that disturbing occasion proved long, worrying and distressing to both my mother and father in the loneliness of the forest. We, the children, apparently slept peacefully through the night's dramatic ordeal. The episode was never divulged to us younger ones, but I vividly recall overhearing family members visiting us that Christmas discussing it around one of our log fires in the studio, the flames throwing ominous shadows on to the studio ceiling's wooden beams.

The story was of a mysterious phone call from a far-off figure, phoning from Glasgow, in the middle of the night, warning my mother that someone was coming to get her. This was followed by a call, received by my father, from an officer at Scotland Yard: a man had been detained under suspicious circumstances in a London phone box with a slip of paper with my mother's name on it. This at some time in the early hours of that morning. The final outcome was that on a cold blustering night a whole contingent of policemen trudged their way nervously and apprehensively through the darkened forest with truncheons at the ready to protect our family home from some mysterious gangster figures. Where they had got my mother's name from, nobody ever knew.

I never did hear any more, but I do remember discovering a large hammer beside my parents' bed, proving perhaps as Mackey always maintained that his own pacifism would only stretch so far if he felt his own family was in danger. It seemed at moments like that, my father may have felt much the same!

Chapter 6

The Second World War Era

Without "Sprad's" constant flow of correspondence, an ever flowing river of ideas and debate – conveyed through Britain's once dependable and efficient postal service to his ever loyal and most compassionate of friends in the Yorkshire Dales, I have to charter my father's life at this point through my own memories and the letters, articles, speeches and documents left in my hands after his death. With my own movement around the world from the mid-seventies onwards, it is more than fortunate that these papers and other things have been retained!

Walter Spradbery's life after the sudden death of his beloved Dorothy in the spring of 1952 became very much that of a dispirited and deflated man. Predominantly his greatest call as his sight failed and heart had suffered such a loss, apart for the affection for his daughter Rima's children, was his campaigning and championing for the cause of peace on every front that faced him. He was never going to desert or leave his home, "The Wilderness", while he could muster the effort and safeguards to hang on – enmeshed in his precious memories. "The Wilderness" which had been acquired by Dorothy's uncle, a landlord in Somerset, and then left to Dorothy was subsequently left to Walter in his wife's last will.

How miraculous it was that I ever came into possession of past correspondence covering those crucial years before such an offspring as I was even thought of; also covering my earliest years of which I have little or no clear recollection. Fortunate indeed that I still have clear recollections from the war-years onwards and the files of personal papers I have amazingly held on to since "The Wilderness" was – specifically at "Sprad's" wish – returned to its natural forest land after his death.

In those immediate pre-war years – as Germany's threat to the world began to emerge, "The Wilderness" was certainly a unique haven of music, artistic endeavour and lively intelligent debate; warm friendships, laughter and endless romances with many children filling the air with noise, laughter and games. Dorothy's commitment to her music and singing was ceaseless. Walter himself built and moved mountains of earth, simultaneously converting a stone Chinese Summer House into an air-raid shelter against German bombing – and at the same time creating in the upper reaches of the garden a natural arena for Dorothy's opera performances against the forest background. It was perhaps a unique double achievement, building a protective measure against barbaric destruction and in the same instance pursuing a creative outlet for the future. "Sprad" himself suffered from a permanent disability of a ruptured hernia for the rest of his life from his excavating efforts with nothing more than a spade, fork and barrow.

The irony of the declaration of war against Germany, and all that followed, was that it introduced a remarkable episode in life surrounding the hideaway home of Walter and Dorothy's "The Wilderness". With the advent of the imminent danger of aerial bombing, Spradbery's conversion of the garden, in the process of transforming the Chinese summerhouse into an air-raid shelter, provided the garden with a natural amphitheatre which opened up a whole vista of open-air opera, dance and drama within the locality at a time when the war had shut down every activity of cultural pursuit. Probably not the first open-air opera, but certainly a forerunner to much that followed, something unique that emerged from a married partnership involving such unique combined talents. Also a repertoire of work of English opera, that to my knowledge has never been approached or surpassed, even in the topmost reaches of opera to this present day. I quote here childhood memories of others from that never-to-be forgotten era. . . .

Strangely the full extent of "The Wilderness" musical years didn't take hold until the air overhead was filled with the drones of German aircraft – yes, and the bombs falling! After all Epping Forest was not so far away from the centre of London, although it could have been a million miles away by its remarkable naturally wild location.

In those pre-war summers, the locality of south west Essex was an extraordinary hive of musical enterprise, on all levels, both amateur and professional. In the neighbouring town of Loughton was the renaissance garden of the Howard family (makers of aspirin) where the extraordinary Scarlatti operas were performed. Also in neighbouring Woodford where the Mathieson family (makers of Clarnico sweets) held similar musical occasions. Walter and Dorothy were enthusiastically involved, "Sprad" painting settings and my mother directing and performing. Through my mother's indefatigable spirit, it was at "The Wilderness", despite its poorer relationship with the grander homes of the neighbouring gentry, that the focus of musical endeavour took off, drawing enthusiasts from far and wide in ever increasing numbers.

Yet another extract from a rare letter from "Sprad" to Jim Berry at that auspicious moment in time:

10th Sept 1939

…We sent the children away to Westbury in Wilts. Last Monday, feeling they will be more secure there and we ourselves more free to do such things as we are able, to lessen distress or any injuries that may befall those in our neighbourhood.

I was in the L.B.T.B. (London Transport) boardroom ready to submit my rough sketch designs for next season's posters to Mr Pick when the news came through that the London children, mothers and hospital patients were to be evacuated. He saw my works nevertheless, and approved most, and suggested modifications in others, and also a similar set by Fred Taylor – who has done London features while I have done the countryside. Just when these will be completed or issued remains as all things in the hands of providence – anyway as chance offers time I am going on with them.

We have had a number of W.A.C.s billeted on us – they seem quite delighted and Dorothy is kept busy – cooking and looking after them. Yesterday, when a group of people from the Settlement (many P.P.U., Peace Pledge Union folk) called on us, they ought to have been gratified to find several of these ladies in uniform sitting in the garden darning my socks. What could be more peaceful? We have also an Austrian refugee on our hands. And among yesterday's callers was Alf Stone, the tramp whom I tried to get settled into useful life. He was resplendent in a new grey suit and brought a companion who lodges in the same house as he is now in (with his father), and told me he had a good job under the Edmonton Council, trench digging. It's an ill wind that blows no one any good. I was delighted and amused to see him so posh.…

… Frank Brangwyn has prepared his place (we had for our holiday) to receive 25 children, but has now been told to expect mothers and small infants from Rotherhithe – this seems a bit rough on so distinguished and old an artist – Rotherhithe mothers are not too gentle a crowd and he expects trouble. I fear his gardens and orchards will be raided and many of his beautiful things roughly handled. He was invited to go to Bruges if he would.

Well everything still looks as lovely as wild nature can make it here – we have had our early share of excitement in the air at close quarters but no damage. Our electric installation is being completed – we already have light and cooking facilities and heating is now going in. Heaven knows how – in the face of present circumstances we shall meet our commitments – but security is always an illusion.…

"The Wilderness" in the year 1929 when my parents first discovered the place, with its extraordinary collection of outbuildings including the Chinese summer-house, had no hot water supply, no electricity or gas. Only ornate oil lamps and hurricane lanterns and no telephone. It did though have inside and outside lavatories, a bathroom (with no hot water) and a scullery and kitchen.

By the outbreak of war in 1939 however, we had electricity and hot water! Also a telephone laid on much earlier, the number of which I remember to this day, BUC 2360!

The stone summerhouse "Sprad" converted into our first air-raid shelter, piling it high with masses of earth from the upper part of the garden which was leveled off to become "The Wilderness" stage and part of a natural amphitheatre. Later we were allocated a Morrison shelter, a large table made of metal and bolted together which we slept under in one of the ground floor bedrooms in the war's latter days.

Originally, at the outbreak of war, both my sister and I as young children were evacuated to Westbury in Wiltshire, but as fate or fortune turned out, our parents decided that with some sort of protected air-raid shelter constructed in the garden – we should return home. It so happened that the day after the night our father collected us from our temporary homes, some months later – amidst much emotional upset from the childless couple I was staying with – the London blitz began. To this day I vividly recall our father reading the nights away to us as German bombers droned overhead while sound of gunfire and bombs rent the air outside. While we lay awake and eventually fell to sleep in tiered bunks, our father's voice rang out through the nights with the heroic tales of "Ivanhoe", John Ridd from "Lorna Doone" and a wonderful novel "Masterman Ready" – reading these massive novels to us from cover to cover.

I remember my bedroom later on in the war years, in the summer months, becoming a communal dressing room for singers and dancers alike, while I would set out masses of seating for audiences and the musical stands for the musicians. An upright piano was kept covered by a tarpaulin on a wheeled truck in the garden. As a young lad, I recall, the piano tumbled over onto the back of my legs as I attempted, unwisely on my own, to pull off the tarpaulin cover for a rehearsal, and being rushed off to the local hospital to treat and inspect my bruised legs.

Never were there so many musical instruments, (I remember a harp, also a lyre in the studio alongside a double bass for years, grand pianos and a square piano), so many local musical enthusiasts, musicians and families who were drawn in and attached themselves into such a musical fraternity: I recall especially the Newells and Clements, the Roxby-Botts and the Blacks, the Orchards and the Kirk-Sternes from those latter war and post-war years. Days of a more Arcadian and gentle atmosphere, with Spradbery carrying on in his own sublime way and supporting my mother's world of music, equally, to its utmost limits.

Seventy years afterwards, amazingly, a long-standing friend of all those years back, sent me a facsimile of a letter dated 9th May 2008 referring to those remarkable days:

... "I also have memories of 'The Wilderness' with Dorothy and Walter, John and Rima Spradbery, because they were our first friends when my parents moved to Buckhurst Hill! I'll tell you about that. I was 4 years old when we came to live in an old Victorian house in Buckhurst Hill. My father was a musician, pianist and organist but in the 1930's, still the recession years, he was unable to find work in the musical world. Instead, to support his family, he had to take a clerical position with the London Electricity Board. This must have been dreadful for him, but he never complained. My sister was only 2. One day or evening there was a phone call for him from a lady he didn't know: Dorothy d'Orsay, ex-opera singer married to Walter Spradbery the artist, living at The Wilderness quite near our house.

Dorothy was going to put on a performance of Rutland Boughton's "Bethlehem" at the Y.M.C.A. Hall in Tottenham Court Road, the following Christmas. She had gathered her singers, but had no orchestra. She had heard of a talented pianist who had just come to live in the area. Would my father (William Kirk Sterne) play for "Bethlehem"? Well! My father was overjoyed! Somebody wanted his music, someone needed him to play. He said yes at once. There was a problem, however, William would allow nobody except my mother, Rita to turn the pages for him and he was adamant about that. And Rita, newly arrived in the district, knew no one with whom she could leave 2 small children. Dorothy reacted characteristically; "Darling! She cried. "There is no problem, I need 2 more children in my street scene. Why don't you bring Diana and Gillian with you, and they can be in "Bethlehem" too.

And that was how Gill and I, aged 5 and 3 at Christmas appeared in London on what I later called the West End stage and it was wonderful! I knew the music because I heard my father playing it at home, and I can still remember Mary's lovely lullaby to the baby in the cradle. Mary was very beautiful, and I thought Herod was very handsome! We had one dress rehearsal and just one performance....

... I did return to "Bethlehem" when I was perhaps 15 or so. Dorothy needed another dancer for a scene at Herod's court! On that occasion my costume was far more glamorous than that of the street child, although there was much less of it....

...We used to go to see the Spradberys at The Wilderness after "Bethlehem", and grew very fond of them. Walter was always gentle and quiet, and Dorothy vivacious and entertaining.

... I lived in Buckhurst Hill for 67 years ... I believe you were a Belisha Beacon in a Road Pageant as I was? And also a moon maiden on the grass stage at The Wilderness, a little later? I was taking A levels just after the Moon Maidens, and crouched in the bushes desperately studying Latin, while awaiting our entrance!"

Diana Tredinnick (Kirk Sterne), May 2008

Equally as remarkable as Diana Tredinnick's reminiscences to long-standing friend Ishbel, over a year ago now, is a similar reminiscence published in a local monthly newsletter in my childhood parish of Buckhurst Hill. This newsletter, called "The Chronicle" is surprisingly the voice-piece of the branch of the local British Legion. It is featured under the caption of "Walter Spradbery – Memories of a young Girl". A message of a bygone era penned by a local woman, herself a personality and locally celebrated figure for as long ago as I can remember; her name, although the piece was written anonymously, is well known in Buckhurst Hill today in the year 2009, as Heather Thirtle.

Memories of a Young Girl (April 2009)

"I was very young when I met another young girl, named Rima, and we soon became close pals. I was taken to her home to meet her parents. Home was The Wilderness – I considered this a strange name but soon realised it was a very apt description of the house in which Rima was growing up.

The Wilderness was situated in the forest just off the High Road, Buckhurst Hill, almost opposite Gladstone Road. On my first visit I was introduced to Rima's parents, Walter and Dorothy Spradbery. The house was very remote and sparsely furnished and a memory which I always retain was the stripped floorboards in the living room. I had always been used to mats and carpets and this I found very unusual, though today it's in vogue and the norm.

I was captivated by Rima's Dad, a majestic-looking gentleman with a beard, who was well known around Buckhurst Hill for his gait and floppy hat. Walter took us into the living room and there I spent many happy hours in the following years, watching Walter at his easel, painting those familiar pictures, one of which hung in the Roebuck snug for many years. Dorothy, whose professional name was Dorothy d'Orsay, had her own orchestra which performed musical works throughout the district. Dorothy always looked so different on these occasions, in her black evening wear and sporting her baton. She liked to take us to the concerts and always reserved the front row seats for Walter, who was so proud and supportive of Dorothy, Rima, Brenda Booker (who later became a well known artist herself, having been very much inspired by Walter and his work) and yours truly.

Whilst visiting The Wilderness I was introduced to Walter's friend, Bernard Bowerman, another artist, who lived at the top of Princes Road. He also had a beard, a red one this time. This was my first experience of men with beards, though I know a little more about them these days.

The garden of The Wilderness provided a stage for many of Dorothy's productions,

189

and Walter was a great help to her on these occasions. We youngsters were quite a help too, fetching and delivering props. Summer days and evenings playing, plotting and chatting in The Wilderness garden was a great part of my childhood and early teens. I learnt to appreciate art and music through this unusual couple who were great characters. I think my love of gardening was enhanced by the lovely plants which grew in The Wilderness garden. The sight of daffodils, snowdrops, primroses, violets and bluebells remains a lovely memory.

If only The Wilderness had been listed, preserved and kept for future generations to enjoy but this was not Walter's wish. A walk through this part of Epping Forest today gives little indication of the happy home filled with music and art which existed there. The wonderful music would echo from the garden through the forest and real paintings were produced within.

The Wilderness could only be described as an artist's paradise."

Heather Thirtle, April 2009

In the same British Legion newsletter of April 2009 is yet another similar recollection, a reminder of those Wilderness years, this by Tony Oliva, Chairman of Buckhurst hill's Residents' Society.

Dorothy d'Orsay and the Wilderness

There is a little piece of Epping Forest in Buckhurst Hill with the intriguing name of The Wilderness. A visit to this strip of woodland shows that it is similar to the rest of Epping Forest, with lopped hornbeam and oak trees standing amid holly and brambles. There are some fairly open grassy glades and by one there is a small flight of stone steps. This part of the forest was where the house stood which in 1929 became the home of Walter Spradbery, his wife Dorothy and eventually their family. The house was originally a four-roomed cottage but had been extended and added to over the years. The rooms were arranged in roughly a square, with steps where necessary due to the sloping ground. There was a single upstairs room with a verandah facing St. John's Church. In one corner there was a large studio room.

Dorothy was a singer with a wonderful contralto voice who was already well known in Opera, preferring Verdi and Mozart, and also as a concert artist, including appearances at the first proms under Sir Henry Wood. During WWII she formed the Wilderness Opera Group and Orchestra, which rehearsed in the studio and performed in the open-air theatre in the garden. Many operas were performed, with sets painted by Walter, including Dido and Aeneas (with children from a local drama school as cherubs), Acis and Galatea and Sir John in Love – for the latter Walter overcame the problem of a daylight performance of a scene meant to be night by giving the audience cardboard glasses with blue celluloid lenses. At this time Dorothy's brother-in-law, Dick Williams, also used the open-air theatre to stage plays by students of Greenleaf Road Educational Settlement, Walthamstow. (Dick Williams continued this tradition with an open-air theatre at his home, Willow Cottage, Stapleford Abbots and this has continued since his death in 2007).

The garden was also opened to local people for community events: the Buckhurst Hill Branch held at least one garden fete there.

Dorothy died in 1952 and Walter in 1969 and they are buried together in St. John's churchyard. The inscription on their grave is from the Rubaiyat of Omar Khayyam:

"and thou beside me, singing in the wilderness, and wilderness is paradise enow".

Following Walter's death the house was demolished and the land incorporated into Epping Forest."

Tony Oliva, April 2009

"The Wilderness" orchestra conducted by Dorothy d'Orsay

Pastoral delights.

"Sprad" miming the role of the one-eyed Polyphemus in Handel's Acis and Galatea" while the role was sung offstage behind the trees. The singer cast in the role found it impossible to sing in such a head-piece.

Members of 'The Wilderness Opera Group'. Never was their womanly charm more apparent than in moments like this!

Whether it is entirely accurate that my mother sang in early proms under Sir Henry Wood, I am not entirely clear about. She had certainly worked under many of the great conductors of the day, including Sir Adrian Boult. There were certainly figures in the B.B.C. in its early years on the musical side of things who put a fair amount of singing work her way.

Unlike myself, I was never aware of either my father or mother indulging in reminiscing over the past. They had this extraordinary enthusiasm looking to the future.

Also that my mother preferred Verdi and Mozart to others is not at all evident as I remember! Her great passions were singing the works of Rutland Boughton, Ethel Smyth and Purcell, and later, especially with her musical activity at "The Wilderness", English pastoral music and opera, notably Vaughan Williams.

Rutland Boughton was her early mentor and she was a great upholder of Ethel Smyth's work. Vaughan Williams and other English composers were very much part of the Wilderness Opera Group and Orchestra's repertoire. My own very first stage appearance was as a cherub in Dido and Aeneas where I plucked a bow symbolising the flight of an arrow to Aeneas's heart. My mother was portraying Dido in that performance, as in many others. A role for which she perhaps never got the recognition she deserved.

The most recent of the recollections and reminiscences quoted here, remind me of nearly forty years back working in Edinburgh with long-standing working colleagues, Lindsay Kemp and Jack Birkett (The Incredible Orlando): when the radio, by chance, was broadcasting an early morning programme of classical music, my ear suddenly caught the names of Epping Forest, and "The Wilderness", the war years and the commentator's words, speaking of sounds of music breezing through the trees, reminding him of musical occasions past.

It is perhaps only now, looking back to when I listened quite by chance to that early morning radio programme in Edinburgh, that the full realisation dawns of the impact and pleasure those long-lost years at "The Wilderness" must have meant to so many music lovers from near and far who were drawn to those unique summer events.

When I reach out and look through old programmes and photographs, I am reminded of the extraordinary repertoire of English music staged with full orchestras, chorus, costumes and scenery in such a pastoral setting, a remote forest garden, so far yet so near to London's almighty urban life. Not that many – if any – of these rarest English operas had any complete orchestral scores! Looking back I can bear witness that my mother's nights and days were endlessly spent writing out individual instrumental scores. One has also to remind the reader that those professional musicians or singers charmed and drawn into partaking, received little or no payment, other than the love, reward and satisfaction of participating in a creative communal effort – engendered and brought about by a shared love of music by all. It seemed a natural process for Dorothy's friends and children, I being one of them – to be turfed out of bedrooms for singers and dancers to invade as improvised dressing rooms; for the house to be overrun on those summer weekends with masses of human musical endeavour and activity was seemingly the normal course of events. Dorothy d'Orsay was a much adored woman, both from the professional ranks and locally where her musical activities held sway. Never was I or my sister going to match up in any artistic sense to such prodigiously talented parents, consequently it is perhaps only in these fading years of my own life that I can now look back with astonishment at their unaided and separate achievements in a detached way.

It is amazing to realise that my mother blazed such a trail of rare quality music, which even today is so infrequently heard. Dorothy d'Orsay in her lifetime created her own world of music. It didn't establish her with any place in musical history, but through her indefatigable efforts, she left a legacy which must have inspired and renewed hope in the many devotees of opera and music who came in contact with her. Besides her wide following among local enthusiasts, she was also uniquely admired by such musical figures already mentioned as Rutland Boughton, Dame Ethel Smyth and the conductor Sir Adrian Boult among others.

For myself, I have to admit my own recollections were not so pure and innocent! Discreet as I was as a young lad, struggling with the first stirrings and signs of puberty and sexual awareness, "The Wilderness" and its whole enclave of activity in opera and music released a high octane of such feelings within me at an early age. My mother and father surrounded themselves with such enthusiasm of the arts and innocent passions of music within an atmosphere of pastoral delights, happening with such close proximity to my daily life that hidden thoughts of frustrated feelings and lusting were not so very far from the surface of my body and mind!

My mother's closest and dearest friend, Kathleen Beer, known as "Fluffy" from the west country, a regular visitor through all those childhood and youthful years was a particularly entrancing woman who as I grew older became more and more the innocent target of my infatuations. A Sylvia Harrison, a local girl, who danced in a number of Wilderness productions was someone who stirred the chords and emotions of "Daphnis and Chloe" within a boy in the growing stages of puberty! The very nature of the whole world of opera, dancing and the spirits it aroused could not help to restrain such emotions and feelings which enveloped and frustrated me at "The Wilderness" at that time. If it was not young passionate dancing girls performing in their transparent chiffons in such pastoral delights as "The Moon Maiden", there was the elegance and coolness of the older singing women: Winifred Gould, the wife and outstandingly womanly figure of neighbouring Loughton's leading farmer, the forever untouched elegance and sophisticated air of her countenance has strangely remained implanted in my mind to this present day! One of a number of serene-looking local ladies. What made it so frustrating and hot under the collar for me, hidden away in my own agitated little world, was that everything was so perfect, civilized and full of natural enchantment – encouraged by the glorious warm summer nights and all the other miracles that the forest, birdsong and cool breezes evoked.

Elinor Pugh

It seems in the mid-thirties Walter Spradbery's massive correspondence to James Berry may have tailed off to some extent, however I cannot be absolutely sure of this. There must be reams of correspondence lost, other than what was miraculously returned to me. Jim Berry himself always maintained he received over a thousand letters from "Sprad" in his lifetime!

Incredibly though, in the mid-thirties there emerged a significant correspondence to an Elinor Pugh, the niece of Arthur Heygate Mackmurdo, and which takes over here from "Sprad's" earlier letters to his bosom pal, Jim Berry. A series of letters, strangely in contrast to them. These letters maintained a very formal nature throughout their friendship of some 25 years or so before her death in the sixties.

Elinor Pugh was a spinster of evidently great charm and not unattractive, whom I recall meeting on rare occasions. My father held her in the highest esteem. She very much handled her uncle's diary and affairs later in life and was a figure greatly involved in the pursuance of the final establishment of the William Morris Gallery.

19th Aug 1935

Dear Miss Pugh

I am very glad to hear that you are having a pleasant holiday and staying a little longer than you first intended. We all send greetings and trust you will benefit from the change.

The Brangwyn Bequest matters are going ahead – two committee meetings and the draft deed made out! Brangwyn expressed the wish that you should be made a Trustee, but Mr Mackmurdo would not agree to this according to Mr Roebuck (Walthamstow's Chief Borough Librarian), who went to Witham to see him in company with the Deputy Town Clerk. Since our committee meetings however Mr Mackmurdo has written to say "we would like her associated with the enterprise –

Arthur Mackmurdo, Frank Brangwyn and Elinor Pugh.

she might be a Trustee or on the Committee of management". I have communicated this to Roebuck and am now writing to you as in the first place it is for you to decide if you are willing to stand. I shall be very glad if you will. Brangwyn's executor has also been nominated but Mr Mackmurdo says that both he and you would be only trustees at the start and appoint no successors – whereas the Town Clerk would function for all time; a Trustee appointed by the Director of the V&A (Victoria and Albert Museum) would also figure prominently, and after my decease or resignation, another artist nominated by me, only the P.R.A. would carry on my responsibilities and duties in relation to the work.

There is a little discussion too as to what the exhibition (museum) shall be called – otherwise all is progressing without difficulty. I may be able to see you and tell you more on Sunday evening – but I leave for Bath 6 am – Monday (an exhibition of his own work in Bath's Pump Room). Am "up to the eyebrows" in work and preparations of various sorts. My Art Class Exhibition opens a few days after my return and I have had to select work, catalogue it, and write a report of about 2000 words. I hope you and Mr Mackmurdo will be able to see the show when it is up. Again kind regards.

Yours sincerely Walter E. Spradbery

19th April 1936

… It has been recommended that the Historical Exhibition at the local museum shall be closed for a year, during which the drawings, etchings and lithographs recently given by Brangwyn as an addition to his bequest are to be shown. It is proposed to have it ready and open on Saturday 27th June at 3 pm, and at my suggestion G.K. Chesterton is to be invited to open it – failing him Laurence Bunyan – failing him Hilaire Belloc who opened the Brighton show you will remember....

What these early letters to Elinor Pugh reveal is Spradbery's commitment from the beginning to Brangwyn and the whole business of exhibiting, not only Brangwyn and his own work, but those of other lesser artists and his own students, some of whom went on to develop their own professional careers. These are subsequent extracts to Elinor Pugh from letters written from the war years onwards.

3rd Dec 1940

… I must tell you that the canvas folding case you gave me has already been put to a good use. Some few days ago I was asked to give a talk on some aspect of art to a women's meeting at Highams Park – the organiser suggested "Paul Cezanne" as a subject, but I would not have this, and at first felt art-talk in these days, to women from and in a bombed area and folks of little experience was a bit futile – unless one could follow it up with some practical craft work – or give a series of illustrated talks. But thinking of what might really be useful and of interest, more than the mere passing of a pleasant hour or so, it suddenly became clear to me that I must talk of Frank Brangwyn again and his gift to Walthamstow, so long in finding a proper home in the place for which it is intended – for (as proved to be the case) I guessed few would know anything about it, and the more who know and look forward to it the better.... And so I went forth and gave my talk which was received with great pleasure – one woman saying one felt as if she had met the artist herself. And I impressed on all their duty to see that after the war, no matter who of us most concerned was alive or dead, that the gift had its proper place and appreciation.... I think it would be a good idea to give a few more talks like this to various groups in the town if I can manage it – not that there's any fees attached to the job – but it will help to spread the interest during a period when it would otherwise lie dormant and can be worked up to greater effect as the time to get busy again comes along....

...We still stand intact to date – still sleep in the dug-out which is not so cold as you might imagine, and where every night I am reading passages of "Lorna Doone", a grand book suited to the taste of all the family, and in the adventures of John Ridd we lose all sense of any danger that is our own living adventure in these times.

> Extracts from letters to Elinor Pugh in 1941 were always formally addressed "Dear Miss Pugh". I am particular selecting passages from these communications, mentioning kind deeds and sad losses in those anxious and worrying years, where a cloud hung over the country, living under the threat of a German invasion and bombing from the skies.

9th Jan 1941

Christmas, with its blessed freedom from raids passed very agreeably.... With us were Mr and Mrs. Bowler, the caretaker of the Settlement, who have been bombed out of their home and spend their nights on the platform of the Friends Hall, and the jovial Miss Jeffries, who declares she has never enjoyed a Christmas so much, and her only fear is (as she told some visitors) that she is being led into temptation – the temptation in The Wilderness – Pressed to explain she said she feared she was being led into "light-mindedness" – at 86!...

...I had two letters from Frank Pick. As you will have seen from the press he has resigned the position of director General to the Ministry of Information after only 4 months in office. In his first note he said "I find I am unable to cope with politicians, diplomats and civil servants" and spoke playfully of having attained "freedom, incidentally one of the things for which we fight". But in the second letter he said that he had been practically summarily, dismissed. One day I must show you the correspondence we have had – probably not concluded yet….

> In this same letter is a long account of his summons to the Epping Police Court for the overdue payment of his rates. In court Spradbery detailed forthcoming modest items of income and was able to convince them that his rate payment obligations would be met as soon as possible. In his appeal he mentioned his work for the National Gallery Committee dealing with a scheme for recording Britain for which he had a guarantee of a £24 payment from the Pilgrims' Trust. The letter goes on to list payments that had been paid and not paid. He was asked by the court, which included a panel of five or six local dignitaries, if he had anything to say. I quote on from "Sprad's" same letter of the 9th January 1941 the words he addressed to the panel….

… "I am an artist. I think I may say that I have contributed to the fame of British posters by my work – indeed they have been shown and are known all over the world – but just now there are no commissions for poster design to be had! As a painter of watercolours I exhibit in the principal galleries including the Royal Academy and have works in various public collections, but the sale of pictures has practically stopped by reason of the war conditions! As an art teacher I think I have rendered useful service in Essex but students have been evacuated or called up, and the classes at my centre have come to an end! However, this morning I have received a message from the National Gallery saying some eight of my drawings will be selected for purchase at £5 each, and when that £24 comes to hand I may be able to spare six pound five shillings to meet these demands!" This seemed to cause a little sensation and certainly the faces on the bench looked more embarrassed than I felt. A moment's whispered consultation took place, and then the presiding magistrate said – "The case is adjourned for 3 months". I said thank you and came away.

A day or so later I had just finished writing a letter to Sir Hubert Llewellyn Smith to tell him that the National Gallery Committee had offered to purchase a selection of my sketches, and to thank him for his part in calling attention to my work, when to my surprise I saw Lady Llewellyn Smith at the door, bearing flowers for Dorothy and a book for the children.

She took Dorothy aside and asked her to accept an envelope with a little present which she hoped we would accept as ready-help, as she had heard we were in some difficulty – indeed a report of the proceedings at Epping had come to her. It was not until she had gone that we found a cheque for £50 inside. Of course I wrote at once and said that while one of the joys of adversity was that it disclosed the great goodwill of friends, I felt I could not lightly accept such a gift, but would, if she would consent to accept it as a loan, and, since in the uncertainty of present conditions the likelihood of repayment was remote and highly precarious, begged her to take my winter picture as a sort of security so that she might have something against her fifty pounds – and then, if and when I was in a position to repay it she could let me reclaim the picture if she felt disposed.

And to this course she agreed – which I think is altogether delightful of her and the very essence of kindness and courtesy and ready helpfulness.

In fact, had I not a life time's experience of good nature and the unexpected blessings in it, with the help that Providence brings, I should say it was like a fairy story. But then life is like that I think....

... I have always had a prejudice against security – believing it unattainable by man – an illusion he hankers after – and a famous philosopher said – "Live Dangerously" – Well these are the days! We do. Planes are overhead as I write....

> Lady Llewellyn Smith's husband, Sir Hubert, was once described by Sir Winston Churchill as one of Britain's finest civil servants. He was also Chairman of the country's National Association of Boys' Clubs and was instrumental in appointing Walter Spradbery as the Art Adviser to the Association. As a boy, I accompanied my father to their summer camp courses, which first introduced me to the thrills of drama and acting.
>
> It also seemed at that anxious period of wartime, that besides the worry of death from the skies, dear friends such as Mackmurdo (later) and others were passing away from more natural causes.

18th Jan 1941

Dear Miss Pugh (or may I say Nell as those near you do)

I have just received a letter from Frank Brangwyn in which he tells me that your aunt has passed away and bids me write to you again, which of course I should have done in any case; and I must attempt a word or two of sympathy to your uncle, a matter of even more difficulty, and requiring skill more than I can command for I would indeed if I could say the sustaining and comforting words to hold him, whom we love so much, with us, at this time....

... We have had to greet death here and I have lost a loyal and excellent friend in Frank Hall, who assisted me at the Settlement Art Classes and who was an active and valuable member of the Essex Art Club. He was killed by a bomb on Sunday last, as he was returning from visiting his wife and young children, evacuated to Hertfordshire, and on his way to stretcher-bearer duty at Connaught Hospital....

Another letter to Elinor Pugh on the 11th November of 1941 reveals the death and sad loss of another of Walter Spradbery's friends of that time, also one of his great benefactors and from the higher echelons of society, Frank Pick.

While quoting from "Sprad's" correspondence at that time, in addition to sombre news of death, these letters are filled with family news and my own mother's incessant and never-ending musical activities, conducting orchestral performances and continuing singing engagements with her arm in a sling, following an injury.

4th Feb 1941

...There is no fresh news I think since last I wrote. Sir Hubert and Lady Llewellyn Smith came to tea last Friday and selected another picture instead of the proposed winter picture which was too large for their house. They decided on the Hollyhocks which hung in the Central Gallery of the R.A. at the United Artists Show, and which just fills a panel in their home, and they seem very pleased with it. And it is a suffi-ciently important work for me to feel satisfaction in it being in their possession.

Costumes, props and scenery, gathered, made and designed for numerous operatic productions of my mother's amongst all the wartime chickens (reared and looked after for producing wartime eggs and Christmas dinners for my uncle's family butcher's business) were stored in the accommodating old garage in the lower depths of "The Wilderness" garden. These same props and costumes helped out the London Philharmonic in their hour of need in those difficult years for art, music and theatre; on one occasion as far away as the Welsh Eisteddfod Festival.

In those trying times loss of life was as regularly anticipated for civilians as for those servicemen serving overseas. The Wilderness in those torn war-struck years was an extraordinary domain and local outpost of music, art, social and cultural survival amongst the mayhem of civilian existence, probably holding on to what Walter Spradbery might have described as the last vestiges of civilized sanity! Meanwhile at the most unexpected times, German Hienkel bombers prowled eerily in the skies on summer afternoons, while music could be heard coming through the trees from the vicinity of "The Wilderness".

Two other incidents dealing particularly with the background of the war in those anxious years and concerning life and death make poignant reading. In "Sprad's" own words:

24th April 1941

... As you may know the night before (this, after attending the funeral of Miss Jeffries, the 86 year old woman from Canning Town whom "Sprad" and my mother had given a home to in those unsettling days) had been a terrible one with air raids all through – planes following planes incessantly, and gunfire and explosions as bad or worse than anything previously. We learned while talking to the Rector and Mr Kibble after our return from the funeral that great havoc had been made in Maybank Road and Maybank Avenue in South Woodford. As several of my relatives lived there I set off to see them and found my sister's house uninhabitable and condemned although I am glad to say they (my sister, her husband and daughter) were alive although suffering a bit from shock – and I hurried them and returned home to get the room Miss Jeffries had occupied ready for them.

By 8 pm we had them all tucked in. I do not mean to say that they were prostrated and had to take to bed. They are very much alive – in fact I am up mornings at 5.30 to get my niece's early morning tea before she leaves for nursing duties at East Ham....

> At some time later in the war, my mother lost one of her sisters, Muriel, when struck by a piece of shrapnel from a bomb which exploded in the bottom of their garden in Higham's Park. Muriel often sang and took roles in many of my mother's operatic productions. She was one of a quartet of sisters – my mother being the eldest. A vivacious quartet of ladies with their own individual charms that all succumbed to happy marriages in an era when marriages were a highly prized attainment!! Dorothy's other sisters, Freda and Edna, were popular and attractive girls. Freda married her childhood sweetheart, Dick Williams, a young actor and musician of indefatigable energy and spirit who went on to encourage and influence generations of young local actors and musicians. A huge Williams dynasty seemingly survives today. Edna married a successful bank manager and was very much on hand to support my father in later years.

F.B. (Frank Brangwyn) writes that he has been commanded to appear at Buckingham Palace, but that it is impossible for him to go – rheumatism being among the obstacles – and that he hopes 'lese-Majeste' will not land him in the Tower. It will be interesting to see what happens – "If the mountain won't go to Mohammed etc." He also asks me not to address him as Sir Frank – because he feels it is not friendly enough – What is one to do in these dilemmas!

11th Nov 1941

…The news of Frank Pick's death came to us over the wireless on Sat. morning just as I was leaving for Bristol. It was a great shock – especially in view of a letter I received from him about 3 weeks ago – which I will quote to you. It came with a copy of his new book "Paths to Peace" inscribed "To Walter E. Spradbery with the writer's warm regards, Frank Pick 1941". The letter read thus:

15.10.41

My Dear Spradbery

My tract is finished and I send you a copy. I have not seen it since June but now I read it again I feel thoroughly disappointed with it. All the joy of creation has gone out of it. However it sets out a point of view not much regarded so that I can only hope that it may provoke discussion so that someone may make a better job of the business. It is a little way towards your point of view, but only a little way. However I may enjoy just a corresponding little approbation on that account.

I begin to feel half dead. Life seems empty and unreal. I cannot even reflect on Nature and enjoy its beauties as you do. I cling to this civilisation of ours which yields poor satisfaction. I try to conjure up faith in its rebuilding only to be continually disheartened by fact.

I ought to retire resolutely and not linger on neither in work or out of work. It is a hard decision to go down to Dorset for good. I am glad you continue with serenity at Buckhurst Hill. I am pleased at your activity. Life is still full for you. With my good wishes for the future.

Yours sincerely

Frank Pick

Is it not a sad and portentous last letter! I was filled with anxiety when I received it and wrote at some length to cheer him up and restore his confidence in himself – Reaffirming his achievement and my faith in the part he could play in restoring the world to sanity.…

The Continuing War Years

The early forties brought forth endless sad news. A letter to Elinor Pugh on 24th June 1942, recognises the loss to "Sprad" of her uncle, Arthur Heygate Mackmurdo. Elinor Pugh's uncle, Arthur Mackmurdo died some time earlier. This is an extract from a later letter, where "Sprad" reminds her of his own feelings and admiration for Mackmurdo.

24th June 1942

… Before posting this I will get a copy of the Guardian (local paper) with account of Private View and opening of the Essex Art Club. This is what I said in the course of my opening remarks as Chairman, in reference to your uncle:

"Our saddest loss this year, is the passing at the age of 91 of that distinguished and picturesque figure who has so often graced our platforms and enlightened and enlivened our proceedings with his wit and wisdom – Arthur Heygate Mackmurdo – friend of Ruskin, Morris, Brangwyn and an inspiration and source of enthusiasm to all with whom he came in touch.

He carried from youth to old age burning convictions of the power and purpose of art as a means to life abundant, and he certainly lived himself abundantly in his many works and interests. I cannot here and now pay proper tribute to his memory, nor detail his claims to fame, but you who met him know that his spirit and influence will not pass: that in part it will be enshrined in the Gallery that is to contain the Brangwyn Gift and William Morris Memorial in Walthamstow.

Not only did he leave us indebted to him for the public-spirited service of his life's work, but he has actually by his Will bequeathed to Walthamstow examples of his art and craft, furniture made from his designs, metal work, pottery, architectural drawings, and also many things of artistic value done by his distinguished contemporaries and friends, largely through his inspiration and encouragement."…

Many letters flowed from "Sprad's" pen to Elinor Pugh in the aftermath of Mackmurdo's death. Mainly informing her of operatic events at "The Wilderness" and subsequent tours of both his training courses and my mother's singing engagements under the government's wartime C.E.M.A. scheme. Despite the limitations imposed on all and sundry, Dorothy and Walter Spradbery maintained a large local programme of open-air performances in the garden with all their other commitments around the country, besides the odd garden party. Her Wilderness Orchestra played at one time for Robert Atkins' Regent Park Players in "A Midsummer Night's Dream" in Leyton. Also "The Taming of the Shrew". There were wide-ranging activities in the field of exhibitions, teaching for adults, and my father's teaching and training for Britain's up and coming generations of young men with the National Association of Boys' Clubs. Also his links with the well known east end Crown and Manor Boys' Club in Hoxton. He journeyed up faithfully every Tuesday evening to teach young East End lads the art of painting and engraving in those war years. These are things that stood out in my own young mind at the time.

9th May 1943

Dear Elinor Pugh

I don't know whether Dorothy has found an opportunity to write to you since we received your letter telling us of your adventures with the fallen plane just outside your garden hedge, but things move so fast that she may not have had time, and now she's in hospital and was operated on Wednesday last. The operation was successfully performed I am told, and her progress is good. We saw her on Saturday when she was still in pain and weak and this morning the nurse told me over the phone that she had been singing a little "just to see that they had not cut out her voice". We shall visit her again tomorrow....

... She is conducting various musical enterprises from her sick bed – I being the agent to convey her wishes and instructions. She has arranged a concert at Pollards Loughton in "Aid to Russia week", another at Mrs. Tavener's on Friday May 8th and a performance of "Thomas and Sally" on June 26th at a Garden party given by Mrs. Butler Harris during "Wings for Victory Week" at Loughton. She will be in hospital at least 3 weeks and will be very shaky when she comes out – somehow I must keep her from over exerting herself....

... We hope you are keeping well and that the shock of the crashing plane has not upset your nerves....

... Unfortunately we have lost a dear and brilliant young friend in an air crash. I attended his funeral at St. John's on Friday. The news of it was a great shock. I don't know if you ever met him – Eddy Rix – but he was a charming fellow, full of promise. He was a regular visitor at "The Wilderness" from the days when he left school and first submitted work for the Essex Art Club. I enjoyed discussing modern books, music and art with him and he often sought my advice in his own work and concerning his private affairs. He married young and romantically and leaves a beautiful young wife to mourn him. I felt a great deal of affection for him and was amused by his pose of modern cynicism. He seemed like a personification of the Aldous Huxley type of intellectualism – very alive, appreciative and full of ideas. He had made a way for himself in advertising and although quite a lad was sent by Lever Bros to be their advertising manager in Buenos Aires....

... He was fond of "The Wilderness" and always came to see us when on leave.

Now he lies under the trees beyond our fragrant hawthorn hedge in the little churchyard – it is most grievous – our loss – and the world's less aware.

He was a wit, a poet, an artist – a creative spirit. He was one welcomed with joy and parted from with regret but refreshed by the happy exchange of ideas and the prospect of meeting again. He was 27 years old: a short life but one full of alert appreciation.

This is a sad story with which to end a letter. I wish it were a merry one, but except for verdant nature these are sombre days.

> Eddy Rix was the creator of the great Persil advertising slogan "Whiter than White". Elinor Pugh was someone both my father and mother felt deeply towards; with "Sprad" not least because of his own past closeness to both Brangwyn and of course her late uncle, Arthur Mackmurdo. There was a desire to keep her informed of their own activities and also not to allow the momentum to be lost with the "Brangwyn Gift" and progress towards the opening of the William Morris Gallery, in which Arthur Mackmurdo had played such an instrumental part in negotiating and initiating.
>
> Particular letters illustrate the energy and incessant musical activity of my mother, Dorothy d'Orsay, during those exceedingly difficult times. Today I marvel at what went on around her and the devoted and dedicated people who endorsed her efforts. A spirit I frankly find impossible to think of in today's present climate. This all transpired under the everyday threat of imminent destruction from Germany's bomber planes, the terror of the droning doodle bugs or the unseen soundless rockets which gave no warning whatsoever.

3rd July 1944

Dear Miss Pugh

We are all very anxious about you because it is a long time since we had word from you, and we fear that with the pressure of work and the harassing conditions of the times we have been very neglectful ourselves and indeed owe you letters.

I have been up and down the country from Carlisle to Plymouth and Dorothy has been incessantly at work on rehearsals for her various concerts and productions, but now things are slowing up a bit as no one will come to rehearsals, classes are closing down and flying bombs make havoc all about.

However the weather held good until Dorothy's last productions were over, and not only sunshine blessed her but no alert was sounded during either show.

I send you a programme, from which you will see the high Gods have been walking in our garden and contending in musical competition: and since Phoebus was awarded the lyre by Mercurias, as victor, you will understand why sunshine for the occasion was inevitable.

About 200 people came to each performance despite the alarms and excursions of the preceding days – which have grown more frequent since….

… I hope to catch up a bit this summer, if I am not too exhausted – as the usual summer courses of the N.A.B.C. (National Association of Boys' Clubs) have been abandoned.

Did I tell you that I have been teaching for some time for the Polytechnic School of Architecture: Partly in the South Kensington Museum where my students work from the casts and other exhibits, and more recently in outdoor sketching in Kensington Gardens. But all that has also come to a sudden stop owing to the new danger of the "pilotless plane"….

…The children and Dorothy and I are all well – though tired like everyone else – having to spend many hours of the night in the shelter – and you can guess how exhausting the days round about the opera were with the preparations, mishaps and disappointments and filling in gaps in orchestra and cast, and every sort of anxiety and difficulty – we are just recovering and Dorothy is surveying the situation with determination to carry out her plans for the other productions.

One rings round to friends every few hours to know if they've survived the latest high explosive. However material damage to masonry is greater than casualties as a rule and the Civil Defence Services are earning high praise for promptitude….

25th July 1944

… Dorothy is off to Blandford to sing this week-end, but Dick Williams is giving the "Midsummer Night's Dream" in the garden on Saturday – despite flying bombs – so I am remaining to see the house is not destroyed either by the visitors or the uninvited….

PS: Have got a poster idea and submitted to the London Transport – Showing the Rose Willow Herb growing from the ruins of bombed buildings (as it is all over London, in Bond Street, everywhere) and with the dawn breaking behind the stricken masonry and the word "Renascence" on a scroll across the foreground. The Advertising heads were enthusiastically keen….

21st Dec 1944

… Dorothy is giving a performance of "Bethlehem" in church on Christmas Eve at 3 p.m. and we are in the throes of preparations. I succeeded in getting my six posters of "The Proud City" – London since the bombing – done and four of them are now on the hoardings and the other two are in the hands of the printers and should soon follow. They have met with considerable appreciation. The "Daily

Renascence 1945. The Rose Bay Willow-Herb
growing from the ruins of bombed buildings.

Sketch" reproduced the "St Paul's" as did the "Evening Standard", also the
Advertisers' Weekly reproduced two – "St. Paul's" and "The Tower", and I understand the world's press did the same. The editor of "Art and Industry", a studio publication, has written to say that he will be reproducing four in the February issue
published on Jan 10th … so the whole household as usual at this season is working
to the point of distraction almost. But we keep cheerful in spite of rockets and
occasional fly bombs. Arthur Nunn (Muriel's husband) has been bombed out of his
home for the third time. And we have had Mr and Mrs Vandy, the artists' colourman
of Walthamstow, who were among the first victims of the rockets staying with us
for some time – they have gone to relatives for Xmas.... I still carry on my
Polytechnic classes, and the Settlement and the Boys' Club work, and so am even
more busy than in the past – but it is wonderful to be alive and able to do it – all in
tune with my heart and spirit – How your dear uncle would have rejoiced! Poor
old Clausen (the artist) has passed away. I went to the memorial service at
St. Martin's-in-the-Fields and was the youngest among the white headed and bald
there assembled....

St Paul's Cathedral and the Tower of London, 1944.

These posters were part of a poster series commissioned by London Transport towards the conclusion of World War Two. The series entitled "The Proud City" was a commission fortuitously awarded to Walter Spradbery who had already been designing posters for London Transport and the country's provincial railway companies for over thirty years. It was a series of posters to celebrate London's enduring spirit, surviving the German air blitz and still standing triumphant. A series of posters to be displayed in many countries and in different languages around the world. It was a prized commission to be awarded and was perhaps Walter Spradbery's greatest recognized achievement in

the field of art – certainly as a designer of posters. How he obtained this commission, probably desired and coveted by many of the country's finest artists, is something to ponder over. Was it anything to do with Spradbery's truly astonishing past history in World War One? It was such a prestigious international commission that could someone in high government office have brought some influence to bear on the choice of Walter Spradbery? Difficult to imagine with his whole history of pacifist beliefs and radical views. Frank Pick, his greatest advocate, had sadly already passed away. However, it was undoubtedly the most important poster design commission of its time.

211

Lino-cut. Cascading Waterstream adjoining Katherine Bruce Glasier's cottage in Yorkshire in the 1920s.
Lino-cutting was a notable feature of Spradbery's craftsmanship, executing some of the first posters for London Transport in an engraving process which at one time was a popular pastime with young amateur artists.

Lino-cut. Ely Cathedral – Exhibited at British Institute of Industrial Art stand at British Industries Fair in 1929.

Chapter 7

Post Second World War

27th June 1945

Dear Miss Pugh

It seems a very long time since we had heard from you and we are hoping you are keeping well and in good spirits now that the menace of flying bombs and rockets has passed … at Whitsun Dorothy fell into the disused well and she thought she had broken her back. I had great difficulty in getting an ambulance or a doctor, everyone seemed to be out holiday making, but at last I got her shifted to Claybury Emergency Hospital where she remained for a week. X ray revealed that no fracture has occurred and you may guess how relieved we all were. Severe shock and bruising however made things painful and she was in plaster for a few days. However she came home again within a week, and before another had passed was conducting an orchestral concert at Epping and singing a few days later at another concert at Walthamstow.

Rehearsals for "Acis and Galatea" were carried forward and the open-air performances take place this coming Saturday and Sunday. Is there any chance of you coming over to see one? Prof. E.J. Dent will be among the audience on Sunday I think.

It is proposed that I take the part of the one-eyed Giant Polyphemus, as the bass singer is rather small and objects to wearing the headdress (made round a waste-paper basket) which I have constructed for it.…

I saw Sir Frank Brangwyn yesterday. He looks a little worn and tired. I am trying to stimulate the Walthamstow Boro' Council to get busy setting up the Water House as the Morris Art Gallery and Brangwyn Gift now. There seems no point in further delay. Brangwyn would like to see it in being while he is still alive.

Roebuck (Chief Librarian) is all for procrastination but the new Town Clerk seems likely to press things forward. Some of the Council fear criticism as so little has been done yet to rectify bomb damage to the many small homes in the town – but to put this right will take years and criticism grows fiercer with the passing of time. Now the opening of the Gallery might be taken as a gesture of thanksgiving that worse has not befallen us and a relief and interest for war weary folk.…

23rd Feb 1946

Dear Miss Elinor Pugh,

You must be thinking that we are ungrateful, forgetful and neglecting of old friends....

... Just how to tell you briefly all that has happened is a problem requiring some literary skill and art in condensation....

... My visit to Brangwyn was to take down for his inspection a wonderful bound volume (bound by Cockerel) of manuscript letters written by William Morris to Bruce Glasier, dealing largely with his early Socialist activities and going on to the very last he penned before he died. These have been formally presented to Walthamstow for inclusion in the William Morris Gallery & Brangwyn Gift and were given by Mrs Bruce Glasier herself who made a remarkable effective and emotional speech when she handed them to Alderman Ross Wyld in the presence of the assembled Boro Council and some specially invited guests.

The story of how she came to make this gift to Walthamstow and the inevitable rightness of it is another tale of the slow working of destiny towards a desired end.

Many years ago, immediately after the 1914–18 war I visited my friend Jim Berry in Earby Yorkshire and while there made a drawing from which later I made a lino-cut of a cascade in the garden of Mrs Bruce Glasier. I did not meet her although I knew of her as an early pioneer of Socialism and a worker in the Labour movement – my friend was too shy to press on her acquaintance – she seemed to him too distinguished a lady to call on without a formal invitation.

Very recently a Capt. Malcolm Bruce Glasier became enthusiastically associated with the work of the Wilderness Opera Group and invited us to his house to dinner. While there I mentioned William Morris and found that he (Malcolm) was the son of Bruce Glasier, and when I imparted to him all the information about a proposed Morris Memorial he was of course highly delighted. I loaned him a copy of the booklet about the Brangwyn Gift, gave him a copy of my lino-cut and one to send to his mother, and later met her when she was on a visit to her son in Woodford.

She at once became a friend and entered with her abounding enthusiasm into all the projects, artistic and musical with which Dorothy and I are associated. She was herself born in Walthamstow: her father the Rev. Samuel Conway was a great social and religious reformer of his day, associated with Stopford Brook in an endeavour to get the 39 articles revised into acceptable form for an enlightened clergy. Marsh St. Church was built especially for him by sympathizers with his convictions, and the Conway Hall was built in Walthamstow as a memorial to him and his work. It was at Conway Hall I first saw and met my Dorothy, when she organized her first series of concerts in 1920....

... Mrs Bruce Glasier has had a distinguished career herself being the first woman graduate of Newnham College to be recognised by the University on the attainment of her degree. She is a well-known speaker in the North of England and an early friend of Bernard Shaw (who sent a message of affectionate greeting to her in response to the Council's invitation to attend the presentation of the volume of letters)....

… However the effect of my little booklet on the Brangwyn Gift was that she at once wrote to me and offered to give them to Walthamstow – to "my gallery" as she insisted on calling it – and so in January of this year I was able to arrange the formal presentation, which her son, very rightly, insisted on....

… At the presentation Alderman Ross Wylde told us that the necessary permits and licences to go forward with the reconditioning of the Water House for a permanent Gallery had been received from the Ministry of Health. So I hope ere long to be able to report progress and that we may see the Gallery in being while F.B. is still alive to rejoice in it – possibly in the autumn.

> This letter of "Sprad's" to Elinor Pugh of the 23rd February 1946 amounting to 14 long pages must have some significance in the William Morris Gallery's emergence. Today, in the recent scandals of the museum's survival, just over fifty years onward, where are those beautifully bound William Morris letters? It is also a letter full of many aspects of Spradbery's multifarious life at that time, and his links with a variety of outstanding individuals, men and women lost to history in the huge scramble for wealth and notoriety that blurs our lives today. Lives very much out of the public arena in the sense of their idealism, social insight and stoic principles. Let their lives at least be recalled and remembered and touched upon here in this chronicle of writings which have survived to the present day; remarkably so as my own existence, although married for 40 years, has been very much that of a wandering troubadour!

23rd Feb 1946 *(continued)*

…The occasion of the presentation of the volumes of letters afforded an opportunity for revising interest in the Press in respect of the Gallery and its early establishment.

Possibly the next item of news that I should impart is of my resignation from the N.A.B.C. (National Association of Boys' Clubs).

Had I replied earlier to your letter of Oct 19th 1945, when you commented on the death of Sir Hubert Llewellyn Smith, I should have probably said that his passing would make no difference to the continuance of my work in this field of social endeavour, but indirectly it has, for had he been alive he would certainly not have allowed a great injustice to be done to B. Faithful Davies, with whom I have worked most closely in the schemes for Senior Boys' Training, and probably my effort to correct this injustice would not have been necessary, or the outcome of it more successful.

I have a great many kind letters from him expressing his confidence in me and the highest appreciation of my work, and I value these very much as coming from one who has been described by two Prime Ministers (Lloyd George and Winston Churchill) as one of the greatest Civil Servants the State has ever had....

... Briefly the story of my resignation is this – from the beginning of my work with the N.A.B.C. I have been closely associated with B. Faithful Davies, a man whose influence and intimate understanding of boys made him a leader and organizer of great power. During the war he organized and developed a system of Senior Boy training which gave new life and purpose to the movement. I attended as Art Adviser and instructor some hundreds of these courses and all the special summer National Courses and so saw his capacity, sincerity, originality and qualities in every respect.

> Bernard Faithful Davies was an Australian; I was in awe of Australians ever since meeting him as a young boy. I remember a magical moment around a huge camp fire in the Gloucestershire countryside as dusk fell. F.D. (as he was known), was spellbinding us with his camp-side stories. One in particular told of the Hollywood film star, Errol Flynn, whom he purportedly saved, through nursing him back to health when he discovered the young man ill and adrift in a boat on some deserted beach on a pacific island! This was before Flynn's Hollywood fame. F.D. was one of the earliest people to have truly encouraged me and influenced my own life.

I also saw all those who from time to time took part as members of his staff – area organizers from all over England, Wales and Scotland – and those of the Headquarters Staff who also attended as lecturers in various capacities and so I got to know their worth and qualities too – for conditions were often very tiring, as also was travel and everyone was called on to show enterprise and initiative, goodwill and honest work not only in their own sphere of interest but in the running of the communities so briefly established in improvised conditions.... It was always accepted that his main scheme, the end to which he worked, would be the establishment of a permanent centre for Senior Boys' Training.... Just recently three great mansions have been acquired through various charities and gifts....

> One of these mansions was Ford Castle near Berwick, which to Faithful Davies made an exciting venue for the centre of Senior Boys' Training. The crux of everything was that F.D. was going to be overlooked for the principal role of

warden; something that smacked of injustice and conspiracy to my father and brought on first Faithful Davies' own resignation and later "Sprad's". This extract of Sprad's letter to Elinor Pugh may very well be the sole reference to Bernard Faithful Davies, however he was such a man as to leave a lifelong impression on Walter Spradbery and myself. Subsequently F.D. opened and ran a "Holiday with Purpose Centre for Young Men" in the Lake District at Brathay Hall by Lake Windermere. As an aspiring young man of the theatre, I was amazingly given my first chance to direct there. The most beautiful miniature stage was constructed in the drawing room of the hall, where for a whole summer I produced shows for the students, young men from colleges, universities and even Borstal institutions on a weekly basis. We rehearsed and performed a new production every week. I was only seventeen at the time. Bernard Faithful Davies disappeared out of my life until he appeared at my father's funeral over 20 years later.

Again in this same letter, there is an intriguing paragraph relating to the whole affair surrounding the dealings and plans for the N.A.B.C.'s proposed National Centre for Senior Boys' Training which involved a luncheon with the country's Prime Minister of the day.

23rd Feb 1946 *(continued)*

… But to explain all about the lunch with the Prime Minister and the scheme for raising funds that was going on at the same time is too complicated to put into a letter now and must await some opportunity for me to discuss it all with you.…

… Well since my resignation I've been mainly employed in preparing the scenic setting for Dorothy's production of "Hansel and Gretel". This proved our biggest success – each performance crowded – said by knowledgeable folk to be better by far than the Sadler's Wells production and general West End standards. 300 school children were held spellbound for the matinee – except for the intervals. You could have heard a pin drop throughout the performance – overture included.…

… Rima is now at boarding school – Sunny Hill School, Bruton, Somerset. She is very happy there and writes frequently. John has had one or two misfortunes this year – first he sprained his ankle and cracked the tibia jumping over a vaulting horse – hardly got over that when we discovered his chest had taken on a bad shape – this proved to be due to food deficiencies and he has been having special vitamin foods and special exercises – and a week or so ago he got his right hand crushed in a printing press. This is making good progress and is unlikely to prove a permanent injury. He seems to like his work at the printers – but I am hoping to find a better outlet for him than prospects at the West Essex Printing work offer. He remains very cheery, very unmanageable and rude – but we hope time will soften these latter characteristics.…

Disturbing words to read of myself. In those early formulating years I was somewhat of a monstrous young fellow! Without the father that I had I might very well
have ended up on a different route in life!

The Brangwyn Gift

The William Morris Gallery and Vestry House Museum

Reading through "Sprad's" pre- and post-war letters to Elinor Pugh is a short-cut
to comprehending and realising his sole initiative and influence in both the saving
of Walthamstow's Vestry House Museum and the eventual establishment and
opening of the William Morris Gallery a few years later in the borough. Spradbery was truly an isolated figure in the wilderness and labyrinth of negotiating
and creating Walthamstow's monument to its finest son, William Morris, as
widely held or recognised in the international world of arts as such other English
icons as Dickens, Shakespeare, Constable or Turner are today.

Without exposing readers to the endless reams of papers, documents and
initiatives – sufficient to say that W.E.S. pursued and pressurized, primarily the
Borough's Council, Library services, local newspapers, antiquarian societies, even
the government itself, also any person or organisation in a position to help and
encourage the process of bringing the museum's opening forward, almost a
quarter of a century after its first seeds evolved in his mind during the days of the
Great General Strike of 1926 and 15 years before first agreements were ever
drawn up.

"Sprad's" overcoming of constant obstacles, apathy and sheer bloody-
mindedness that confronted himself, Brangwyn and Arthur Heygate Macmurdo –
before his death – was remarkable. As evidence of all the intrigue and
frustrations that constantly confronted the spirit, passion and endeavours of
these men, quoted here are brief extracts from some of Spradbery's flow of
correspondence to Macmurdo's niece, the designate womanly figure who took
on the role of fulfilling her uncle's dreams and wishes. This correspondence
which I have held on to, going back seventy years or more, very much hints at the
immense mountain W.E.S. and his fellow artists had to climb. Spradbery himself
was a true son of Walthamstow if ever there was one!! This quite independently
of his role in saving the Vestry House Museum and opening the William Morris
Gallery, jewels in what is left of London's remaining cultural and historical
heritage today; his art classes alone in the borough's Greenleaf Road lasted
nearly fifty years under his tutelage – and as I have already indicated, produced
many artists of professional distinction. The Essex Art Club was another

embodiment of local artists, whose exhibitors included such diverse figures as Sir Winston Churchill and Sylvia Pankhurst. The club was a vital influence within the borough which "Sprad" was a driving force in for the best part of his life.

Within his letters to Elinor Pugh one cannot fail to catch the irony, concerns and worries that constantly had to be confronted and acted upon as the years stretched by.

2nd May 1946

Dear Miss Pugh

This is a great blow to the smooth execution of the plan to place a representative group of Selwyn Image's work and collection of prints into the hands of the Borough Council for the William Morris Gallery, but I don't think we should be deflected by what is probably a little nervous reaction on the part of Mrs Image at the prospect of signing anything....

18th July 1946

... I shall have to fix up one day next week to go down to see F.B. and show him the second instalment of the Selwyn Image Collection. He will be delighted with the manuscripts. When can I fix up the Town Clerk's visit and the formal handing over I wonder....

12th September 1946

Dear Elinor Pugh

It is splendid news that you will be in the party on Tuesday – for that is the day the Town Clerk (Mr Blakeley), Mr Roebuck, the new Borough Librarian (Mr Leyland) and I travel down to see F.B. We leave by car from the Town Hall, Forest Road, at 9.30 a.m. That should get us there by about 11.30 or 12 I imagine.

The occasion is the presentation of Mrs Selwyn Image's bequest to the Boro' Authorities – and it is an opportunity to press matters forward and hear authoritatively what has already been done and when we may look for an opening....

26th Oct 1946

... The visit to Brangwyn proved useful in rousing Leyland's interest – he got vigorously to work and drew up a whole scheme for the arrangements to open the Water House – estimating money that could be spent on various necessities – resident caretaker, attendants, hours of duty, hours open, a very complete and practical survey of the whole situation....

19th Feb 1947

Just how things are going with the William Morris Gallery and Brangwyn Gift is difficult to say. I think things are moving – but with much difficulty and dangerous aspects, because of Roebuck's awkwardness and jealousy and the acute feelings that exist between him and young Leyland, the new Boro Librarian and curator of Boro galleries etc. They seem to hate each other bitterly … Leyland is regarded as too "go ahead" and personally ambitious, and Roebuck seems to set everyone on edge. As James Laver said after the Trustees meeting "If I was made Director of the V. & A. I should not think it necessary to submit my draft plan for improvement to the late director and it is ridiculous that we are not allowed to consider Leyland's plan because Roebuck thinks he should have been consulted first"….

10th May 1947

Enclosed is a copy of a letter which I have sent and is published in the Walthamstow Guardian. It gives in the briefest terms I could manage a statement of the situation that has arisen in regard to Vestry House (the Walthamstow Museum), the Water House and the relation of the two places to the Brangwyn Gift.

It is deplorable that this step has been taken to present as it were the Trustees with a fait accompli (if I may risk the term) when they are in the course of shaping recommendations to the council, and is largely I fear due to the bitter feelings that exist between the recently appointed Boro Librarian, Eric Leyland, and his predecessor George Roebuck.

It seemed the only thing to do – to make the whole thing public in a reserved but emphatic way….

…The question of Vestry House and the Water House is still unsettled. A meeting of Brangwyn Trustees and the sub-committee appointed by the Boro' Council takes place on the 30th. After that I may be able to tell you more. It will be a difficult occasion and I hope to rise to it – or must pronounce myself a failure.

Yours sincerely,

Walter E. Spradbery

21st Dec 1947

…The battle to save Vestry House and to get forward with the William Morris Gallery and Brangwyn Gift has taken considerable time and effort and I hardly know how to tell you briefly on the progress made…. After my opening the matter in the press, I was adopted on to the Museum's Advisory Committee and its first meeting was in Vestry House, which had been stripped bare….

…The Committee met in gloomy spirit, annoyed by being checked by outside protest, giving some lip service to the past but afraid of a breach in their own ranks and of making a decision open to criticism for or against.

Therefore when a proposal was made that authoritative bodies should be approached to give an opinion on, 1. "Was Vestry House of sufficient architectural and antiquarian interest to justify its preservation, and 2. If so was it suitable to house a local museum", this was agreed to and the Society for the Protection of Ancient Buildings was one authority decided on, and the Museum Association the other.…

…The report of the Society for the Protection of Ancient Buildings was a most able and thorough one. It wholeheartedly confirmed all I had claimed.…

… I gave a lecture at Romford to an Art Society on Brangwyn and his work. At the end of it I told them all about the bequest to Walthamstow and how it had been in store for 12 years and the excuses that the Council had made about shortage of labour and licence difficulties – how only a grant of £450 was available to date and so on.

At the end of the meeting I went to the house of a builder who is also an amateur artist, to have coffee, and he had other builder friends gathered there also, and they offered to give their labours in the leisure of their week-ends to put Water House in condition. They pointed out that labour costs were 2/3 of expenses at least and so much more could be done.…We considered a plan of action – and (with great difficulty for he was as nervy as usual at the prospect of meeting strangers) I persuaded Brangwyn to see them and discuss it all.

Brangwyn was of course delighted and enthused by their devotion and good will. His suggestion was that the leader, a Mr Wastell, and his wife (who also came with us and quite conquered F.B. by her enthusiasm) should visit Ross Wyld, the leader of the Council, and make their offer to him, so that he might get the credit for taking them to the Council and promoting the matter.

He fell for this and the Council received them with every show of gratitude and appreciation.…

9th Feb 1948

… In regard to the Selwyn Image Manuscripts – they were handed over into the care of the Walthamstow Boro' Council when we made the presentation to Blakeley the Town Clerk and Eric Leyland … two men have been at work in the Water House for some time – Council employees – and the partitions have been taken down and the extent of exhibition room is now more evident and looks encouraging.…

… So far as the voluntary group of builders are concerned, although I have written to them three times I have had no reply – which is strange.…The situation as I last heard is that they were welcomed, promised every assistance in the way of materials and equipment, subject to the Labour organisations to which Council employees belong offering no objection. Perhaps they have objected....

... Indirectly, through press reports, I have heard that the Vestry House and the Museum there is saved, and that the proposals of the Society for the Protection of Ancient Buildings that some £1,600 shall be spent to recondition it has passed the Council's approval....

... Life today is full of frustrations, and as precarious as ever, progress is dreadfully slow and aggravatingly difficult, but we do not lose hope. Time slips away remorselessly I know – but, please God, we may ultimately have some accomplishment to show....

A Black Face in "The Wilderness"

The following letter was sent to Elinor Pugh in South Africa while visiting her sister in Cape Town. One of a number of vignette tales that peppered "Sprad's" correspondence over the years. A true account of the discovery of a young black African in the garage building in the depths of "The Wilderness" garden, used as a store for costumes, props and scenery, as well as storing (at one time during the war) the feed stuff for the chickens reared for my uncle Ewart's butcher's business in Walthamstow and, even earlier, offered as premises for some local boys to form a club. That is, until they got into trouble with the law!

Strange that I am quoting this particular letter on the day of the 4th November 2008, the day America elected its first black Afro-American President, Barack Obama! This incident was very much the era of the great influx of the Caribbean community to Britain. It was I suppose just around the time when the beginnings of a new multi-racial and multi-ethnic society in Britain was about to emerge.

Today, nearly 60 years on, I still number some of those early Caribbeans amongst my closest friends.

Looking back to 1949, it must have been an occasion when my mother was in "The Wilderness" alone. I would have been away doing my National Service, and my sister away down in the west country.

25th Mar 1949

Dear Elinor Pugh

We were most delighted to have your letter from Cape Town and to know you arrived safely, found your sister's health improved and so much to enjoy and interest you in South Africa – in fact what with bathing beaches, fine old Dutch buildings, magnificent drives, expansive country, sunshine and pure air it should all prove most exhilarating and your graphic descriptions carry us along with you and make us wish very much to be there in actuality.…

…We have also had an unexpected visitor who came from South Africa but did not find it attractive enough to stay in. That is another story.

A few weeks ago Dorothy was collecting costumes and properties for loan to the London Philharmonic Orchestra's production of Rutland Boughton's "Immortal Hour" which is to be given for a week at the People's Palace, commencing 4th April, and went down to "the Garage" to look for some details. This, as you know, is a store of theatrical and operatic scenery, old furniture and things which may "come in useful", so packed and piled that the dilapidated doors have long since collapsed, and indeed had to be taken off to get the larger pieces of scenery in, and is open on one side except for a very ragged tarpaulin that keeps a good deal of the rain out. Well – when she eased her way into the deeper recesses, she noticed a number of animal skins and curtains in a pile on the floor, and exclaiming about the carelessness of the dramatic group who had, she imagined, returned and dumped them so, she stooped down to pick them up, when, from underneath, a head emerged, and a startled face (black or at least warm dark coloured) gazed at her. Momentarily bewildered Dorothy asked "Where are you going?" "Home" said the face. "Well where's that?" asked Dorothy. "Scotland" said the face. "Where have you come from?" said D. "South Africa" said the face. "Good gracious, did you walk" said D. "No I came in a ship. I only walked from London" said the face. "How long have you been here?" enquired Dorothy. "Since about 5 o'clock yesterday" said the face. "Have you had any food?" said D. "Not for two days" said the face. "Well come up to the house and I will get you a cup of tea and something for you to eat" said Dorothy – and with that the young man rose from among the pile and followed her up to the house, arriving close on her heels as she entered and told me – "Another adventure – a black man in the garage!" He was an incredible figure in relation to his tale. Clad in a trim lavender grey suit (no waistcoat) very smart, a striped shirt and grey silk tie, thin brown boots, he looked like a dance-band leader or a "spiv". I asked him in and gave him a cigarette to break the ice as it were, sat him by the fire and began to question him while Dorothy heated some Scotch broth (from a tin) as appropriate for one bound for Scotland.

His story was that his home was at Arbroath, where his mother lived and where, as a lad, he had been farming until the war took him into the army. After the war, having heard that there were great opportunities for farmers in South Africa, he went out and tried his luck in Johannesburg. But, he said, people from England are not very popular in S. Africa, and unless you speak Afrikaans you are at a disadvantage – the farmers are sons of men who fought in the Boer War. Most of the work is done with oxen, very primitive and the pay was £14 month, the day commencing soon after 4 a.m. and going on until 7 p.m.

"Black boys do most of the work" he said, apparently unaware of his own woolly head and dark complexion – one just saw the animals harnessed, and superintended things. Anyway by the time he had saved £80 he longed to come home, and paid £77 for his fare, arrived in port of London with only five shillings and the hope that his mother would meet him. He received letters from his mother saying that she could not come, but had sent £2.10.0 to the dock superintendent and £5 to the head-quarters office of the Union Castle Line. No-one was there.

He got off his trunk to St Pancras and went on to London and called at the Head Office. No letters for him had arrived. He called again on Monday and Tuesday – no luck. He felt beaten, and determined to walk out of London till he came to a farm to seek employment to earn his fare to Scotland. He walked as far as our patch of forest, and had seen no farm, was exhausted, entered the wood, heard singing and a piano in the house, saw the shed, entered it, saw a camp bed, and feeling he must rest, put it down, covered himself with the skins and curtains and fell asleep and stayed there until Dorothy found him. He said "it seemed a queer place to me – there were spears and swords and all sorts of strange things around." He produced some crumpled letters from his mother telling him she was sending the money, advising him to label himself with his name and address and come up by coach, first to Edinburgh, and thence to Dundee and Arbroath.

By this time the food and tea was ready and he quietly consumed it – while we debated the next move.

Dorothy's first idea was to phone the Bailiff of Woodridden Farm, Epping where John had been happily employed before the call-up to the army. It belongs to Sir Thomas Buxton. But Mr Tine, the Bailiff, said he was finding it difficult to employ his ordinary staff at this time, but he was sorry for the chap and if we could find nothing else in the meantime, if we phoned again in two days time he would see if anything was possible!

Then Dorothy had another idea, and phoned the head-quarters of the Union Castle Line to ask if the letters had arrived since Tuesday (this was Wednesday) and she got the right man straight away, and he said letters had been forwarded from Tilbury and arrived a few minutes after the chap (whose name was Douglas Hutchinson) had gone. He said if he could reach the office by 5.30 he could have them. It was now about 4 p.m. So with speed we got him on his way again; I accompanying him to Buckhurst Hill station where he could now get a through electric train to "the Bank" and be at Fenchurch Street in good time. We gave him 4/6 for immediate expenses and I gave him a card with our address and asked him to send a postcard when he was reunited with his mammy. On the way to the station I said "Was it not cold in the garage last night (we were having sharp frosty weather – bitter). "Oh no" said he "I was more cold on the other two nights". "Where did you sleep then?" I asked. "In bombed out houses in London" he said. "Good heavens" said I "with no other covering than that thin suit. Why did you not go to the police – they would have found you shelter, indeed if you had told them your story they would have verified it by phoning Arbroath and getting in touch with your mother, and probably got you a ticket or advanced money for you to get home. "Would they really?" he said. "I didn't know that. I felt I knew nobody and was sunk".

Anyway he got on the train – and so far that's the last we have heard of him. He was a simple sort of lad – about 25 perhaps – and had I not been fixed up with a teaching engagement I would have gone to London with him and seen him on his way. I hope he was not ill. He seemed calm and alright after his feed. He spoke English with an impediment and a Scottish intonation. I am told there are Jamaican Scots, so I suppose he was one of these – for anything less like a Scotsman to look at I have never seen. Whether his mammy was a coal-black mammy or not, I did not enquire – in fact of course, I made no reference to his colour – but I am told it probably accounted for his not getting on well in South Africa. He thought that engineers and folks with a trade stood a better chance in S.A. than young farmers.

I wish we had news of him – he was only in the house about a couple of hours (excluding the time in the garage) and we regret that we sent him at once, but as Dorothy said, she also had to go out on the Wednesday evening, so we felt we could not put him up, but that it was best to get him in touch with his money and on the way to his home. I gave him the telephone number in case he got into trouble but I did not take his mother's address and doubt if "Mr Hutchinson, Arbroath" would find him. Of course once home he may have been ill from exposure – or have lost my card – or forgotten all about it – or just take it as a detail of the stages of his journey – and not know that we are anxious about him – this lost soul travelling twixt Africa and Scotland and settling like a bird in the Wilderness!…

Back to The Brangwyn Gift

After the William Morris Gallery's eventual opening in 1950, Spradbery's dis-illusionment must have set in. I suspect he felt, once the museum was established, that his presence and guidance was tolerated rather than appreciated, both in the circles of the museum's curatorship and administration as well as the borough council. Some time in those ensuing days, months or years, he was also deeply affected by Brangwyn's own estrangement from him, due to Spradbery's reluctance to take on a major role in Brangwyn's own affairs. He seriously felt it was a role for a younger man; "Sprad" was then in his sixties. This all coming at a time of my mother's break-downs and eventual sudden death in May 1952. I quote here from "Sprad's" further letters to Elinor Pugh, emphasizing more of his concerns and involvement surrounding the museum.

19th Nov 1948

…There are so many things to tell you, so much we should have liked to discuss – but there seems no pause in the things requiring immediate attention here, follow-ing in too quick succession, and so the opportunity seemed to have escaped us.

In particular I should have liked to tell you of matters relating to the Brangwyn Gift – and I have been attacking the Council on their neglect, in the press, through personal letters to members, and recently in an article in "Friendship" the Settlement journal. This letter was quoted in full in the "Walthamstow Guardian"….

A reminder that "The Settlement" was what became the Walthamstow Adults' Educational Centre which sprang from Spradbery's and Haydn Mackey's early art classes at the Quaker Friends' Hall Meeting House in Greenleaf Road, E.17.

15th Sept 1949

…The Water House is now being fitted up with heating etc. – the outside has been painted, caretaker installed, some structural alterations and repairs completed and a new librarian and Curator Mr Overall appointed – a nice go-ahead chap a bit more reliable than Leyland, I fancy. Miss Rappatort, curator of the museum at Vestry House has compiled a catalogue and checked work with me….

16th Aug 1950

Dear Elinor Pugh

You will be glad to know that it has been provisionally arranged that the Prime Minister will open the William Morris Gallery and the Brangwyn Collection on

Oct 21st between 4 and 6 at Water House....

This same letter goes on to acquaint Elinor Pugh with the arrangements of transferring the Brangwyn collection from the vaults of the Town Hall to the Water House itself, meeting the newly appointed staff, detailing their salaries and referring to the thousands of pounds spent on the fitting up and restoration of Water House. "Sprad" goes on to tell of the new librarian's enthusiasm and concludes with the comment "Pray heaven another World War does not interfere".

The same letter goes on to report on both "Sprad's" and my mother's activities at "The Wilderness" and further afield: the Essex Art Club Annual Exhibition at the Royal Exchange with a work by Sir Winston Churchill to be exhibited; my mother's production of "Orpheus" in the garden and productions of "Dido & Aeneas" and "The Beggars Opera" in Wansfell College, Theydon Bois and at an opera school in Cambridge, before going on up to Llangollen to play her role in Rutland Boughton's "Immortal House" at the International Eisteddfod with the full Philharmonic Orchestra of 120 and over 8,000 in the audience. Incredibly the costumes were supplied from my mother's costume stores at "The Wilderness". This same letter of some six pages of faintly printed ink also goes on to refer to an invitation from the Yugoslav Ambassador to a display of Yugoslav Folk Dancers at London's Scala Theatre and rubbing shoulders with Sir Stafford Cripps. It also briefly mentions me being accepted as an acting student at both London's RADA and the Webber Douglas School in Kensington!

26th Sept 1950

Dear Elinor Pugh

Mr Blakeley, the Town Clerk, is now preparing a list of invitations to send off at the week-end, for the opening of the William Morris Gallery & Brangwyn Gift at the Water House on the 21st Oct. Can you give him the names of important people to invite, in particular in connection with your uncle Arthur Heygate Mackmurdo and Selwyn Image? Is Mrs Image still alive: if so can you let him have her address?...

A further letter of the 27th Sept goes on to list all the arrangements and plans for the opening day's ceremony, the numbers of guests and various dignitaries from other neighbouring boroughs. So many last-minute details, including presenting copies of the original booklet regarding the museum published in 1936 to the 400 guests. Strangely though no mention of the address "Sprad" purportedly delivered at the Gallery's opening and quoted in earlier pages.

"Sprad" describing an exhibit to Prime Minister Clement Attlee
at the opening of the William Morris Gallery (1950).

29th Oct 1950

Dear Elinor Pugh

Thank you very much indeed for your very kind appreciation which I shall value most highly and place among the papers I am collecting concerning the opening of the Gallery. I have also had a most kind and appreciative letter from Brangwyn himself. He seems to think I was responsible for the telegram sent from the meeting. I must let him know definitely that it came from the Mayor and on behalf of the entire assembly.

The press has been most disappointing. "The Times" is the best and only notice of any length and good general statement that I know of. "The Chronicle" was pitiable in its brief comment and half-disparaging report….

… It is evident that we all have a lot of work to do yet to get the Gallery well known and the collection fully and properly displayed….

> "Sprad's" letter goes on to make much criticism of things that had to be improved, including publicizing the gallery, space more effectively utilised, including an additional annexe where years later I discovered a scribbled drawing he had made, having in mind an added facility. The sad truth has to be that over the many decades since the gallery's inception, little or nothing has been achieved or undertaken by the borough to match its growing international reputation and interest from around the world. Today it has acquired a unique legacy from overseas and other eminent sources. Despite Spradbery's ensuing disappointments, his enthusiasm never wavered for Morris, Brangwyn and its whole artistic and social significance and influence. Although he must have still felt these disappointments, he did give the first public lecture at the gallery on Brangwyn which was published in a booklet and remarkably still exists.
>
> Yet another letter to Elinor Pugh on the 5th November refers to the recent gallery's opening and the death of another momentous figure in Spradbery's life….

Dear Elinor Pugh

Having just written another in my long series of letters to the press in our Peace campaign, I turn with some relief from the serious matter of threatening annihilation and damnation to all those who are not kind to communists, coloured people and all, to the more light-hearted matter of telling you that, having decided to accept your present in the generous spirit in which it was offered, I have blown it all on the preservation of my health and the improvement of my comfort and appearance, having bought a new overcoat and paid up the arrears in my National Health insurance with it and managed a box of cigarettes into the bargain….

… Of course Dorothy enjoys the excitement of purchasing things so much that one is in grave danger of every form of extravagance in her company – bewildered shopmen, bewitched by her enthusiasm and surprising familiar merriment, pile the whole stock before her and unearth forgotten bargains. It was with difficulty I escaped huge herring-bone tweeds or checks distinctly racey and firmly held to my decision to have an ample woolly black one – something I could wear anywhere and on any occasion – pointing out that in these latter days I am constantly attending funerals or funeral proceedings where a grave note is desirable and proper, and that I am always a little at a loss what to wear from the variety of gay Harris weaves that are the joy of all the young moths that abound in our forest home or which I destroy myself with holes made by sparks or hot ash from my cigarette ends. I capped it by saying that I should want to attend the memorial service to Bernard Shaw and that settled it.…

… I am sending you the rather comic report in this week's "Guardian" which progresses from complaints of the stink from the moat in the Water House garden to the raptures of a literary visitor to the opening ceremony of the William Morris Gallery who appreciated my words in the brochure and my appearance on the platform, and is based with an almost unrecognizable snapshot of me discoursing to the Prime Minister about a picture I can't recall. It is the nearest thing to enthusiasm I have so far encountered – and I am duly gratified – but determined to secure something better from everyone's point of view, if I can beat it up.

Anyway it is opened and the house looking happily restored, and on that basis and the interest of the young ladies in charge and Overall, properly worked upon it, it may yet do some of the things we hope of it.…

… You will know all I feel about the passing of G.B.S. (George Bernard Shaw) one of the greatest spiritual (and witty) forces of our time. It is grand to have met him as well as know the major part of his work.

It is a problem for those in high places who praise him and yet condemn communism out of hand to square their praise with his well known opinions. Ironic – like so much more today.…

6th Oct 1951

Dear Elinor Pugh

Yesterday Queen Mary and the Princess Royal visited the William Morris Gallery. They came as a result of reading Hector Wiles's new book "William Morris of Walthamstow".… The Royal party was received by the Mayor Lord McEntee & Lady McEntee and introduced to Ald. Ross Wyld (leader of Council), Ald. Fitt (Leader of opposition), S. Overall (Curator and Boro' Librarian), Hector Wiles (Proprietor Guardian group of newspapers and author of the book), Walter

Spradbery (described by the Mayor as having had to do with the "arrangement of things"), Miss Weaver, Miss Halford and Miss Bennett.

They inspected the ground floor, McEntee who knows nothing of art taking 'em round with Overall putting in a word or two at intervals.… I followed the Mayoress who was with the Princess, (who seemed fairly knowledgeable) and was able to give her a number of points of view of interest. They were both very taken with your uncle's cabinet and the jewel case, and opened the drawers of both. The tapestry, furniture and such craft work and designs naturally interested the Queen who does a good deal of tapestry and embroidery herself and they looked at every-thing very thoroughly.… I pointed out your uncle's portrait by Haydn Mackey and Brangwyn's by Augustus John. They then had tea and afterwards were pho-tographed grouped round the big bust of William Morris in the hall.…

When I rang up Brangwyn and told him they had been – he said "I don't care two bloody hoots."

A Devastating Blow

"Sprad's" greatest and most devastating blow irrespective of his concerns for money, the development and expansion of the Water House, his own failing sight and the constant cold war between eastern and western powers, was the sudden death of my mother in May 1952. Here it is simply expressed in a short communiqué again to Elinor Pugh who seemed at that time to be Spradbery's most sympathetic ear and arbitrator of all his deepest concerns.

"The Wilderness"
12th May 1952

Dear Elinor Pugh

My dear Dorothy died on Sunday afternoon at 4 – the final stroke of a series of break-downs from nervous tension.

That bright flame – its radiance cannot be forgotten: – that spirit voice, melting or dramatic: that kindness, humour and understanding humanity –

Oh grateful memories yet not grateful enough for the bounty of uncounted giv-ing – for the joy, loveliness and companionship.

There will be a service at St John's Church, Buckhurst Hill at 2.30 on Thursday 15th – the family will go on to the cremation in accordance with her expressed wish – and I will scatter the ashes in our garden to be enshrined with trees, flowers and fragrance and bird song. Rima and John are with me – they are shaken as young things are at such (here the ink is smudged, possibly with tears, and unreadable).

Despite this overwhelming tragedy in "Sprad's" personal life at a time when the scope of things beyond the perimeters of "The Wilderness" had lifted his spiritual optimism to new heights, he did remain an indomitable character, determined to live on at "The Wilderness" surrounded by his memories and heirlooms that kept mother's memory alive and vital to his existence. He never in any public sense dwelt on her memory, but her spirit was always present. That summer though, a lasting gesture was a huge memorial concert within "The Wilderness" garden, dedicated to her memory.

Enough has been recorded in this chronicle of W.E.S.'s involvement and part in the extraordinary municipal establishment of the William Morris Gallery; however I must quote one last passage from a later letter to Elinor Pugh which seems to suggest how things were very much forced to be left by Spradbery in the aftermath of the Gallery's opening and initial years.

My mother's death in the spring of 1952 must have made the most profound and devastating impact on Walter Spradbery's life. It took place on a quiet peaceful day at "The Wilderness". This was on a weekend I happened to be staying there while fulfilling an engagement which had run some three weeks previously in St. Martin's-in-the-Fields; a play entitled "The Vigil", in which I was playing the part of a gardener, brought to trial, supposedly for stealing Christ's body before his resurrection. The play had transferred and was concluding that very weekend in a small theatre club just off the Charing Cross Road, known as the Watergate.

My mother collapsed and died very suddenly in my father's arms and mine. As I remember visitors were about to arrive. My mother was struggling to recover from an overburden of work that as ever enveloped her life. In her last moments I just pray I did reveal some glimmer of my true feelings towards her.

Those early fifties must have been a shattering disillusionment to all my father's dreams and hopes. This especially after the end of the War, the opening of the William Morris Gallery, his ever-blossoming love and marriage and "The Wilderness's" growing uniqueness as a local centre of summer opera, music and artistic activity. If his paintings and poster commissions were not providing him with a sufficient income, then other compensations filled his life. Dorothy was his greatest!! Above all his belief in peaceful co-existence with the east and the communists. His ambitions for a continuing sense of peace among all men, races and religions were always there for him to serve and take up the rallying call.

With his beloved Dorothy's sudden death, his spirit and countenance took a desperate blow, which many others settled into his style of life would not have recovered from; he was then in his sixty-second year of age. Spradbery's very existence epitomised the essence of the simple things and delighted in a rural life surrounded by nature itself.

Later letters and subsequent communiqués to Elinor Pugh relating to Brangwyn and the William Morris Gallery:

3rd Feb 1953

…As soon as this W.O.G. (Wilderness Opera Group) opera is over I must stir up the Water House curator and the Boro' Council to call a Trustees Meeting in furtherance of the plans for the development of the William Morris Gallery. I am determined to have a permanent Brangwyn room at least – there is a tendency to let the Morris side overshadow all, even gratitude to the donors who made it possible….

12th Oct 1954

I have been asked to give a lecture (without fee) at the Water House but can't think what it would best be to talk about or how to put it over. – I am regarded with distrust, if not hatred, it seems by the entire curating staff including Overall – because I have been and am critical and have stressed the importance of Brangwyn and the finer works he has given to the collection, wider in range than the Morris group exhibits. This hostility upsets me – and I have worked disinterestedly for the public good, and in the terms of the Trust, which I aim to see properly fulfilled and developed – and am grateful to Overall and the girls who have also done good service according to their light. But they so obviously resent my suggestions, or, as they view it as interference; and the Boro' Council and Officers would like, I fancy, to quite ignore the trustees, and their dependence on the Brangwyn Gift for the realisation of the project of a Gallery at all. The idea – its breadth and scope as conceived by F.B., your uncle, and myself is regarded as an effort to overshadow Morris whom they want to worship, not for his socialist principles and purpose but in a middle-class Victorian kind of adoration, undiscriminating, such as rather engulfed his broader intentions, and characterized the less vigorous, weaker side of his artistic output – a weakness that reached a point of some exhaustion in many of his lady followers and some of the more anaemic men….

One has to imagine that anyone with a hint of pacifism or even worse, a hint of sympathy for communism or the principle of its ideals was distrusted or, more so, shunned. This was an attitude which must have haunted Spradbery all his life. Spradbery had no fear of being branded a Communist or fellow-traveller or whatever, because he was in fact the most liberal-minded of men, prepared to consort with one and all. He in fact suffered the most outrageous aspersions throughout his life.

There was no less evidence of this prejudice in the suburban circles of the Borough of Walthamstow than anywhere else. Again, without Brangwyn's gift, it is impossible to imagine that there would ever have been a William Morris Gallery. The sheer short-sightedness of the Boro's appointed staff not to allocate some adequate exhibition space to the whole Brangwyn collection caused great anguish to Spradbery and subsequent problems with the museum administration. It was in fact a betrayal of the council's original promises and agreement.

Warm letters continued to flow between W.E.S. and Elinor Pugh detailing life at "The Wilderness" with a house full of my sister's growing family, myself and a Wilfred Clifton who had found residence there; also a Danish gentleman, a Mr Frederiksen who was living in his Gypsy caravan in the garden. Also news of "Sprad's" own exhibitions at the local Community Association's "Bedford House", a Community Association that has thrived and which to this day remains an outstanding centre of adult classes and activities within the Buckhurst Hill community. There was in addition the work of the Wilderness Opera Group, Dorothy's great legacy, still continuing to flourish with many of its faithful and stalwart members.... Yet another death in Spradbery's latter years – that of Brangwyn himself, not unexpected....

14th June 1956

Dear Miss Pugh

Thank you for your letter. My first intimation of the passing of Frank Brangwyn was through John who phoned me up to say it was announced in the evening papers of Tuesday. I immediately sent a telegram to Robert Massey his executor and account-ant and adviser saying I would give any help or advice on artistic matters should he need it, despite the recent change of plan in the will, and phoned Ditchling where Edgar Peacock (son of Mrs Peacock, Brangwyn's longtime housekeeper) answered me and told me the funeral will be tomorrow, Friday, at St Mary's Catholic Cemetery, Kensal Green at noon; that no ladies (as is often the case if not custom-ary) would be present but that he thought that it would be better for me to take any floral tribute I might be sending to the graveside as so many had already arrived that it seemed certain many there would have to be left behind. So I shall do that.

Some representatives of the Essex Art Club will accompany me and Dan Gladwell will convey us by car.

I phoned the Town Clerk, who, before I could say what I intended said "We know all about it. The Mayor has written to the local paper and I cut out the information about the funeral from yesterday's "Times" but I could not say whether the Mayor will attend, it depends on engagements". Edgar Peacock told me F.B. passed away very quietly and peaceably; but for a little over a fortnight he had been quite unable to see and this was the final darkness that most afflicted his brave spirit.

Before I went to Yorkshire to take charge of décor again at the West Riding

Summer Drama school on 19th May I wrote to Brangwyn asking him if I could see him for a little while (before I left for Yorkshire) on Thursday 17th and got a dictated letter back, the first letter from him not in his own handwriting, telling me he could no longer see…. This was to me appalling news, which together with the sudden death of Austin Spare after an operation, remained a preoccupation in my mind while devising sets and making properties for Greek Drama – "Antigone", "Oedipus Rex" etc where the tragic fates and treachery of destiny are the unrelieved theme….

17th July 1956

Dear Elinor Pugh

Herewith a copy of the Quarterly bulletin of the William Morris Gallery & Brangwyn Gift. When we were at the graveside at Kensal Green, Mr Overall, who was there with the Deputy Mayor of Walthamstow (Lady McEntee) asked me if I would write a few notes for their next publication, concerning Brangwyn.

I have taken the opportunity to reassert the nature and value of the Gift and the generosity (that should never be forgotten) of the Donors and their high and comprehensive purpose.

I had no acknowledgement of my script (nor of my letters to the Major, or for that matter of that to Sir Gerald Kelly) but at least it is published….

…There is far too much to tell you about all my anxieties and determinations now but rest assured that while life and energy lasts I shall endeavour to pursue and fulfill the promises and aims we all had (and those living who remember, still hold), that the creative purpose of art is a means to transform the world and realise in actuality the visions and aspirations that have inspired the keenest and most appreciative minds throughout the ages.

Protest and the Peace Movement of the Fifties

What one has to remember today, fifty years onwards, is that the whole world, East and West, just years preceding the Cuban missile crisis, was facing a growing madness within the realms of world powers to build up large masses of nuclear weapons, and play awesome games of threatening one another with nuclear annihilation.

The emergence of the Campaign for Nuclear Disarmament in the late fifties into the most popular protest movement of the post-war era was of even greater impact than the Anti-War Alliance against Iraq of recent years trying to prevent the Iraqi War. At the height of its effectiveness, the Aldermaston Marches attracted support from nearly 500,000 marchers on the streets of London, and contrary to misleading political and media propaganda, it was a popular movement of protest that must have held some sway, if not in the House of Commons itself, then certainly in the adjoining corridors of West-minster. Unlike Britain's more recent Prime Minister, Tony Blair, being sucked into a scandalous war with the Iraqis, regardless of the peoples' enormous protest in 2003. The CND was headed in the fifties by such well known figures as Bertrand Russell and many others – To this day I remember the names of Pat Arrowsmith and George Clarke. Eventually it was the CND's overwhelming popular support, although ridiculed and mocked, (by the typical tactics in certain sections of Britain's conservative society), that did affect the government of the day's recklessness and impending approach to outright nuclear war; something too awesomely awful to contemplate. Though never publicly admitted by govern-ment or anybody else, a caution and sanity prevailed which saved the world from inevitable destruction, leading surely from the foundations of protest laid by the earliest of those CND protesters, among them my own father, Walter Spradbery.

"Sprad" was above all else in his motivation through life a pacifist, a man of peaceful resolutions. Looking back, it's possible to imagine there has never been such a voice as his in the field of protest and argument against war and its diabolical arsenal of weapons; its futile fighting, resulting in annihilation and unwarranted destruction throughout the twentieth century. His words and stance have never been widely heard or appraised because he never ventured openly into that political arena which commands such attention. Yet his own particular blend of human and political fortitude and aura of simple trust and spirited self-belief in his own rightness was impossible for more formidable minds to contradict.

Spradbery set the ball rolling with an unpopular non-combatant soldier's rebellion in the First World War, hidden from public scrutiny. Amazingly he survived to eventually enjoy the fruits of his beliefs at least in his art and love for a woman – and still take up the cudgels of anti-war protest to his dying day. Was he a saint? A visionary spirit or just a simple man with goodness in his heart? A misguided fool or someone just too trusting of the world around him?

"Sprad" wrote reams of letters to the press and politicians on why the virtues of peace rather than war should pave our future course; he wrote articles and even a fictitious short novel, a premonition of the future as it might be. He was forever at the forefront of decrying and protesting at the development of the atomic bomb, German re-armament, napalm bombing and fire in Korea and the constant "cold war" propaganda. He led his local Peace Committees, amongst which were such stalwart women campaigners as Olga Leventoff and Sybil Morrison. Spradbery marched on all the Aldermastons and participated in anti-nuclear demonstrations to the very end of his life. He also participated and advised nationally within the peace movement and as an outstanding campaigner for peace was selected to partake in international post-war events in both Poland and Bulgaria in the fifties.

"The Isle of Sinisfree"

A fictitious story Spradbery wrote for the pacifist newspaper Peace News in 1953.

As a famous author wrote of another place, it might be claimed that the fabulous island continent of Sinisfree had passed from barbarism to decadence without gaining the wisdom of experience of practicing the arts the older civilisations achieved in their progress.

It had, however, acquired and used with vigour a great deal of their scientific knowledge and technology and the financial system of usury of their decline, and was, through the latter, in possession of the most expensive works of art produced by other nations.

It had also applied the scientific knowledge to gadgets and inventions for speed and streamlined efficiency, and to the making of diabolic instruments of destruction, so that its leading statesmen came to believe that they were a people of special merit, destined to rule lesser humanity and spread the principles of the Sinisfree way of life by the use and threat of their acquired powers of mass destruction.

They had the biggest, noisiest, most stinking bomb ever – so they thought, somewhat fearfully.

The principles of Sinisfree, as its name implies, were that men were free to exploit each other; that competition to get all that can be grabbed is a stimulus to vigorous well-being; and that what the age of faith regarded as deadly sins became when allowed free play, admirable; that Pride, Greed, Avarice, Sloth, Idleness, Lust, and Envy can all be agreeably dressed up to great effect – in fact will hardly be

237

recognised by the simpler exploited when the trappings that advertisement can put upon them are used or propaganda proclaims their high qualities; that cleanliness and cosmetics are united for the benefit of mankind, particularly the manufacturing combines of soap, powders, and health and beauty preparations; and that beauty may thus co-habit with deception and is not as some believe inseparable from the truth – and anyway when it comes to diplomacy or getting one's own way, what is truth.

Being "tough" was a manly virtue, "glamorous" a womanly attraction, and maudlin sentimentality was "romantic", while wealth and extravagant luxury were distinctions that put you in the news and huge incomes a measure of worth and importance.

Socialism, of which it seems almost certain they knew nothing, would, one suspects, have been anathema to their governors. Indeed even those folk among them who ventured to suggest that the islanders' way of life, or foreign policy at some points, transgressed the humanities, were represented in a Press that reduced whole forests to pulp, as dangerous criminal revolutionaries were removed from all positions of administration, or lost their humbler jobs, for "Anti-Sin activities" and were represented as being inefficient dictators.

Some think this may be considered at times as revenge (or a reaction) to their Puritan ancestry; but, of course they were of very mixed racial origin really, and seem mainly to have been drawn into a unity by the widely held conviction that money makes the man.

The President chosen under these circumstances was a General, experienced in total war, popularly known as Tyke, a name which conveyed certain bluff qualities and a doggedness that endeared him, with his wartime record, to the majority of voters.

The noisiest of his advisers was a certain Senator Daft, whose hysterical reactions at the mention of socialism or similar ideas reached an apoplectic frenzy, felt even among some of the islanders to be a bit dangerous and ridiculous, while in a good position in the background, as an influence on foreign affairs, was a General by name MacAskey, who failed to achieve that reputation for good heartedness that the name somehow recalls.

As isolationists they aimed at a controlling interest in all the world markets with as little opportunity as possible for the world to get back at them.

Jack Notso Bright was another well-known personality in a privileged position, and all members of the government pursued a policy of mutual security that many who noted results felt less certain of themselves.

Now what was the fate, do you think of this fabulous island continent?

Some say it is like Atlantis and lies beneath the depth of the seas where it sank at the explosion of its own arsenal.

Others say that it awoke from its dream of power and perversion and returned to a nobler idealism that inspired its earlier days – that its people were neither entirely submerged by atomic explosions nor its voluminous press propaganda of Sinisfree ideas; that among them were healthier thinkers with a more humane and better idea of man's needs and responsibilities and that it gave up its pretensions to leadership by force and threat and joined simply and humbly in the Council of the Nations for reconciliation through understanding and goodwill, and an age of peace followed.

Some even say, that after all, it was infiltrated and in economic confusion became Communist – but that seems a very doubtful story....

That "Thy Kingdom Come on Earth as it is in Heaven", be no hopeless prayer but a promise ultimately to be brought to realisation and fruition.

> "Sprad's" ensuing life at this time was intermingled with his growing activism and obligations to peace, a visionary and idealistic objective paramount in his heart and soul from the bitter lessons of two World Wars. Something at the time that was looked upon with distrust, apathy and misguided judgement by the majority of a population seemingly forever hell-bent on nationalistic chauvinism and led astray by temptations, false promise and the assertion of some hypocritical kind of righteousness and bravado. This in a world of political posturing and ever-changing horizons, with little imagination or visionary perception to match its changes.
>
> It was in the fifties that Spradbery's activities increased in proclaiming the message of peace and peaceful co-existence with the ever impending threat of confrontation between the Eastern and Western powers. Voices had to be raised, and "Sprad" was amongst that little band. In 1951 he was approached and selected for a Peace Mission to Poland. A Body of individuals representing 500,000,000 of the world's population. Many in the West viewed it as a propaganda stunt and typically showed their disdain. Spradbery was not to be diverted from any such reactions: in an earlier dated letter to Elinor Pugh in the course of a planned visit from her to the gallery, he mentions such a trip to Poland. Perhaps to a man in his sixties, travel behind the so-called "Iron Curtain" must have appeared an awesome undertaking....

28th July 1951

... How I was invited to Poland and given the most wonderful tour of my life – going and returning by air in itself was a marvellous experience – and what I saw and experienced behind the "Iron Curtain" is too long a story to embark on now. I am giving a lecture here in the garden on Sat. 4th August at 3 p.m. when I shall hope to put it over pretty effectively with the aid of my sketches and photographs. I gave a short talk (2 hours) on Thursday at Harlow.

In short what I have seen is the rebirth of a nation from the most awful devastation war has inflicted – the resurrection and the life in progress, and heard the voice of the dead speak from the great memorials erected to them, and the trumpet of victory sound from the tomb of the 5 million martyrs that died in the gas chambers and concentration camps at Auschwitz.

As "Sprad" painted what he saw with honest intent, so he wrote those words with honest intentions and believed and felt the genuineness of his contact and connection with the Polish people. Western political propaganda was at its height then. Communism was never going to be allowed to be given any credence or good word against the West's capitalism and so-called freedom. Natural greed and avarice has been at the heart of everything in the West and has encroached everywhere in the world today. Views that I have privately held at the back of my mind, ever since I saw my father, amongst a straggling bunch of people, marching down Whitehall in the very first Aldermaston to London march.

Following on in these chronicles are extracts from two of the last letters I have traced to Elinor Pugh, dated December 1957 and December 1958. Letters written at Spradbery's most apostolic moments of uncrowned achievement in campaigning for human rights. Pacifist to the core, he battled on as a last lost soul with the remaining pivotal elements of his gentle and unequivocal vision of a better world.

12th Dec 1957

Dear Elinor Pugh

I found your letter waiting for me when I returned by air last evening from Sofia, Bulgaria, where I have been entertained for a fortnight following my attendance at the celebrations at the William Blake bi-centenary there at which I spoke to a crowded hall of over 1000 people (and more turned away) on November 25th, his birthday (and my dear Dorothy's) and to which I took the Blake prints which we collected from Mrs Selwyn Image, and the Image manuscripts on Blake (which we saved from being burned up that were given as the Selwyn Image Collection to the William Morris Gallery – These have been Photostatted for the records of the Bulgarian Peoples' Republic Central Library (a marvellous collection of Eastern books but few English ones) where they will be available for students' study – the prints are now back with me here and will be returned to the William Morris Gallery to whom (the Boro' council) thanks and appreciation will be conveyed.

I have also made a recording for broadcast in the cause of peace and international understanding and with particular reference to Blake's message and ideas on that. It has been a terrible undertaking and difficult but highly exciting and I have a large number of new friends among leading Bulgarians and their leading artists by whose enthusiasm and understanding I hope further to ease world tension and by the international language of art and the vision which is the contribution and particular quality art brings to the world, avert the annihilation that H-bombs and new guided missiles threaten for all humanity.…

Optimism and what would seem naïve and innocent words from a figure such as Walter Spradbery, growing older, now in his late sixties, suffering from approaching blindness, the continued encumbrance of a double hernia and life dependent upon a few friends; Rima, my sister, and her family in temporary residence, and other miscellaneous human beings!

In those last approaching years, his crumbling home "The Wilderness" and overgrown garden around him, I look back and think where was I? At that time still trying desperately to consolidate my theatrical future. I cannot entirely be sure who was around at "The Wilderness" then. Not even the enigmatic figure of Wilfred Clifton who had made some effort to help me through those personally barren years. One particular relative I have to pick out was my late mother's younger sister, Edna, and her husband, Derric, a stern banking type of a gentleman who did help "Sprad" with the everyday domestic running of his house. Edna was another of those angelic Horsey sisters who was never too far away to assist in any moment of crisis or cry for help.

The very last letter I can trace to Elinor Pugh was dated in faded ink 23rd December 1958. His words in this frail physical period of his life take on a determined belief in his own convictions; there is as much positive evidence as ever of his deepening pacifist beliefs. The epic protesters stand at Swaffham must have been a landmark in the history of Civil Disobedience. "Sprad" inevitably was there.

23rd Dec. 1958

Dear Elinor Pugh

Your present of a fine bottle of port has just arrived, and amid the labour of trying to get off over 300 cards and fulfil numerous other duties and cope with the two extraordinarily vigorous grandsons, I have paused to give a sip to those assembled here and we have toasted you with grateful appreciation, find it inspiring and excellent, are refreshed for a further session of inscribing cards and addresses and shall spread its ruby treasure with discrimination and among only the most honoured guests.

I should write you a long letter now and tell you all the news, but every day seems to have been packed with incident and experiences moving and tragic – old friends pass away in such quick procession – and the political, economic and social

situation of the day needs such continuous watching and is so perilous; and responsibilities, commitments and urgent duties pile up – that I fluctuate between states
of exhaustion and exaltation of spirit in the struggle....

... I was at the first Swaffham demonstration though not among those man-han-
dled nor soaked – but I got a close-up view of most of it and many young friends
were among those who endured the reception and stopped the work for some
notable time and at least got the headlines – with effect likely to be as valuable as
was the Aldermaston March – in which I also had the joy of taking part....

It is impossible not to recognise these last fulfilling years of my father's life without citing his uniqueness and making a place for him in the history of twentieth
century pacifism.

Given the workings of political surveillance with its secrecy and hypocrisy, it is
easy to believe that "Sprad" was a fellow not entirely unknown. From his earliest
stand in World War One, against the removal of his red cross insignia, following
which questions were asked in Parliament; from his penned letters to succeeding
Prime Ministers and Foreign Secretaries, his controversial post-war visits to
Poland and Bulgaria, his articles and public debates on peace and the madness of
nuclear weapons. From the earliest days of non-violent protest, demonstrating in
Swaffham, from Aldermaston, Trafalgar Square to the banks of the Clyde and
Dunoon in demonstrations against the American nuclear submarines; from the
tiniest peace gathering to the greatest gatherings in London. Surely even if he was
not known to any political figure, he was on some sinister black-list of M.I.5 or
Scotland Yard. These were the movements and essence of non-violent protest.
Let time not blur one's memory: old "Sprad" was not alone among protesters of
all ages. The legend and history of Wanstead and Woodford (Churchill's parliamentary constituency) will remember the names of local campaigners, and on a
national scale the name of Pat Arrowsmith is forever enshrined in that period of
civil unrest and martyrdom.

These were the restraining influences against world war three and four. Today,
half a century onwards, through the emergence of such a ridiculous American
President as George Bush and such a British Prime Minister as Tony Blair, international war and destruction became as terrifying and threatening to the human
race as ever.

The first Aldermaston March
The first march was from London to Aldermaston in 1957.
A snapshot of the marchers, somewhere en route.
"Sprad" can be distinguished strolling along.

Chapter 8

"Sprad's" Last Years

Walter Spradbery lived on at "The Wilderness" to his dying days. As referred to earlier, my sister, Rima, and her family stayed on at "The Wilderness" where her husband, Ken, became a postman. "Sprad" found some latter-day happiness and solace with Rima's growing children, Laurence and Nicolas. For "Sprad" those post-Dorothy years became embroiled more than ever in the rising tide of protest and peaceful civil disobedience from a growing minority of Britain's population.

In the fifties and early sixties as today, the politicians and the press barons were always willing to ridicule and underplay the threat of the reckless build-up of nuclear weapons, which the majority of a gullible population were always readily happy to believe. Perhaps it is only in these recent early years of the twenty-first century that the realisation of the fallibility and untrustworthiness of politicians has been brought home, not only to our own little country, but in the world as well.

Spradbery was a part of this small band of campaigners with such local heroines as Sybil Morrison and Olga Leventoff. There were local peace movements, foreshadowing the "Campaign for Nuclear Disarmament" (CND) which had at one time the leadership and voices of luminaries such as Canon Collins and Bertrand Russell. They were at the forefront of a commitment to a peaceful future and existence which shows itself today as a visionary alternative. Without that minority of restraining voices, recent history has proved what ominous signs await us in the future. A consequence of the hypocritical attitude this country has lived under, is the adoption of arms on the streets, closed circuit observation, torture and other barbarous acts of inhumanity, happening in collusion and prevailing within our own country right now.

As a young fellow myself, eternally struggling as an unemployed and un-recognised actor, I was never going to openly emerge with the growing sym-pathies I held for the CND movement and all it stood for, although I gathered with the vast crowds on a number of the big occasions of national protest that swept the country in the late fifties and early sixties, being arrested and charged on at least two massive protest meetings.

Sometime in the late fifties I took a small flat in West Hampstead in pursuit of my theatrical career, and really neglected my father and "The Wilderness" shamefully. A time of misplaced endeavours and exposure to the fun, trials and errors of a young actor struggling to find an agent, a foothold and become a new young Brando of the English theatre!! Instead my years were eventually spent working in nightclubs, revue bars and even one notorious strip club.

Walter Spradbery hung on at "The Wilderness" surrounded by his memories. Besides his daughter and her family, he was apt to draw around him various lost souls who needed a roof over their heads. It was also a time where the frailties of age were mounting; his blindness amongst other disabilities. I recall a young insecure fellow by the name of Wilkins he gave a roof to live under, and there was always Wilfred Clifton! He had as a child been in the maternal charge of another of my mother's greatest friends who died suddenly and left him on his own. Wilfred was something of a wanderer and loner, but not without a certain enterprise and skill as an electrician from his earlier days with the B.B.C. at Broadcasting House. He was a help to me in my direst hours, finding me some employment opportunities in crucial times as a "resting actor". A Danish gentleman, Mr Fredrickson, arrived into the garden and household with his home, a traditional old Romany caravan. He stayed in "The Wilderness" garden for some years. In the meantime, as the years passed by, so "The Wilderness" and the garden suffered and was constantly encroached upon by the surrounding forest.

Spradbery's sight so deteriorated in the sixties that writing must have been an irksome task for him. I have discovered copies of rare later letters to Jim Berry, almost impossible for my own eyes to read. One dated 18th October 1962 in fact says very little, apart from commenting on the gathering autumn weather and what he is able to distinguish through his diminishing eyesight from the sunlight outside.

18th Oct 1962

My dear Jim

Sitting here, in my customary seat, before the open door looking on to the garden, with the setting sun shining in, so that when I lift my eyes I am dazzled by the dappled light penetrating the gently swaying foliage; with birds twittering and fluttering to and fro to pick up crumbs, and peck off berries from the hawthorne hedge or maybe pulling at the orange hips or tearing a petal from a belated rose, moist with the veiling mist: and with my kittens and their alert little mother-cat watching, and sending all scurrying away in regular interludes in their constant teasing play.

The grass and paths are littered with fallen leaves that gather again however often they are swept away: and in the background all the fading glories of the season at their most colourful. But for the occasional barking of the dogs, so enthusiastically alert and ardently affectionate, the seclusion is tuneful with notes graciously in harmony with autumn's passing; and the wood pigeons cooing in lullaby, lamenting it, and soothingly assuring that ere winter's frost grips the earth, and Christmas draws us round the flickering fire, the promise of the New Year is being encased in sticky buds that carry the colours of autumn, in sweet refinement, into the delicate hues of spring, and assure the summer's resurrection.

Friends, neighbours, relatives and the family, now moved away to their own new home, drop in, drawn back to the place, to partake of its fruitfulness, bottle it, and gather windfalls for more immediate consumption; and I almost expect you (or your spirit) in the hands of the postman (nervous of the dog) who pops the letters through the open window or with cautious haste into the letter-box, (before I can get there to thank him and pacify the dog), to greet me too....

> There is another letter to Jim Berry on "The Wilderness"-headed writing paper with the motif of the flute-playing youth and his lover under the chestnut tree, dated the 17th March 1964, penned in the tiniest writing on foolscap pages.

17th March 1964

My dear Jim

I am hoping to write you an amusing and interesting & informative letter on the much abused plant, the DANDELION, that is so annoying to gardeners such as yourself. In the creation of life, the sustaining of it, the enriching of it, the development of it, it has played an important part, and cannot be so lightly dismissed, it should never be so ignorantly abused. The world would be a very different place without it. Artistically it is richly endowed, marvellously shaped, constructed with variations of functions that lend it a usefulness few other plants possess so fully. It supplied the humus so many other valuable plants need to nourish them and make them fit to serve human needs. It penetrated and broke-up with its sensitive tap-root the seemingly dead hardrocks, and by its own decay among other decaying matter, produced the substance on which the nutrient for them came into being. They became fodder and food-stuff for animals including primitive man, and self-conscious, intelligent life emerged and took control of natural unconscious forces that had no idea where it (or they were) was going. Its construction so complicated, its shapes and parts so various in texture, substance, and form.... It was the plant I chose when I did my first competitive sheet of designs – a square, a circle and a rectangle filled with differing patterns, for the Board of Education's Examination for the Art Class Teacher's Certificate; which I did at 16 or 17. I could draw and describe every detail of it ever since – as also countless other plants and trees that I

have studied since, or had then. Think of it in all its variety of surprising charms –
The delicate fluffy ball of its tiny seeds that look so ethereal amid the grasses and
buttercups and daisies that rival its golden glory, and, as one looks, sends trails of its
fairy-like parachutes floating away on the wind, to carry new life far and wide. Is
anything in nature more poetical and lovely to behold! – Full of joy and promise.
Which you appear to appreciate differently....

In this same letter, its final paragraph refers to a brief visit from me. It describes a
meal we had together at a local restaurant. Sadly, it seems I was rude and abusive
and my manner attracted other customers' attention.

I have to realise that to my father I must have been a bitter disappointment as
a son. With his early tortuous years with his own mother, Emily Spradbery, and
his concerns for his brother Joe, I must wonder if the same thoughts of me
drifted through his mind. Was there some wilful hereditary gene that found its
way into our family strain, connecting and showing itself in the cases of "Sprad's"
mother, Emily, his brother Joe and perhaps myself?

It is difficult for me to recall too much of the feelings between us when we
actually met up in those latter days. When he saw me at the George Inn
Southwark playing the title role in Shakespeare's "Macbeth", he did mention it
around with some pride, although earlier, not long after my mother's death, he
had been witness to a terrible debacle of mine – when partaking in a staged
performance to a crowded congregation in London's St. Martin-in-the-Fields –
when I forgot my lines completely. An occasion which left me utterly
demoralized. With and before "Macbeth" I possibly redeemed myself a little in
his very much sightless eyes, visiting me while in weekly rep in Great Yarmouth.
A place that must have brought back poignant memories to him from his own
childhood.

One of his last letters to Jim Berry is dated 7th February 1969, congratulating
him on his own remarkable literary piece surrounding the times and history of
the "Yorkshire Luddites". Illustrated by his own remaining son, David (who went
on to study and teach art).

7th Feb 1969

My Dear Jim

I cannot find words to say how delighted I am to receive your long and newsful letter of Feb. 3rd the first four parts of your admirable and effective work on "The
Yorkshire Luddites 1811–12" with the honour of your dedication at the head of it
... (more than I deserve)....

Nothing could be more fitting than David's illustrations that catch the depression and anger of the time, and faithfully records the period. They must be a further source of pride to you. He has always shone like a star for you! It is a united effort which will become famous, and nothing can give you greater satisfaction, and in time to come … you should send a complete set to the Prime Minister and if, on enquiring into your life and work, he does not recommend you for an O.B.E. at least I shall be surprised and disgusted.

I shall be going by ambulance (not that I could not quite easily get there without) to the North Middlesex Hospital, Edmonton, for a check-up by Dr V.B. Levison on Tuesday 11th Feb 69 at 1.45 p.m., and hope that at length I may be permitted to have a bath again. "It is such a perfect relaxation! It is nice to be in bed and think what an awful thing is work, but to be in a bath is even better"….

Of course there was no longer at that time a useable bath at "The Wilderness". As I recall the floor of the groundfloor bathroom had collapsed from decay and dampness. Nevertheless, bath or no bath, "Sprad's" indominatable spirit always shone through.

If Walter Spradberry was never recognised metaphorically as a giant figure of a man, he could certainly easily walk with such men. He was undoubtedly ignored, ridiculed and despised by sections of the human race that unfortunately will always prevail.

Nevertheless there was this invincible aura surrounding his physical presence, surely crying out for some wider recognition. However, his ideals which were never seemingly broken, were not going to be unnoticed. James Berry, Haydn Mackey, Faithful Davies and others saw and experienced this moral fortitude which must have left them with a unique legacy of hope and faith themselves.

There is also evidence in my possession of other correspondence from a number of eminent figures who were not unappreciative – in fact, hugely sympathetic and admiring of Spradbery's views and his lifelong moral stance. Josiah Oldfield, humanitarian and friend of Gandhi, Frank Pick, the doyen of London Transport's greatest era, and the distinguished civil servant, Sir Hubert Llewellyn Smith, certainly recognised qualities differently from others.

With "Sprad's" constant flow of letters to the country's succeeding Prime Ministers and Foreign Secretaries (not unacknowledged by various private secretaries), it is possible to imagine even such a monumental figure as Churchill being conscious and perhaps even respectful of a "fellow artist's" totally opposing views! From as far back as 1916 when Churchill returned to parliamentary duty, this awareness may have been so. Especially with "Sprad's" stand at the time over the removal of the red cross insignia, seemingly treated without any great public awareness. As in the secrecy of affairs hidden from today's public; even with television cameras and leaking parliamentary sources that now exist, much is hidden from public knowledge, scrutiny and debate. Acts of pacifism in World War One were as embarrassing to politicians then as acts of torture from their own military personnel are today.

"Sprad" the Writer

The enthusiasm of compiling this account of a man's life was doubly encouraged by having returned to me his original hand-written correspondence to James Berry. As Walter Spradbery's son, I was from my early teenage days aware of his capacity and facility for writing. From the days of undertaking my National Service and serving in Germany, it was letters from my father that largely kept my spirits and hopes alive!

His writing, less known and recognised than his painting however, was prolific and must have had some impact and impression. One has to imagine James Berry was the greatest receiver of his letters. His literary skills, though, were not confined to writing letters. He wrote many articles, features and essays, notably on art and peace. A few have been published in local newspapers and specialist periodicals. Some unpublished texts on art and designing posters lie waiting to be revealed in print, while a beautifully designed illustrated booklet, with an accompanying text on rambles in Epping Forest still awaits an enterprising publisher today!

Besides corresponding with the humblest, "Sprad" has also written to the mighty! Succeeding prime ministers, foreign secretaries and others in high office have not been excluded from the reach of his pen.

Sir Winston Churchill

I think in particular it is worth quoting here from letters that he wrote to Sir Winston Churchill at No. 10 Downing Street. By the nature of at least one particular response from Downing Street, it is likely that Churchill may well have read one of these letters himself!

Two men could not have been further apart and from such different strata of life. However, Churchill was our local constituency member of Parliament for Woodford and he did come to exhibit as an artist with the Essex Art Club under "Sprad's" chairmanship! One also has to imagine before the age of internet and emailing, that it was not unusual for commoners to write letters, delivered by a reliable postal service to politicians in high places! There were no high metal gates protecting the prime minister's residence then from a marauding and prying public and certainly no army of bureaucrats surrounding him as would happen

249

today. "Sprad" himself, despite extremely opposing points of view on war, certainly perceived Churchill as an awesome figure and politician.

It was on the streets of London, as a child, that Spradbery first glimpsed Churchill in the flesh. The great man was pointed out to him by his father. I quote again from "Sprad's" diary:

… One day in the city with my father among a crowd I suddenly found myself looking at a startlingly proud, arrogant, implacable and haughty face – a pale young man in a carriage, folks were cheering – I had read of "Nero" and the fall of Rome and I immediately thought of him – the face I looked at seemed a significant mask. My father said "that is Winston Churchill" and I was haunted by the memory, and felt I had seen a man of destiny – implacable, terrible. I had.

These are extracts from drafts of letters Spradbery wrote in later years to Churchill, in particular after his visit to Poland, after the death of my mother and the almost forgotten ceasefire in Korea. A war which fortunately for me, happened just after my demob from National Service. No sooner had I left for my return to civilian life, than my regiment in Germany was posted to Korea and subsequently suffered many casualties.

His letter to Churchill following the visit to Poland was prompted by the reactions of apathy and virtual ridicule which he encountered amongst the ordinary members of his own community on returning home and attempting to spread some enlightenment about what he had witnessed behind the "Iron Curtain".

To the Right Hon. Winston S. Churchill P.M., O.M.
R.A. Extraordinaire

Dec 1951

Sir

I write as an artist … on the Eve of Christmas.

That was a happy day, I think, when you took a brush and first began to praise creation in paint – a way must have opened to new experiences in vision. Words you already had, but this medium can be more broadly instantly comprehensive and comprehensible and you felt the impulse to impart the joy you found in it to encourage others to become amateur painters and, I remember, wrote describing a hesitant beginning and Lady Lavery's demonstration, from which you decided the first necessity to be – audacity. …

… Last June-July – I spent three observant and memorable weeks touring Poland as a guest of the Polish Peace Committee and there saw that war had inflicted appalling malicious devastation far greater in extent and intensity than that endured by Londoners — from Warsaw, where 75% of the buildings had been destroyed, through hundreds of miles of countryside and many cities damaged in lessening intensity as one got to the Tatra mountains at last and the Czech border.

I moved freely among people, so like the folk I knew in Britain that the different language seemed little barrier to understanding — a mere safeguard and prevention of the distractions of argument. It seemed to me these people and what they had done and were doing since the war, should be an inspiration to the world.

They had come back to the cities and homes, to ruin and rubble that beggars description and had set up and were still ardently setting up historic features restored to original design and had built new buildings, roads and bridges to new designs with comprehension and forethought such as the past had not arrived at. Without the machinery the West can command they had achieved in civil reconstruction more, conceived more generously, more devotedly laboured — a spirit unconquerable in its patience, and determination seemed to me to be among them — something in quality such as Kipling aimed to describe in "If" — it made one feel pride and emotion in being of human kindred — If this be Socialism in practice it is a vital faith. And I thought of what were practically the last recorded words of Bernard Shaw — "A war on Communism is ignorant blazing nonsense"….

To the Right Hon. Winston Churchill, P.M. O.M.
10 Downing Street, Whitehall

21st May 1952

Concerning the death of Dorothy d'Orsay

Dear Sir

I am sure that amid your many heavy burdens of State you will yet desire to be informed of the passing of one in your constituency who has contributed greatly to the musical life of the country and particularly in this area, and one beloved by all who knew her.

I write to you because she conducted the orchestra that played on the occasion of your receiving the Freedom of Woodford at the Bancroft School, and it was noted by the press and all those present at that time, that you observed her vitality and enthusiasm in giving you the best welcome her orchestra could express….

To Sir Winston Churchill P.M., O.M.

27th July 1953

Dear Prime Minister

At this time of thanks giving for the Cease Fire in Korea, let me join those who desire to express to you and to Mr Eden (who have so great a responsibility in carrying

"Sprad" studying a catalogue at an exhibition of posters
in central London in the sixties.

forward the British contribution to World affairs) congratulations on your returning health and strength, by which, with the grace of God you can be vital instruments in shaping a lasting peace among the nations – your coveted "last prize" – to
attain which all concerned will need to forgive things done in the past and to be
forgiven: and in pursuit of creative purposes fulfil and accept the promises and gift
of life abundant that our age can realise....

... It is courage with art and inspired by vision, that when conflict and destruc-
tive attacks with lethal weapons are abandoned, may strive to shape to unity of purpose, or bring to mutual service, delight and harmony the diversity of effort and
the varying attributes of nations, in the Great Design for giving that is humanity's
abiding desire.

Such contributions as I could make to these endeavours in peace or war, have
been pacifist, compassionately and aesthetically practical and intellectually persua-
sive – or so I strive. My sympathy is much with Socialist and communist idealism –
the achievements of which are underestimated and little known by the prejudiced.

I regard the World Peace Movement and still more the Gandhian peace movements as of the greatest significance and importance for the salvation of civilisation
and common humanity in the crises of today.

But I am not writing particularly to tell you this, but because this seems a fitting
occasion and opportunity to express regards, appreciation and good wishes to
those of differing opinion who yet give their energy, skill and very life to serve their
fellows – and so I take it....

The Last Chapter

"Sprad" lived on at "The Wilderness" almost to his dying day. His very last days
were spent in the home (situated locally) of my sister, Rima. I was there with him
in those last days. Although life was ebbing away from him, he seemed to
maintain a great inner will to live and hang on to life. Strangely his lips murmured
the names of friends from earlier years: the Reverend Dunning, Schwab, Edwards
and others. My mother's name was never heard.

From the letters to both Jim Berry and later, Elinor Pugh, I have tried to
convey to the reader the life he led, the friends he surrounded himself with and
what kind of man he was. His own personal ambitions really lay no further than
his art and giving the benefit of his art to others.

With his beloved Dorothy, in his humblest way, he supported her in keeping
music and other local artistic pursuits as alive as possible under the dire
circumstances of the depression, the approaching war years, war itself and post-
war years and the little income available to them. By the time of the Second

World War, Spradbery was in his fifties and never going to be in uniform again. I do recall him designing and creating a huge local battle-plan of Buckhurst Hill for the local Civil defence force with cut-out models representing bombed or burnt-out houses and local landmarks for placing on the plan to show where damage was being inflicted from the air-raids.

At the outset of war, ATS girls were billeted at "The Wilderness" while troops dug entrenchments in the surrounding forest.

However, as the war dragged on, my mother took up performing for C.E.M.A., a government organisation to further sustain music and opera within the limits imposed on the country by the constraints of the war. At the same time "The Wilderness" garden continued to provide a number of musical events which probably set many precedents in the world of arts and has already been commented on.

The presence of Nazism, casting its shadow over Europe, must have tested "Sprad's" pacifist ideals of "thou shalt not kill" like nothing else before. Nevertheless he was always there to defend a conscientious objector's right not to take up arms if called upon. His moral stance and belief against taking another man's life was as unwavering and as unshakeable as ever.

Walter Spradbery was never going to be a man on any international stage, his service was always towards his local community and fellow men. The founding with Eric Southwell of Buckhurst Hill's local Community Association was and is still today a prime example of his public spirited efforts. The Community Association half a century on at Bedford House is a striking testament to both him and Eric Southwell, a remarkable man in his own right. Today the Community Centre functions under its own financial income and support.

His teaching at the local Harts Hospital and Wansfell College were all works of faith and goodwill in the same charitable vein.

After Dorothy's death, his blindness handicapped him severely, especially with his embracing of the peace movement and concerns for nuclear war, which hung ominously in the balance at that time with the west and east adopting such provocative and aggressive postures towards each other. The world of capitalism and free enterprise was ever opposed to the ideal of communism being recognised in any form. Communism in its own desperation to withstand the west was at the same time destroying its own fundamental ideals and succumbing to the worst forms of a totalitarianism and suppressive rule that the west was only too pleased to exploit and condemn.

In its own little way, Spradbery's participation in peace missions to Poland and Bulgaria were extraordinary adventures and achievements for a man into his sixties and suffering the first signs of blindness and other ill-health. Haydn Mackey had always maintained this early blindness was from the attacks of mustard gas he had suffered in the 1914-18 war in France. Although he received treatment at London's Moorfield's Hospital, his sight did deteriorate later.

Today as I struggle to assemble this last remaining chapter, I myself have just returned from the miraculous hands of my local eye surgeon, Dr Paritosh Shah, with my own sight restored. A fearful and apprehensive experience initially, but under the local anaesthetic administered, it became something of a heavenly experience as lights flickered before me in a kaleidoscope of colour under Dr Shah's exquisite hands. Of course in the days of "Sprad's" operation, things could not have been so sophisticated, nevertheless I vaguely recall my father expressing the same delight and relief that passed through my own mind and body only yesterday. Walter Spradbery would of course have admired the work of the eye surgeon above all others, as at this moment I do myself. Thankfully, the invaluable work of eye surgeons and other surgeons rises above the hatefulness and stupidity of the world today.

Spradbery's return from Poland encouraged him to lecture and write en-thusiastically of the Polish people's quick recovery from war and his lecture to a thousand Bulgarians on William Blake in 1957 in Sofia must have been utterly unique! These occasions were very much in the latter days in Spradbery's life, as were his letters, articles, marches, demonstrations and support of the whole peace movement, including the rising popularity of the Campaign for Nuclear Disarmament in the late fifties and early sixties. In those latter years he moved within a dedicated group of local campaigners for peace and an end to the cold war. Their efforts were derided, but there were as many madmen in power then as there are today without any realisation or vision of what the consequences of another international misunderstanding might bring on. A hand on the button of world destruction was not just a fantasy with such war-mongering figures – as we have so recently experienced today.

"Sprad" made few concessions to his moral conscience in his later years, very much as in his earlier days. He decided that "The Wilderness" should return to forest land rather than leave it to his son and risk it being sold off to some property developer. He had nothing else he could leave equally to both myself and my sister Rima anyway.

Fortunately the Ministry of Transport were looking for land adjoining the forest to purchase and offer the corporation of London's Forestry Commission in exchange for forest land required for road development. A modest deal was struck that after his death "The Wilderness" would revert to forest and a nominal sum of money would be shared between his dependants, namely my sister and myself. This is how it is today, a forest glade with not a sign of its earlier existence as a haven of music and the arts, as it had been in some of the country's most desperate years of wartime crisis and other more idyllic days....

In "Sprad's" final years I was becoming increasingly involved with a young mime troupe led by the irrepressible Lindsay Kemp. At the same time Steven Berkoff was someone I helped in his earliest years. I also had to earn some alternative money to maintain a marriage and a small Victorian terrace house backing on to the Grand Union Canal in Islington.

Perhaps unforgivably, I saw little of my father in those later years of the sixties where it seemed revolutionary happenings were afoot in theatre for myself and certainly others around me.

Today I look back on my father and my mother and realise my good fortune as a child growing up in such an environment as "The Wilderness".

In Spradbery's long descriptive letters returned to me years later by the recipient's daughter-in-law, Elaine Berry, he wrote glowingly, lovingly and warmly of my mother, her talent, zest and indefatigable spirit. As someone myself who has worked in one capacity or another in the world of theatre, both internationally and in the humblest of circumstances, I can only recall the uniqueness and prodigious capacity of her talent. As a woman in love, she made such sacrifices, as Walter Spradbery himself made such sacrifices for his moral, social and artistic conscience. In the twenties and thirties she sang up and down the country for regional broadcasts for the BBC, the only broadcasting company at that time, yet there is absolutely nothing in the BBC's sound archives of any voice recordings of her work over all those years.

The scope and depth of Walter Spradbery's life was very simple, but breathtakingly brilliant and spirited to the very end. His morality, his uncompromising stance against hypocrisy and ineptitude, and above all his pacifism, made him an uncomfortable figure in some authorities' and establishments' eyes. I understand the Royal Academy itself was openly uneasy at his active part in affairs outside the realms of his professional work and spoke to his great artist friend, Haydn Mackey, to have a word in his ear! Of course Mackey never did. Only recently I received from Elaine Berry a handwritten message "Sprad" had sent to James Berry on the occasion of the anniversary of Berry's birthday in 1961. Despite what other men may still predominantly think, I believe it is worth reprinting here (right).

At "Sprad's" funeral in St. John's churchyard within sight of "The Wilderness", I remember it was Mackey, himself in his nineties, who, stumbling by the graveside, threw a rose onto the coffin as it was lowered into the open grave; fellow mourners grabbed him before he almost fell into the grave himself. I cannot recall the funeral service now. I remember it was a cold January morning in the year 1970. Faithful Davies was certainly there. He spoke to me at my sister Rima's house in Debden close by — where sandwiches and tea were provided afterwards. I often wonder what became of that man; I never heard from him again — a great Australian!

1918 — 1961

Happy memories of our years of friendship and how we travelled together through the havoc of Flanders in the 1st World War, doing what we could as R.A.M.C men to rescue and tend the wounded; your unfailing cheerfulness and courage; your invaluable comradeship; your integrity and character, strengthened by the "Advice to young men" by bobbett, who has helped so many to this day, and whose influence like your own, still helps to keep sanity and good will active among humanity and the nations; under the Nuclear threat.
    Every Blessing attend you.

Copy of "Sprad's" letter to James Berry.

Walter Spradbery as far as I am aware never entered a church under his own volition other than for a relative's wedding or funeral. He had though read the bible most assiduously and was not too shy in quoting from it.

Perhaps it is apt to quote from the bible in the Epilogue as a lasting acknowledgement to "Sprad's" own sense of morality, his artistic beliefs, his love of nature and his efforts for peace.

Epilogue

It seems that nothing has ever been written or little recorded in print of Walter Spradbery's life; and it has been such contrasting events in recent times as the momentous political treachery, ineptitude and short-sightedness surrounding the Iraqi War and the whole Middle East, the continued immoral banking crises, the even more scandalous exposures of the country's politicians' expenses; but more poignantly, in my parochial mind, the seemingly less important issues, in worldwide terms, of the threatened closure of the London Borough of Waltham Forest's great monument and homage to William Morris, the Art Gallery in E17's Lloyd Park, that brought home to me a necessity to attempt some personalized account in print of my late father's life.

At "Sprad's" death, his great and enduring friend and comrade, Haydn Mackey, wrote a eulogy which I have kept to this day. Whether it was spoken or read out at "Sprad's" funeral service at St. John's Church in Buckhurst Hill I have failed to recall. It was written out by Mackey on four large sheets of blue card. Haydn Mackey himself was then in his late eighties. Some of the handwriting, although clear in parts, is crisscrossed with deletions and some indistinguishable words; however some of Mackey's words on "Sprad" can justifiably be included in any final tribute to my father:

"I admired his unbreakable integrity, even in the abominable conditions of the Great War; and an indomitable physical courage; of which he often produced examples – he seemed to regard adversity as a trial of strength. And I never knew him to utter a vicious or malignant thought. His was a truly great character. William Morris once defined "Ornament as an expression of joy in the work" – and I always feel that "Sprad's" best work, whether in art or behaviour, always seemed to have a feeling of joy – or at least gaiety in the work. And I never knew him to entertain any mean thought or action…

Spradbery was a friend of Brangwyn's – and a life trustee of the "Brangwyn Gift", and Brangwyn was an apprentice of William Morris and destined to become the most brilliant decorative artist since the great Venetian G. B. Tiepolo. As a craftsman

259

Brangwyn regarded certain of Spradbery's watercolours as comparable to those of the great English watercolour school which arose in the 18th century and continued into the 19th century....

Also Spradbery was a brilliant teacher – he knew that by merely teaching it was not just the imparting of verbal information and knew the advice of Albert Durer – "In art never heed him who cannot prove what he sayeth with his hand."...

Spradbery's character, as I have tried to describe it, explains his pacifism. It was innate and supremely part of his nature, and it was, I think, the only real and perennial disagreement we had of any lasting nature – throughout a lifetime – we have discussed it before, during and after the wars – and we were always content to leave it like that – it rested on the methods of changing the minds of government or the minds of men....

Your sight might be blurred - as it was on one occasion after a gas attack in the war – or by the poison of criticisms, but you took it all in your stride....

I am not the only one, I feel, there must be myriads, who will experience a gap he once filled in one's life.

Ave Atque Vale, Old comrade"

Haydn Mackey

All his life "Sprad" rode against the tide and flow of popular choice and opinion, certainly gravitating towards some of the deepest thinkers, writers, artists and missionaries of thought and conjecture of his time. He was not a great man in the category of a doctor, surgeon, scientist, philosopher, or a writer – or a miner, a postman, a bus driver or a care worker, but certainly as a human being.

Belatedly this review and account of "Sprad's" life really requires giving a great deal more prominence to a body of artists, known as the Essex Art Club, than I have done in the preceding chapters, and which I feel I must mention now. A Club which took shape from various groups of artists that emerged in the early part of the twentieth century. The Essex Art Club was not exactly the Royal Academy of Arts or the Royal Society of Watercolourists or any other fashionable group or school of artists, but a club located in the east end of London and its outlying districts. The Club's history is recorded in a tiny booklet: "One Hundred Years of the Essex Art Club" by the Club's present exhibition secretary, Sandy Connor. It is today (in the year 2009), still very active. Its Chairman, for as many years as I can remember, was "Sprad", who was finally honoured as its President in his very last years. It was a Club with an elected body of artists that forever threaded its way through Spradbery's life from the post-First World War years to almost his last years; the Essex Art Club was very much at the forefront of "Sprad's" commitment to his whole world of art. Many of its future members sprang from his Greenleaf Road Settlement classes with Haydn Mackey – and others, indeed, went on to distinguish themselves nationally in the professional ranks. Among the Club's members in its earliest days were two sisters, nieces of Joseph Lister, the famous surgeon and inventor of anti-septic techniques. Both his nieces were students of "Sprad". One of the sisters, Edith Lister, he recognised as a truly fine artist. I think it is fitting that some of "Sprad's" final words on Edith Lister should be quoted here. It surely encapsulates Spradbery's own feelings, ideals and approach to art itself in the most simple and fundamental words. A tribute I came across not so long ago, surviving today in the hands of the present-day Essex Art Club.

Edith Lister's Art, a tribute by Walter E. Spradbery (Essex Art Club):

"To make a complete and just statement in any medium requires, in addition to an appreciation of the possibilities and limitations of the chosen medium and ardent practice in its use, a breadth of vision and the inspiration it imparts; a joy in the work; a serenity of mind; a philosophy and a religious faith which begets awareness of relative values essential in the quest for truth and beauty and a comprehensive praise of creation.

A study of the work in watercolour of Edith Lister reveals her to be an artist of this calibre – working as she did in comparative retirement, through a long life, with the advantages of travel and a great measure of economic security, accumulating the great collection of sketches, jottings and lyrical little pictures that she so happily made and which so few but her intimate and sympathetic friends ever saw. She was content in the making of them, in the search to encompass and record effect, impressions and the loveliness of things seen; and sought no profit or fame, seldom exhibited them and then most often for charitable ends.

She was humbly grateful to those fellow artists of the Essex Art Club who recognised her subtle perception and the exquisite skill of her little pictures and bequeathed a selection, which it was my privilege to make, of one hundred and six works to their care. These are being preserved and will be placed on exhibition from time to time for the benefit of art-lovers and students of the art of sketching in this atmospheric, limpid medium, and it would be hard to find such another collection so completely inspiring, so variously instructive and throughout so masterly.

Miss Pollard has spoken of those studies of Pre-Raphaelite intensity which combine with the searching detail, the essential basic breadth, appreciation of effect of light and air: but more arresting is her power of swift summary, the encompassing unity with the illusive suggestiveness of broad masses and direct washes, giving the

essence of the chosen subject – the skill in composition and happy emphasis, recalling the influence of masters she was fortunate enough to contact in her studies –
Wilson Steer, William Nicholson, James Pryde – and the earlier masters such as
Cotman and Turner. In my opinion her work, while imbued with her own personality, ranks with these."

> Perhaps some of the final words in an epilogue to Spradbery might be left to one
> of the country's most famous and renowned northern socialists of her day,
> Katharine Bruce Glasier, whom "Sprad" met and became a friend of fairly late in his
> life. These are her words quoted from an article written in "Labour's Northern
> Voice" in the year, 1946:

"But I must hasten to my special subject of the month. The treasure came to me at
Christmas-time from a newly discovered friend and comrade, Walter E. Spradbery,
a wholehearted disciple of John Ruskin and William Morris, with all his boyhood
and most of his working life spent in the Walthamstow where William Morris was
born and spent his happiest holidays. Even before the first World War, Walter
Spradbery's genius for getting on to coloured posters the very soul of the natural
unspoiled beauty of our English home counties or the star-lit poem of an Ely cathedral, was transforming the drab walls of many of our Southern Railway stations.
But it will always stand to the credit of the managers of the London Underground
Railway, in the worst of the blitz that, seeking to hearten the citizens of London,
who by hundreds of thousands were finding shelter in the safety of their stations,
they sent for Walter Spradbery and won from him his magnificent series of posters
"The Proud City".

How I wish I could bring them all before your eyes as I write. Many of my readers must have seen and rejoiced in them.

But amongst countless others, Canadian soldiers saw them and told of them to
their folks at home. Thus, caught by their enthusiasm, the firm of W.H. Bosley and
Co., Toronto, Canada, obtained permission to reproduce them on a small scale in a
luxuriously attractive white-papered booklet, suggestive of Canada's wealth in
such material, called...

THEIR FINEST HOURS
A Tribute to the People of Great Britain

"This is the story of Britain's finest hours. They came with Dunkirk, they ticked
away their last anxious seconds when the fury of the V-bombs lessened and finally
stopped early in 1945. They were the hours when Britain fought alone, her people
and her leaders indomitable in the face of their unequal contest for survival.

They were the rallying hours of freedom, hours that wove the miracle of Dunkirk, the epic of the Kentish aerodromes and the Battle of Britain into one glorious tapestry of courage, sacrifice and valour....With the night the blinds went down in 12 million homes. Britain was lost in a sea of darkness. Men and women worked 70, eighty and 90 hours a week in the factories.

Over seven million women stepped into overalls. Sturdy grandmothers toiled by the sides of girls of 18. In the little gardens, vegetables replaced the flowers. Famous landmarks crashed into tangled ruins. St Paul's Cathedral, the Tower of London, Big Ben – symbols of Empire, they stood bathed in the light of burning buildings. But they stood – and still they proudly stand."

> I think it is apt, proper and logical to quote "Sprad's" own words published in the same article. Included here are two extracts in response to Katherine Bruce Glasier's revealing him yet again as the controversial figure he was:

OUR FINEST HOURS ARE YET TO BE

"For to me, despite my appreciation of your tribute of the bravery and endurance of our people, these were only our most precarious hours in the inescapable logic of events, when a policy of mutual destruction had been adopted by the peoples of the world; and that precariousness has not passed, but been increased by later inventions, such as the atomic bomb and the continued pride of those who achieve power among men ...When all homage has been paid to the brave, there remains this: The finest hours were not in the folly of pride, but in the wisdom of humility and thankfulness. Youth has too often been commended to the glory of dying, but it is in the joy of living, the importance of living, that its rightful inheritance remains, and it is not in the wild excitements and adventure of destruction, but in the patient labours of beneficent creative endeavour its most god-like attributes lie.

I hope our finest hours are yet to be – when Charity fills all hearts anew and the wars of the world are but the dramatic nightmares of a bygone age – for the glamour of war is in essence theatrical, a dressing up and pretence: its reality largely a merciless horror, the sum total of human folly and confusion. We have now to escape the delusions and havoc it has caused."

Walter E. Spradbery, February 1946

> This is a letter "Sprad" wrote to his nephew, Ronald Spradbery, in the first days of the second world war, which has only just become known to me in the year 2010. A letter whose contents at this late stage I feel are worth revealing as testament of his beliefs – in a time of the direst of threats, cast by fellow human beings against humanity.

7th November 1939

My dear Ronald

I had some difficulty in getting into touch with Mr Deal, the headmaster of the Chingford Senior School, (who I told you I thought could help to find agricultural employment for you), as he was with his evacuated school children in rural Essex, but today he came back to Chingford and rang me up to say how happy he would be to help, and suggested you should go over to see him so that he could make a personal recommendation to the farmers and influential folk he knows in Essex. He told me he knew a farmer in a big way who runs an instructional farm. I at once went over to your home, and found that you had been successful on your own initiative in finding an opening. I am very glad indeed. It is always most satisfactory to achieve things by one's own efforts. However, I will tell Deal, and his advice or help may come in useful some other time or on a later occasion.

I should like to take this opportunity of saying how proud I am of you. I read your statement before the tribunal and thought it excellent in its brevity and directness – incontrovertable.

It requires no little courage and spirit to face up and hold your views in a world so confused as we see it today, but nothing gladdens the heart more than to know that youths of integrity have faith and goodwill towards their kind, and pluck to maintain their faith; and work towards human understanding and a happier world. One is aware how full of problems and difficulties life is for the young in any case, who have no long experience to guide or comfort them nor support their hope. But theirs is the future and the making of it, and to know that there are among them those who are inspired by love for their fellows and determination to do no ill to them, but work towards a better order, is a grand assurance to us older folks who have tried to do our bit to this end also and rejoice to know that the light still shines and is maintained in the threatening darkness of these present hours.

I am glad to know you have undertaken agricultural work. Nothing is more vital nor nearer to the fundamental necessities of man. When civilisations pass away there remains the meek, humble, industrious and truly happy peasant, who inherits the earth, and who, near her, knows something of her vital secrets and taps the source of life in contact with the very elements.

At such times as these we are drive back to basic truths. All the pride of man's inventions and the power he has harnessed by his collective integrity cannot save him when he departs from social goodwill – indeed the very mechanism he has created but hastens his destruction and threatens terrors more afflicting than the catastrophes nature herself inflicts in her more violent moments.

Humanity's accumulated injustices, thoughtless greed, efforts to exploit and enslave its own kind, rise up in succeeding waves of retribution in the history of wars and revolutions, and seem likely to culminate in ever greater conflagrations until today the world seems on the brink of Armageddon itself. Yet all through the ages there has persisted truth and goodwill – the effort of human beings to cooperate and help each other, whereby civilised life is in ebb and flow, from the small groups of families, to tribes and then states and nations, and then groups of nations, covering ever-widening areas, empires, leagues, commonwealths, and on towards, we have hoped, at last a world unity of civilised endeavour.

All this progress is based on (whether recognised or not) the ever-extending application of the simple principle 'Do unto others as you would they should do unto you': and all its weakness, insecurity, falls back, and confused conflict results from misunderstandings, greed, short-sighted selfishness, pride and unthankfulness.

Literally and truly Christ brought salvation to the world when he summarised all wisdom into the injunction to man 'Love God with all your heart and strength and your neighbour as yourself". Stated so simply the humblest intelligence can put it to the test of experience, and after all the researches of science and the deepest of philosophic and theological discussion one can come to nothing better or more workable.

To some, the first part is unintelligable – they have never explained the spiritual basis of their experience, and to all, the other part presents difficulties that are unending in variety and complication. But faith is a joyous thing – the very opposite to fear, which is rooted in doubt and distrust – and it is by faith we go on, and in it is our only security in a world where reality is like a dream and by change of mood or temperament may become a very nightmare. Keep faith.

Well, my dear Ronald, my nephew and kinsman in thought, feeling and idea – good luck and good spirits go with you and support you in whatever lies ahead. Acquire the wisdom of the soil – be wise in vegetation stock-raising and all farming lore – if this war fever grows and spreads or if the civilised powers engaged in it break up in revolutions and social disruption, only those who can bring the earth to fruition will survive – if they can find shelter in the earth as well as raise food from it – and we look to you brave conscientous young fellows to preserve the truth an the spirit and carry it on to happier times that may lie ahead, when the obscuring clouds of war have passed away.

Write to me when you have the chance, and if you are not too tired, and I will try to find time and words to answer you, in fellowship, fellow feeling and as

Your affectionate uncle
Walter

Dorothy joins me in salutations and affectionate greetings and good wishes. We hope you will enjoy the work, even if it proves hard, and know you will render your best services honourably. Again Cheerio and God bless you.

This extraordinary letter, revealed to me some years after his nephew, Ron's, death, even at the time of Hitler and Nazism's dire threat to Europe, shows real if not mystical belief in his profound opposition to war, faith in nature and adherence to the principles of Christ.

And finally, these words are the last written by Walter Spradbery. Almost certainly to James Berry:

Let me go out into the sun again, and feel the breath of fresh air, the wind, and even the rain. My brush and pen are not yet laid aside – colour, light, shade, and atmosphere still thrill. Vision remains "Where there is no vision the people perish".

Glossary of Friends

Walter Spradbery's friends over the years were a unique group of people; apart from James Berry in the north, at one time an aspiring local politician, and to some extent Haydn Mackey, Austin Osman Spare and Bernard Faithful Davies, rarely, if ever, in any domain of public attention or focus. There were of course such exceptional figures as his former commanding officer in the RAMC, Josiah Oldfield, the supremo of London's Transport, Frank Pick, Frank Brangwyn and Arthur Mackmurdo and much later his acquaintanceship with Katharine Bruce Glasier. Elinor Pugh became very much a friend, a woman greatly admired, but someone who wanted to stay in the background. Generally though many of his closest friends came from local backgrounds. They were also, perhaps in the mould of Spradbery himself, unassuming, intellectual, charitable and loyal. Some of them have little reference or mention in the preceding pages. Some of them were very much part of "Sprad's" world and others walked into his life from different and less fortunate circumstances. Family and relatives were always close and loyal to his causes, although perhaps too shy to express much openly!

Not so widely touched upon in these pages, but very much part of his early life – and names not unfamiliar to me as a child growing up – were such friends as:

HIGGINS (John) – Higgins it seems was always around. A few years older than "Sprad", but a pal who accompanied Spradbery on many visits to the theatre and concerts. What happened to him subsequently, after my father's marriage, I have no knowledge. He is mentioned in "Sprad's" correspondence a number of times and was someone my father was obviously very close to in the post first world war years.

HAROLD PARKER – Along with Mackey and Austin Osman Spare, a close artist buddy. "Sprad" conveyed a deep personal pride in Harold Parker's early achievements as an artist. He was great friends with his family as well. Parker won the great artistic award, the Prix de Rome, studying in Rome for a year and later designed the motif of the wren on the old penny farthing. As I write these words, I quote from a letter received only a few days ago from Mackey's daughter, Helen, (living in Malta today) detailing an instance she remembers in her life three quarters of a century ago:

"Was Harold Parker the student of my father who designed the farthing? I sat with him when my parents and I went to see your mother in "The Beggars Opera". I went to school the next day and boasted about sitting next to the man who designed the farthing. I recall he was a large man with huge hands. Possibly I thought that because I was a puny child with small hands!"

JACKSON (Ernest) – Not exactly a close friend or pal, but someone who comes into Spradbery's correspondence with James Berry quite frequently. Especially to do with the "Scrolls of Fate", something which was rather a mystery to me, and the "Social Credit" movement which was very much a topic with Jim Berry in the late twenties and early thirties. As "Sprad" said "You cannot really ignore a man who writes you a letter of 40 pages". Jackson emigrated to Australia in the twenties and was, as far as I understand, never heard of by either James Berry or "Sprad" again.

FRED PARSONS – Quoted here, a tribute "Sprad" wrote of another of his closest pals...

Humanist – Philosopher – Enthusiast – Friend
Genial, humorous, kind, generous.

A lover of literature and a literary man; a teacher by nature – guide to the young... a figure of Dickensian quality – lovable, warm, picturesque, cheery.

My personal memories of him are of his qualities and of his artistic skills and appreciation. As an amateur artist he often achieved a very high level, and some of his best work has been exhibited at the Essex Art Club, of which he was an esteemed member.

Generous with his work, few of his friends can be without some prized example given to them – like his letters they are a lively comment on what he has seen and knows – things very worth having, lyrical little treasures.

> Just as Spradbery wrote such a eulogy of his old friend Fred Parsons, so both in pen and voice was he ever praising and in awe of many an artist and friend. He always spoke most glowingly of such a figure as George Bernard Shaw. I believe he actually met Shaw, but typically there is no evidence of it. William Blake, John Ruskin, William Morris were men he admired as much as any figures of his time. Blake, as already noted, he lectured on in 1957 to an audience of Bulgarians in Sofia! Both Frank Brangwyn and Arthur Mackmurdo were forever praised for their art, charity and generosity. Lifetime fellow artists such as Haydn Mackey and Austin Osman Spare were always supported most ardently in their skill as artists of the highest quality. He once lectured on the painting skill of Sylvia Pankhurst and also Edith Lister, as already quoted.

SQUIRE (Albert) – Photographer pal. Very much a visitor with his family at "The Wilderness" in my early childhood. He took many photographs of my father, mother, sister and myself at one time or other; some of them are reproduced in this book.

W.N. EDWARDS (Ed) – Lived with his wife (June) and family in Welwyn Garden City. He held some position in the British Museum. I don't remember ever meeting him. He and my father met up in London a number of times as friends do. Someone my father had a great deal of time and respect for. "To know him, his father and a few of his friends, was to move in an atmosphere of observant, appreciative, speculative and entertaining thought."

ALFRED SCHWAB and his wife, Mary. Before meeting and marrying my mother, Mary was someone my father was very smitten with. When she later married his pal, Alfred Schwab, he felt he'd missed his chance!

ALBERT CORAM and EDDY RIX – Ex-students who subsequently became greater chums. Coram was a medical technician; he caught up more closely with "Sprad" later, when my father was forced to wear a special truss for his double hernia. Eddy Rix's tragic death in World War Two is quoted in a letter previously.

AUSTIN OSMAN SPARE – Fellow artist, he also served in the RAMC in World War One. Probably met in the days of setting up the art section of the Imperial War Museum. Brilliant "artist of the occult". Early student friend of Sylvia Pankhurst, both were dismissed from the Royal College of Art, for some reason or other! An artist who lived in poverty most of his life. His remarkable book of engravings, "A Book of Satyrs" was given to my father in 1919, published both in London and New York; only three hundred copies were ever printed. Along with books of Brangwyn's and Mackey, it is one of a number of books of my father's I have held on to to this present day.

CHRIS MASSIE – Best-selling author. Someone I remember once meeting. Wrote a novel entitled "Love Letters" which was made into a Hollywood film starring Joseph Cotton and Jennifer Jones.

Rev. DUNNING – A vicar with a diocese in Kendal. Over the post-war years of 1914-18 letters intermittently passed between them. Memories of a warm acquaintanceship of wartime years.

PETER TAYLOR-SMITH (Smithie) – The founder and inspiring spirit behind the Maddermarket Theatre in Norwich. Met up while serving in the RAMC. "Sprad" appeared in one or more of his stage productions while serving in the RAMC.

Mr LITTLE – A conductor on the 38A bus route in the thirties and forties. A wonderfully humorous character whom we regularly encountered on our many local bus journeys. He subsequently became a visitor to "The Wilderness".

From his days at The Settlement, the Essex Art Club, National Association of Boys' Clubs and the Peace Movement, many names of friends stood out in my memory. None more so, to me personally than Bernard Faithful Davies. From The Settlement and Essex Art Club, names that I can still readily recall today are people such as Dan Gladwell, Vivian Bewick, Nadia Newmarsh, Frank Hall, Mabel Harris, Dorothy Isons. There was a Bernard Bowerman, an artist who lived very close by, and was a frequent visitor. Also the sculptress, Elsa Fraenkel, a refugee from eastern Europe.

Mr Knight, the owner of the corner shop at the top end of our patch of forest who, during the war years when there was nothing to display in his shop windows, offered "Sprad" to display his paintings in them to sell. Of course many friends were jointly friends with my mother, friends from the world of music. There was also a Mrs Jeffries who sought refuge with us from her home in Canning Town – and who died at "The Wilderness". Siegfried, the beautiful German girl, with whom I recall I was enamoured as a child; she came to stay with us in the mid-thirties, a passionate young admirer of Adolf Hitler! Later, when "Sprad" was living on his own, the Danish gentleman, Fredericksen, and his Romany caravan arrived. He parked himself in the garden and stayed on for years. Alf Stone, a huge tramp-like figure who appeared from time to time. "The Wilderness" it seemed served as a haven for some, even in its last derelict and crumbling years.

GALLERY

OF

PICTURES

FROM

SPRADBERY'S

WILDERNESS DAYS

Walter's grandson, Laurence.

The Essex Art Club's memorial bench to Dorothy.

"Sprad" going over some papers.

Later days

at

The Wilderness

Fredericksen and his caravan.

Fredericksen, his nephews and Wilfred Clifton
enjoying a cup of tea with Walter.

The Vestry House Museum, a unique and quaint Georgian building, surviving today as a museum and reference library in Walthamstow, E.17.

A drawing Spradbery made of the museum and published in the local Guardian newspaper in 1947 alongside an appeal he wrote which played a prime role in saving the museum to the present day.

(Above left) Buckhurst Hill's Bedford House, still the home of the parish's Community Centre.

(Above right) Greenleaf Road's Friends' Hall (known as The Settlement) where Walthamstow's Adult Educational Centre was eventually established and survived in Greenleaf Road into the twenty-first century.

(Right) Walthamstow's old Water House which became, in 1950, the William Morris Gallery and was recently threatened with closure. A gallery of international standing, which was saved by massive local and international support.

Teaching at Walthamstow's The Settlement (above) and Hoxton's
Crown and Manor Boys Club (below).

Days with the National Association of Boys' Clubs and at
Brathay Hall's 'Holidays with Purpose for young Men'.

Walter Spradbery's early designs for London's buses and underground trains.
These designs, depicting rural images of the seasons, went on the overhead
panels above the passengers' heads in the underground train carriages and buses.
The word captions were usually his own.

More designs for London's buses and underground trains.

277

Souvenir of "Fête Galante", December, 1949.

Every coming Christmas-tide "Sprad" designed a Christmas card from The Wilderness.

"Sprad's" distinctive letter-headings motifs at "The Wilderness"

Telephone – Buckhurst 2360.

The earliest letter-heading – featuring the studio, the well and the stone figure of the medieval knight, symbolically guarding the unusual sliding metal gateway. The old gateway was always there as long as I can remember, but the stone figure disappeared probably before I was born.

Telephone – Buckhurst 2360.

A later tiny lino-print of "The Wilderness" silhouetted against the forest trees.

A motif "Sprad" had printed for his headed writing paper after Dorothy's death. Taken from a beautiful pastoral porcelain piece that remained over the mantlepiece fireplace in the "Wilderness" studio as long as I can remember.

279

Epping Forest

Drawings, sketches and watercolours
by Selwyn Image and Walter Spradbery.

1 May – 31 July

Free entry
Wednesday–Sunday, 10am–5pm

William Morris Gallery
Lloyd Park, Forest Road, London E17 4PP
Tel: 020 8496 4390
Email: wmg.enquiries@walthamforest.gov.uk
www.walthamforest.gov.uk/william-morris

Walter Spradbery's painting "Pollard Hornbeams in Epping Forest"
was used to promote an exhibition of his work at the
William Morris Gallery in 2009.